VEGAN *Vittles*

SECOND HELPINGS

down-home cooking for everyone

Jo Stepaniak

and the people and critters of Farm Sanctuary

BOOK PUBLISHING COMPANY

Summertown, Tennessee

Library of Congress Cataloging-in-Publication Data

Stepaniak, Jo
   Vegan vittles : second helpings : down-home cooking for everyone / by Jo
Stepaniak and the people and critters of Farm Sanctuary. — 2nd ed.
     p. cm.
   Includes index.
   ISBN 978-1-57067-200-2
   1. Vegan cookery.   I. Farm Sanctuary (Watkins Glen, N.Y.)   II. Title.

   TX837.S77 2007
   641.5'636—dc22

                       2006035490

15 14 13 12 11 10 09 08 07 06   1 2 3 4 5 6 7 8 9

Printed on recycled paper

Cover art and illustrations: Bernice Davidson
Cover and interior design: Aerocraft Charter Art Service

Printed in Canada

Book Publishing Company
P.O. Box 99
Summertown, TN 38483
888-260-8458
www.bookpubco.com

ISBN 13: 978-1-57067-200-2

Calculations for the nutritional analyses in this book are based
on the average number of servings listed with the recipes and the
average amount of an ingredient, if a range is called for. Calculations
are rounded up to the nearest gram. If two options for an ingredient
are listed, the first one is used. Not included are optional ingredients,
serving suggestions, or fat used for frying, unless the amount of fat
is specified in the recipe.

The Book Publishing Co. is committed
to preserving ancient forests and natural
resources. We have elected to print
this title on paper which is 100%
postconsumer recycled and processed
chlorine free. As a result of our paper
choice, we have saved the following
natural resources:

128 trees

5,972 lbs of solid waste

46,507 gallons of water

11,204 lbs pounds of greenhouse gases

89 million BTUs of total energy

*(Paper calculations from Environmental
Defense www.papercalculator.org)*

We are a member of Green Press
Initiative. For more information
about Green Press Initiative visit:
www.greenpressinitiative.org

SECOND HELPINGS

Vegan (vē´-gĕn)

n. a strict vegetarian who consumes no animal food or dairy products;
one who abstains from using animal products (such as leather).

adj. types of [food or products] suitable for a vegan.

Vittles (vi´-tĕlz)

n. nourishment; provisions; food fit for human consumption.

Other Books by Jo Stepaniak

From BOOK PUBLISHING COMPANY

The Ultimate Uncheese Cookbook

Food Allergy Survival Guide
    (coauthored by Vesanto Melina and Dina Aronson)

Vegan Deli

The Saucy Vegetarian

Table for Two

The Nutritional Yeast Cookbook

Delicious Food for a Healthy Heart

Dairy-Free & Delicious
    (coauthored by Brenda Davis and Bryanna Clark Grogan)

From MCGRAW-HILL

Raising Vegetarian Children (coauthored by Vesanto Melina)

The Vegan Sourcebook

Being Vegan

Compassionate Living for Healing, Wholeness & Harmony

From ST. MARTIN'S PRESS

Breaking the Food Seduction by Neal Barnard, MD
    (recipes and menus by Jo Stepaniak)

About the Author

Jo Stepaniak has been involved with vegetarian and vegan issues for over four decades. In addition to writing and recipe development, Jo is a senior book editor and an international business dispute resolution specialist for a global employment broker. Her award-winning advice column "Ask Jo!" appears on her Web site, Grassroots Veganism, at www.vegsource.com/jo.

Contents

Foreword

Thank you for picking up *Vegan Vittles* and for your interest in compassionate food choices. Choosing vegan food is good for people and animals, and it softens our species' impact on the earth.

Most people in countries like the United States give little thought to how our food gets on the table, and the manufacturers of meat, milk, and eggs are happy to keep it that way. The pastoral farm scenes depicted in children's books and held in many of our imaginations do not square with the current reality.

Farming today is starkly different than it was just one generation ago, as small farms have been replaced by large-scale factory farms. Consumers who buy meat, dairy, and eggs unwittingly subsidize cruel and destructive farming practices. But it doesn't have to be this way. Every day we each can make simple choices that will lead to a world of difference.

By choosing a vegan lifestyle, eating plants instead of animals, we can directly support compassion instead of cruelty. In this updated version of *Vegan Vittles*, Jo Stepaniak provides solid advice for eating well and creating positive change in our world. This tasty collection of recipes and inspiring stories of rescued animals living at Farm Sanctuary provides tools and inspiration for eating humanely and in good conscience.

What we eat represents our most intimate interaction and connection with the earth and our own sustenance. In a very real sense, we are what we eat, as food is incorporated into our bodies. In affluent countries, where we consume diets heavy in animal products, we suffer from widespread obesity, heart disease, and other ailments, while animals experience the brutality of factory farming. By killing and consuming animals, we also end up killing ourselves.

In addition to the physical ills that come with excessive meat, dairy, and egg consumption, the exploitation and slaughter of other animals also hardens our hearts. Slaughter is violent and bloody and requires that we adopt a callous attitude toward other living beings. Cruelty and callousness have become pervasive on modern farms, and most consumers complacently support them.

People growing up in nations like the United States are typically indoctrinated to believe that eating animal foods is necessary and healthful, and we have tended to accept this notion without thinking very much about it. In fact, we can live well and be healthy without eating any animal products.

How we treat other animals says a great deal about ourselves. As Mahatma Gandhi said, "You can judge the moral progress of a nation by the way its animals are treated." It is impossible to reconcile factory farming, which has become rampant across the United States, with humane ideals.

At Farm Sanctuary, cows, pigs, chickens, and other so-called food animals are our friends. Animals who had been exploited, commodified, and even discarded by the factory farming industry become our cherished companions. As these animals' lives are transformed, so are ours.

Farm Sanctuary was formed in 1986 to combat factory farming and protect farm animals from abuse. We encourage citizens to make informed, compassionate choices, and we work on legislation and policy reforms to prevent egregious cruelties.

Our advocacy efforts have led to the nation's first laws to protect farm animals, including measures banning the confinement of farm animals in two-foot-wide crates where they cannot even turn around, prohibitions on the sale of "downed" animals (animals too sick to stand) at stockyards, and prohibitions on the force-feeding of ducks and geese to make foie gras. Despite these successes, however, the vast majority of farm animals continue to suffer with little or no legal protection.

Farm Sanctuary operates two shelters for rescued farm animals: one in Watkins Glen, New York, and one in Orland, California. The animals living at Farm Sanctuary serve as ambassadors, and their stories help educate people about the callousness and cruelty that exist in modern farming. Our first resident, a sheep named Hilda, was literally discarded on a pile of dead animals behind a stockyard when she was too sick to walk.

Thousands of people visit our shelters every year. In addition to sheltering animals, each location has a People Barn—a visitors' center with educational displays—as well as overnight accommodations. Visitors have a chance to meet cows, pigs, chickens, and other animals, and to know them as friends instead of food.

Farm animals are sensitive, intelligent creatures who live in complex social systems. They form close friendships, and they express a variety of emotions ranging from fear to joy. Spending time with the animals at Farm Sanctuary, one comes to understand and appreciate them.

Like all animals, farm animals deserve to be treated with compassion and respect instead of cruelty. Treating animals with kindness is good for them, and it is good for us. Callousness and cruelty can be contagious and spread, but so, too, can empathy and compassion.

Gene Baur

COFOUNDER AND PRESIDENT, FARM SANCTUARY
www.farmsanctuary.org

Farm Sanctuary East PO Box 150, Watkins Glen, NY 14891
Farm Sanctuary West PO Box 1065, Orland, CA 95963

Preface

In the many years since *Vegan Vittles* first appeared, there has been an enormous outpouring of interest in the vegan diet and lifestyle. Retail stores, mail order catalogs, products, books, magazines, and Web sites devoted to the countless issues that concern vegans have multiplied and flourished. Previously, the word *vegan* was shunned or disregarded by the mainstream media, or it was buried in a back-page story. On those rare occasions it was acknowledged, it was typically disparaged, mispronounced, and misdefined. Times have changed! Once relegated to second-class status even among vegetarians, veganism has emerged as the benchmark of healthful eating and compassionate living.

Today, vegan cooking runs the gamut from hearty, everyday fare (the kind that is featured in this book) to haute cuisine. No longer are vegans condemned to an empty plate or a dull diet of lettuce leaves and boiled tofu. The options found in recipe books and on store shelves are limitless and nearly mind-boggling. From fancy appetizers to decadent desserts, and from pressure cookers to slow cookers, vegan fare covers it all— beautifully, deliciously, and healthfully.

Most people who aren't vegan appreciate an occasional respite from heavy meals laden with animal products. Designating one meal per day as vegan, or even all meals one or two days per week, can help broaden and enliven a mundane repertoire. Such an approach will add more fun and flair to mealtime, as well as provide an opportunity to increase your intake of fruits, veggies, and other health-supporting foods. You can do this without any pressure to actually become vegan—ever. But be forewarned that expanding your culinary horizons may lead to a more receptive mind-set and accessible heart, and who knows what could happen from there!

Every day I receive letters and e-mails from people around the world who somehow found their way to veganism. They usually begin with, "I never thought I would do this." Yet due to health problems, or having read a touching article or seen a heartrending film about animal suffering, or simply watching how a son or daughter or parent has thrived physically and emotionally as a vegan, they were inspired to make a personal change

they never believed was possible—one that previously wasn't even on their radar screen.

If you are not yet vegan but are headed in that direction, don't fret about how to do it "right" or be concerned that your practice isn't perfect. Veganism is a journey, a road map—it isn't a destination. As the Vietnamese Zen master, poet, and peace activist Thich Nhat Hanh tells us, "If we want to head north, we can use the North Star to guide us, but it is impossible to arrive at the North Star. Our effort is only to proceed in that direction."

Jo Stepaniak

PITTSBURGH, PENNSYLVANIA

Acknowledgments

My deepest gratitude goes first and foremost to the animals of Farm Sanctuary and all the farm animals who will never be rescued, enduring unspeakable horrors and abbreviated lives for human indulgences. Many thanks to Gene Baur for his courageous efforts in pioneering the movement for public education and legislative sanity on behalf of these magnificent beings. The staff of Farm Sanctuary East and West have been enormously helpful and supportive of this project and contributed their time, research, and writing skills. Special thanks to all of Farm Sanctuary's behind-the-scenes shining stars.

To the countless people who have enjoyed *Vegan Vittles* these many years, I am grateful. Your feedback and encouragement have inspired me and given me great hope and deep satisfaction. I consider you all dear friends. Jeff and Sabrina Nelson of Vegsource.com have always been an incredible pillar for the cause of veganism, selflessly championing the myriad voices and work of so many. Thank you for your cherished support and generosity.

Freya Dinshah of the American Vegan Society and Brian and Sharon Graff of the North American Vegetarian Society ignited the vegan flame throughout North America, and their efforts have rung a clear bell for veganism around the world. Their tireless dedication continues to inspire locally and globally, and I am grateful to know them and have them in my life.

To the countless vegan authors, activists, friends, and acquaintances who have blessed my life, thank you. There are too many to mention here, but you know who you are and how much I love you. To all the guests who have frequented my Web site and discussion board over the years, and to those who have sent in their questions for me to answer in my "Ask Jo!" column, I bow in appreciation of and respect for all of you.

Many thanks to Stanley M. Sapon, Ph.D., for his loving friendship and for contributing his vast knowledge of linguistics to assist with our "veganisms." Appreciation and respect go to my esteemed colleagues—and friends—Vesanto Melina, MS, RD, Dina Aronson, MS, RD, chef Francis Janes, former owner of Cafe Ambrosia restaurant in Seattle, Washington, and chef Mark Shadle, owner of It's Only Natural Restaurant in Middletown, Connecticut, for donating several of their phenomenal recipes.

High praise and gratitude go to John and Rhonda Wincek for their extraordinary layout and design skills.

Special accolades go to Bob and Cynthia Holzapfel of Book Publishing Company, who have been courageous trailblazers in the field of vegan living and publishing for decades. I will always treasure our working relationship and friendship.

And last but not least, I offer endless appreciation to my husband, Michael, who has willingly and joyfully endured taste-testing an infinite number of recipes in various stages of edibility, and never once complained.

A Note about Our "Veganisms"

A society's view of animals often can be characterized by its popular proverbs and idioms. Commonly used expressions and adages throughout the world contain endless harsh references to animals of every kind. Although many of our common sayings have their roots in historical events or customs, too often they reflect our culture's ingrained, unchallenged, and/or disparaging view of animals. To counter this, we have selected dozens of familiar American and English maxims, some enduring for many centuries, that malign or denigrate animals, embrace or advocate the exploitation of animals, or debase the human spirit, and "veganized" them. In other words, we revised some of these sayings to reflect a more compassionate outlook by eliminating most animal references altogether. This is not to say that using animal references is necessarily unacceptable. According to Stanley M. Sapon, professor emeritus of psycholinguistics at the University of Rochester and an internationally renowned authority on the psychology of language, "Animals and other parts of nature can—and maybe should—be part of our similes and proverbs—as long as they are referred to in respectful or appreciative ways."

By incorporating these "veganisms" into our daily lives, we will all become more cognizant of how language can spark and perpetuate both negative and positive attitudes. We hope that they will elevate the awareness of those around us in an upbeat and positive way.

instead of

He that would fish must not mind getting wet.

use

He that would garden must not mind getting soiled.

What is veganism?

Simply stated, veganism is the conviction and practice of compassionate living. Although this way of life has been followed by a number of individuals and groups throughout history, it wasn't until 1944, when the first Vegan Society was formed in England, that the term *vegan* (pronounced VEE-gn, with a long "e" and a hard "g") was coined to differentiate vegans from vegetarians. This was the beginning of the modern vegan movement.

How does being vegan differ from being vegetarian? According to the 1839 definition, still in use by Webster's today, a vegetarian is an *herbivore*; that is, an individual or species that feeds on plants. This designation was expanded ten years later, in 1849, to encompass "[a diet] consisting wholly of vegetables, fruits, grains, nuts, and sometimes eggs or dairy products."

Thus the term *vegetarian* refers only to what someone eats and does not pertain inherently to any other aspect of that person's life. For this reason we can presume the impetus for someone to become a vegetarian may be based on one or more possible factors: ethical, spiritual, religious, health, environmental, political, economic, or any combination of these. Therefore, when people tell us they are vegetarian, all we can reasonably assume is that they don't eat meat, fish, or fowl.

In recent years the term *vegetarian* has been woefully misrepresented by the media, health professionals, and the medical establishment to include particular meat products (such as fish or chicken), or to simply mean "no red meat." The term has even been twisted into oxymoronic malapropisms: *pesco-vegetarian* (a person who eats fish but no other meats), *pollo-vegetarian* (a person who eats chicken but no other meats), *pesco-pollo-vegetarian* (a person who eats fish and chicken but no other meats), and *flexitarian* (a person who hasn't made a commitment one way or the other; someone who may eat mostly plant foods but won't turn down steak or salmon). This distortion has misled the public and caused confusion among food manufacturers, restaurateurs and chefs, and even friends and family.

In contrast to the broad spectrum of motivations for vegetarianism, veganism is rooted in a single, compelling philosophy of "reverence for life" that extends beyond what a person eats. The Vegan Society in England describes it as follows:

> Veganism is a way of living that excludes all forms of exploitation of, and cruelty to, the animal kingdom, and includes a reverence for life. It applies to the practice of living on the products of the plant kingdom to the exclusion of flesh, fish, fowl, eggs, honey, animal milk and its derivatives, and encourages the use of alternatives for all commodities derived wholly or in part from animals.

Thus, in addition to adopting a totally plant-based diet, vegans make a conscious effort to avoid all forms of cruelty, manipulation, and harm to animals, regardless of any presumed benefit to humans or perceived value to society. This includes lifestyle choices, such as avoiding industries that exploit animals for entertainment, and seeking alternatives to animal-based clothing and other commodities. Despite these seeming limitations, most vegans don't grumble about what they cannot have; instead, they view their philosophy, lifestyle, and choices as surprisingly liberating. For example, countless people have shared with me their exuberance about exploring a vast number of new plant foods, which they say they never would have discovered had they not become vegan.

Some people might argue that it is impossible to be totally vegan in today's modern society, and technically they would be right. The use of animal products and the by-products of meat, dairy, and egg production are tremendously and regrettably pervasive. Vegan "purity" in an industrialized society is not only unattainable but unrealistic, and to maintain the impossible as an objective may very well be counterproductive.

Additionally, veganism is not about being "perfect." Rather, it is a means to create a more loving and just society for all life. It is consoling to recognize that the widespread availability of animal commodities and by-products is due to the use of animals for food. If we can eliminate the root cause—meat, dairy, and egg consumption—the by-product industries will cease to exist. For many vegans, it makes much sense to sidestep the policing of minutia in order to adopt a more practical and far-reaching approach.

When you embark on your vegan journey, start with the most obvious changes—food, clothing, and other commodities that are clearly animal derived. Begin where you are at this moment, with love and patience. But do begin. You don't have to be the "ideal vegan," now or ever. Just strive to do your best and you will succeed.

Embracing veganism compels us to confront our attitudes toward all forms of life, including our fellow humans. According to the American Vegan Society, founded by Jay Dinshah in 1960, the prime directive of veganism is *dynamic harmlessness*, the tenet of doing the least harm and the most good. This philosophy encourages vegans to search for options that will protect and improve the lives of all living beings on this planet, eliminate suffering, bring about the responsible use of natural resources, and inspire peace and harmony among people. Consequently, veganism is not passive self-denial. On the contrary, it instills active and vibrant responsibility for initiating positive social change by presenting a constant challenge to consistently seek out the highest ideal.

It is my hope that this book will provide you with an abundance of ideas for alternatives to animal-based food products, and that your vegan journey will bring you lifelong joy, well-being, strength of spirit, and peace of heart.

Dawn

Dawn was rescued from a herd of range cattle being raised for beef, where tiny calves had to rely on their ability to keep pace with the herd for protection from predators and the elements. She came to Farm Sanctuary as a "downer" calf when she was just one week old. Now she is all grown up and has established herself as matriarch of the herd. Perhaps because she herself was rescued as a small calf, she is always the first to greet newly rescued calves when they arrive at the sanctuary. She mothers each new orphan arrival as her own, tirelessly watching over them when they are on the long road to recovery. Like all good moms, Dawn knows that no sacrifice is too great when her "kids" are involved.

Farm animal industry myths

The farm animal industry is increasingly scrambling to address animal welfare concerns, especially when images and information about abused, downed, diseased, or dying animals reach the public. Meat, poultry, dairy, and egg producers typically attempt to represent themselves as "animal welfarists," claiming it is in their own economic interest to keep animals healthy and content. Yet in the "food animal" industry's own words and actions, it is often more "profitable" for producers to neglect and abuse animals. Article after article in livestock, poultry, and United States Department of Agriculture (USDA) publications is filled with glaring examples of cruel animal agricultural practices whereby millions of animals suffer and die because they are considered "acceptable economic losses" rather than living, feeling beings.

There are none so deaf as those who will not hear,
None so blind as those who will not see.

AMERICAN PROVERB

Myth: *It is in the livestock industry's best interest to ensure that their animals are treated humanely in order to maximize productivity and increase profits.*

Fact: The argument that providing animals with appropriate care to protect the producer's financial investment only holds up if the financial losses caused by mistreating animals are greater than the economic benefits gained by it. With the advent of mass production technology, mistreating animals is profitable and has become the industry norm. It is economically acceptable, even expected, for a certain percentage of animals to become ill or die during the process.

FOR EXAMPLE:

- Dairy cows are commonly fed an unnaturally rich diet in order to maximize milk production, despite the fact that this diet causes metabolic diseases that can be fatal.

- Hogs are so severely overcrowded on transportation trucks that tens of thousands of them die each year in transit. This practice persists, however, because the money saved from overcrowding the animals is more than the dollars lost from their deaths.

- Chickens and turkeys have been anatomically manipulated to grow at such abnormal rates that millions die annually of heart attacks. Despite these deaths, the faster-growing birds yield higher net profits for producers, so these genetic strains are the industry standard.

Myth: *Modern farm animal production housing and feeding systems are scientifically designed to meet the needs of the animals.*

Fact: Modern farm animal production systems are designed to maximize profits and produce the most "product" at the cheapest price, even though such systems commonly cause both physical and psychological harm to the animals. The animal farming industry designs feeding and housing systems for economic efficiency, not animal welfare.

FOR EXAMPLE:

- Confining animals in tighter spaces allows a facility to produce more meat, milk, or eggs, despite depriving animals of appropriate space to fulfill their basic needs. Sows used for breeding are confined in two-foot-wide enclosures for most of their lives.

- Farm animal feed contains agricultural and industrial waste products, including by-products of farm animal carcasses deemed unfit for human consumption and manure. Although plentiful and cheap, these are potentially hazardous to the animals who ingest them and, in turn, to human consumers. Scientists believe that mad cow disease was spread by feeding the remains of dead cows to live cows.

- Overcrowding of animals on factory farms contributes to slower individual growth rates and increased incidences of illness. Nevertheless, it is more profitable overall, and therefore has become the production norm.

Myth: *Farm animal producers are committed to raising the healthiest animals possible to provide a safe food source for consumers.*

Fact: Report after report has been issued on the health risks associated with the consumption of meat, poultry, eggs, and dairy products—from widespread outbreaks of toxic bacteria to inadequate inspections. Animals raised in intensive production systems regularly contract diseases—and these diseases, and the drugs used to combat them, can be hazardous to human beings.

FOR EXAMPLE:

- Farm animal living conditions are so stressful and disease so rampant that antibiotics are routinely used, leading to the development of antibiotic-resistant pathogens, which threaten human health. Approximately half of the antibiotics produced annually in the United States are used by the livestock and poultry industries.
- Animals with various diseases are regularly and legally slaughtered and used for human food.

Blatant animal cruelties, such as overcrowding, mutilation, deficient diets, genetic manipulation, sensory deprivation, and severe confinement, are used to increase profits for meat, poultry, dairy, and egg operations at the expense of animal welfare. One look at the victims of farm animal production—the diseased chickens, genetically altered turkeys, downed cows, and dying pigs—clearly dispels all myths created by poultry and livestock producers.

Leyla

Leyla was brought to Farm Sanctuary from a humane society in California. Her family gave her away because they said she was a vicious biter and a troublemaker. Having been told that Leyla liked to bite, the humane society could not give her to another family. Instead, she came to Farm Sanctuary, where she has been nothing but gentle and kind to all. She now spends her days snacking on fresh veggies and burrowing in the straw in her cozy rabbit hutch. When given the space to be herself, Leyla thrives while living contentedly among the other rescued rabbits at Farm Sanctuary's California Shelter.

Whatever you do, do what you can!

No matter where you are or what you are doing, you can find ways to help farm animals, show respect for the earth, and improve your own well-being. Maintaining close ties with individuals, businesses, and farmers in your community can make a tremendous difference. Even the smallest efforts to educate others can have an impact too.

A delicious vegan meal or a few words spoken to your co-workers about factory farms can change hearts and inspire others to live more healthful, compassionate lives. Supporting local sustainable agriculture can encourage friends and neighbors to follow your example toward a brighter future for everyone. Donating your time and money to worthy animal protection organizations can be very rewarding and will maximize your effectiveness for those who are suffering. With very little effort, you can make your daily life—and even the busiest of schedules—into a campaign to improve the lives of farm animals, protect our precious planet, and safeguard your own health. Here are just a few ideas for how you can help:

Everyday Activism

- Help support sustainable agriculture in your community by joining a Community Supported Agriculture (CSA) group in your area, growing your own food, or buying organic produce from local farmers' markets.

- Educate yourself about factory farming and then share what you have learned with others. Consider handing out informational leaflets about factory farming and watching videos with friends and family. Use bumper stickers and buttons to spread your message of compassion, and speak one-on-one with everyone you can about this important issue.

- Reach out to restaurants in your community and ask them to carry more vegetarian and vegan options on their menus.

- Let your voice be heard. Write letters to your local newspaper and to nearby businesses about issues that affect animal welfare, the environment, and your health.

7

- Teach others about the benefits of a plant-based diet by setting up a display at your local library, or donate veg-friendly books and videos to your library's main collection.

- Take full advantage of your civil liberties and the democratic process by staying informed about the legislative issues that interest you. Get out and vote whenever you can and make your opinions count by sharing them with lawmakers.

- Prepare the wonderful recipes in this book for friends and family. Show them how healthful and scrumptious cruelty-free meals can be.

Support Farm Sanctuary

- Become a member of Farm Sanctuary. Members provide the organization with almost 90 percent of its annual budget and give hope and compassion to suffering animals. Your donations support groundbreaking legal advocacy efforts, legislative projects, cruelty investigations, media outreach campaigns, public awareness and humane education projects, and direct rescue and shelter efforts for abused farm animals.

- Take the time to visit Farm Sanctuary. Currently, Farm Sanctuary operates two shelters: one in upstate New York and one in northern California. Both shelters rehabilitate and provide lifelong care for hundreds of animals who have been rescued from stockyards, factory farms, and slaughterhouses. Guided tours of the shelters, overnight accommodations, and special events offer guests ample opportunity to meet face-to-face with the cows, pigs, chickens, and other farm animals who call Farm Sanctuary home.

Dreamboat

Dreamboat was rescued as an older hen, or what the egg industry would call a "spent" hen. Her egg production levels had dropped off, and because she was no longer considered valuable, she was going to be sent to slaughter. Instead, she was taken to safety at Farm Sanctuary. Although Dreamboat is almost completely blind, her sense of hearing is acute. She is usually a quiet, reserved hen, but when she hears music she becomes very animated and starts chirping and swaying to the sound. She especially loves to be sung to. Classical, pop, jazz, or rock, she doesn't care—but she does have a good ear. Visitors to the sanctuary, make sure you sing in tune!

- Encourage restaurant owners and chefs in your area not to serve cruel delicacies by having them sign a *No Foie Gras* or *No Veal* pledge, or by leaving a Farm Sanctuary comment card about these products at your restaurant table next time you dine out.
- Join Farm Sanctuary's Adopt-a-Farm Animal Project and become a monthly sponsor of a rescued animal at their New York or California shelter. As a sponsor, you will help provide the necessary support to shelter and feed a rescued cow, pig, chicken, or other farm animal. In return, you'll receive an adoption package for your sponsored animal and special visitation privileges at Farm Sanctuary.
- Put on your walking shoes and take steps toward a more compassionate future for farm animals by participating in Farm Sanctuary's Walk for Farm Animals events across the United States. Held on or around October 2nd in honor of World Farm Animals Day, Farm Sanctuary's walkathons raise thousands of dollars for the organization's advocacy efforts each year.
- If you care about rescued farm animals and are willing to donate a portion of your free time to make a difference in their lives, consider volunteering at Farm Sanctuary's New York or California shelter. As a farm volunteer, you will have the opportunity to work directly with animals and complete the necessary chores that enable the organization to operate its shelters, conduct educational programs, and initiate campaigns to stop farm animal suffering.
- Get involved with Farm Sanctuary's advocacy efforts by signing up to become a member of their Activist Network. As a member, you will be contacted when Farm Sanctuary needs activist assistance with campaigns, demonstrations, outreach tabling, emergency rescues, and other special projects.

For more information on how you can get involved with Farm Sanctuary, please contact 607-583-2225 or e-mail info@farmsanctuary.org.

instead of

Give a man a fish and you'll feed him for a day.
Teach a man to fish and you'll feed him for a lifetime.

use

Give a man beans and you'll feed him for a day.
Teach a man to garden and you'll feed him for a lifetime.

Alternatives to milk and dairy products

For most people intent on making their diets as healthful and cruelty-free as possible, eliminating milk and dairy products is often viewed as the most foreboding hurdle. Fear no more! Manufacturers have created a smorgasbord of alternatives that rival the taste and versatility of cow's milk and other dairy foods. Many mainstream supermarkets are carrying these healthful products; but if you can't find them in your grocery store, visit a natural food store. You may be surprised at the vast assortment of choices.

You can also prepare many delicious and healthful dairy-free substitutes right in your own kitchen using the recipes in this book. Thus, once you have made the decision to eliminate dairy products from your diet, the only real challenge left is sifting through the vast options at hand, sufficient to satisfy almost any requirement or taste.

When converting traditional recipes into vegan ones, remember to always strive for consistency in flavor. Use plain or unsweetened nondairy products for savory recipes, and sweeter products for baked goods and desserts. Different brands will deliver different results. Let personal preferences and product availability guide your choices. As with most new foods, experimentation is often the best teacher.

"Dairy Free" and "Nondairy" Labels on Packages

Vegans should be cautious about food products labeled as "dairy free" or "nondairy." These terms can appear rather prominently on the labels of certain food products, but, surprisingly, they do not always mean a product is free of dairy derivatives.

No regulatory definition exists yet for the term "dairy free." This means that the Food and Drug Administration (FDA) has not established any regulations regarding the use of this terminology on package labels. While the FDA does not allow the use of false and misleading terms in general on food labels, without a regulatory definition in place, there can be no assurance that foods labeled as "dairy free" are in fact free from any milk proteins or other dairy derivatives.

Some companies use this term to describe lactose-free or low-lactose products for those consumers with lactose intolerance. Alternatively, they may use it on products that are free of traditional dairy ingredients, such as milk and cream, but not free of milk derivatives, such as caseinates (proteins in milk) or whey (a by-product of cheese making). Vegans cannot and should not rely on "dairy free" package claims and will need to scrutinize the ingredient statement for evidence of milk.

A regulatory definition does exist for the term "nondairy." But, incredibly, the regulatory definition actually allows the presence of casein in such products. For example, coffee creamers and soy "cheeses" that are made with casein but do not contain milk or cream are permitted to be labeled "nondairy." The term "nondairy" is a long-standing consequence of the strong dairy lobby that aims to ensure that alternative milk and cream products cannot bear the "dairy" name.

"Nondairy" definitely does not mean that a product is vegan. FDA regulations specifically allow the use of caseinates in nondairy products. However, the term "caseinate" will appear in the ingredient statement and must be followed by a parenthetical explanation, such as "casein (a milk derivative)."

Vegans should not rely on the terms "dairy free" and "nondairy" on product packaging to indicate a vegan-safe food. Careful inspection of the ingredient statement is a vegan's best ally and only defense.

Milk Alternatives

The selection of alternatives to cow's milk is extensive. Packaged products run the gamut from fresh (in the dairy case), to boxed (in aseptic cartons, often in the cereal aisle), to instant powders (in canisters or bulk bins in the dry goods section). You can choose from soymilk, rice milk, soy-rice milk, nut milk, oat milk, and a host of others made from various plant-based ingredients. Nondairy milks come plain (unflavored and unsweetened) or flavored, with a variety of tempting tastes, such as chocolate, mocha, chai, coffee latte, strawberry, spiced, and vanilla. Package sizes range from single servings to pints, quarts, and half gallons. Rich soy creamers, as velvety and luxurious as dairy cream, won't curdle in your hot coffee or tea. They, too, come in tantalizing flavors, such as hazelnut and French vanilla.

Many nondairy milks are fortified with calcium and vitamin D that is equal to the amounts found in cow's milk. In addition, many brands are enriched with several important vitamins and minerals, including vitamin B_{12}. Most nondairy milk products will stay fresh in the refrigerator for 7–10 days after the package is opened.

Yogurt Alternatives

The assortment of creamy, custardy nondairy yogurts, replete with active cultures, has expanded in recent years. As with dairy yogurt, some brands are more palatable than others. If you don't like one brand, try another. Nondairy yogurts come in an array of flavors, from plain to vanilla, and from chocolate to fruity. You can also make your own yogurt using fresh soymilk (or any other nondairy milk) and a high-quality vegan yogurt that contains active cultures as a starter. Homemade nondairy yogurt is incubated in the same fashion as dairy yogurt.

Butter Alternatives

For cooking, vegetable oil is a quick stand-in for butter. Good choices for cooking are cold-pressed olive oil, coconut oil, sesame oil, safflower oil, and organic canola oil. Another option is to use nondairy, nonhydrogenated, trans-fat-free soy margarine; many brands have a surprisingly rich and buttery flavor, and most are also excellent for use in baking. For a lower-fat choice, spray your cookware with nonstick cooking spray or oil (handy refillable pumps are available in most cookware stores and many natural food stores) or sauté food in vegetable broth, water, or even herbal tea. If you prefer to use nonstick cookware, buy a high-quality piece or set (with high-quality products, the nonstick coating is bonded to the cookware and will not scrape, chip, or peel off). With many recipes (other than baked goods) that call for added oil, the oil can just be omitted. Try replacing some of the fat in baked goods with fruit purées, such as applesauce, mashed banana, or prune purée (note that prune purée may darken light-colored cakes or muffins).

Hopi

Hopi was rescued from the property of a San Diego man suspected of buying and reselling diseased and wounded stockyard animals for profit. Suffering from malnourishment and neglect, Hopi was in bad shape when he arrived at Farm Sanctuary. But in no time, caregivers had him in good spirits and well on his way to recovery. Hopi can still be a little shy at times and prefers the company of his friends Jitterbug and Moo to that of humans. Together they spend most of their free time roaming green pastures and mooing contentedly from the hilltops, grateful to be free.

Vegan margarine makes a tasty spread for morning muffins, bagels, biscuits, or toast. Here are a few more ideas for spreads for breads and baked goods:

- vegetable butters made from puréed cooked vegetables (try Carrot Butter, page 87)
- vegan cream cheese, store-bought
- vegan mayonnaise, store-bought or homemade (try Deli Dressing, page 208)
- fruit butters or preserves
- nut and seed butters (such as peanut butter, almond butter, or tahini)
- plain or seasoned mustard

Buttermilk Alternatives

Some manufacturers have created a cultured soy beverage that is a cross between buttermilk and a fermented dairy drink called kefir. These products contain active cultures ("friendly" bacteria) that aid digestion and add a zing of flavor. They are usually fruit-flavored and may be fortified with vitamins and minerals. Look for them in the dairy case.

To replace 1 cup of buttermilk in recipes and baked goods, use plain soy yogurt measure for measure. Alternatively, simply add 2 teaspoons apple cider vinegar to 1 cup plain soymilk (or other nondairy milk). Let the mixture rest for 5–10 minutes before using to give the milk time to sour.

Cheese Alternatives

While there are several commercial nondairy "cheese" products on the market, the majority do not taste very good, and the few that do are high in fat, making them poor choices for everyday consumption. In addition, a number contain casein, a protein derived from cow's milk (see page 10 for an explanation of the terms "nondairy" and "dairy free"). Casein is added because it helps these products melt better and gives them a bit of the characteristic "stretch" that we associate with dairy cheese. If you want to try some of the commercially prepared cheese alternatives, read the label before you buy the product to see if it contains casein (which may also be listed as "caseinate" or other similar terms). Vegan cheese alternatives that are commercially produced include block-style and grated dairy-free cheeses in several flavors, grated Parmesan substitutes, and cream cheeses in plain, savory, and sweet flavors.

It's easy to prepare homemade uncheeses (a term I coined when I wrote *The Uncheese Cookbook*, originally published in 1994), and I have included several uncheese recipes in this book. If you are a cheese aficionado, however, you might want to buy a copy of the current incarnation of this classic volume, now titled *The Ultimate Uncheese Cookbook* (Book Publishing Company, 2004). It includes recipes for uncheese sauces, spreads, dips, blocks, sprinkles, soups, salads, main dishes, and even desserts, all of which taste remarkably similar to their dairy cousins. They are made from only pure, natural, plant-based ingredients and are quick and effortless to make.

In addition to uncheeses, you can impart a sharp, tangy, salty, or rich taste to foods (the qualities most often associated with dairy cheese) by using one or more of the following seasonings:

- nutritional yeast flakes for a cheesy taste (see Ingredients That May Be New to You, page 27)
- small amounts of light miso or chickpea miso, to add a salty, aged flavor (see page 26)
- a dash of soy sauce and a small amount of sesame tahini, to add richness and saltiness (see pages 28 and 29)
- a dash of umeboshi vinegar, to add tang and saltiness (see page 32)
- a combination of nutritional yeast flakes, sesame tahini or cashew butter, and freshly squeezed lemon juice, umeboshi vinegar, or soy sauce to add a blend of cheesy, rich, tangy, and salty tastes
- ripe avocado and umeboshi vinegar, to add richness, tang, and saltiness

Ricotta and Cottage Cheese Alternatives

There currently are no packaged vegan alternatives to ricotta and cottage cheese, but you can make tasty and versatile homemade versions right in your own kitchen. Try Tofu Ricotta (page 78) and Creamy Cottage Cheez (page 84).

Cream Cheese Alternatives

There are a few excellent vegan cream cheese products on the market in both flavored (sweet and fruity or savory) and plain varieties. Be sure to look for products that do not contain hydrogenated fats.

Sour Cream Alternatives

There are several brands of vegan sour cream on the market. In some recipes, plain soy yogurt may make a good replacement. You can also make your own vegan sour cream—it's simple and fast! See the recipe for Sour Dressing (page 209).

Sweetened Condensed Milk Alternatives

There currently are no packaged vegan alternatives for sweetened condensed milk, but you can make a homemade version right in your own kitchen using the following recipe.

Vegan Sweetened Condensed Milk

makes about 2 ½ cups

1 cup powdered instant soymilk or rice milk

1 cup boiling water

¾ cup granulated sugar

2 tablespoons nonhydrogenated vegan margarine

Pinch of salt

Place the instant soymilk powder, boiling water, sugar, margarine, and salt in a blender, and process several minutes until smooth, thickened, and well blended. Chill uncovered in the refrigerator, stirring occasionally. When completely cold, cover tightly. Stored in a covered container in the refrigerator, Vegan Sweetened Condensed Milk will keep for 5–7 days.

Evaporated Milk Alternatives

There currently are no packaged vegan alternatives for evaporated milk, but you can make a homemade version right in your own kitchen using the following recipe.

Vegan Evaporated Milk

makes about 2 cups

1½ cups boiling water

1 cup powdered instant soymilk or rice milk

Place the boiling water and instant soymilk powder in a blender, and process several minutes until smooth and well combined. Chill uncovered in the refrigerator, stirring occasionally. When completely cold, cover tightly. Stored in a covered container in the refrigerator, Vegan Evaporated Milk will keep for 5–7 days.

Pudding and Custard Alternatives

A few vegan packaged puddings and mixes are available in some areas. However, most pudding and custard recipes can be easily adapted simply by replacing dairy milk with soymilk or other plant-based milks. Another option is to blend silken tofu with a sweetener and puréed fruit, fruit preserves, and/or flavorings (such as vanilla extract or cocoa powder). For a heavenly and lightning-fast tofu-based pudding recipe, try The World's Best (and Easiest) Chocolate Pudding (page 227).

Ice Cream Alternatives

This is an area where vegan alternatives really shine. There is a huge assortment of vegan frozen desserts available that includes light and fruity sherbets, luscious frozen soy yogurts, and rich, decadent "ice creams" in every flavor and combination imaginable. You'll find numerous brands and sizes at your natural food store and even some mainstream supermarkets. In addition, there are frozen "ice cream" sandwiches, bars, sticks, and cones—enough options to quell the most ardent sweet tooth and meet the demands of any festivity.

   If you want a simple, inexpensive frozen dessert, try freezing flavored soymilk or fruit juice. Just pour the liquid into a Popsicle mold, partially freeze, insert Popsicle sticks, and return to the freezer until solidly frozen. Another delicious treat is a frozen banana. Just peel ripe bananas and cut each one in half horizontally. Insert a Popsicle stick into each cut end. Freeze the bananas until they are solidly frozen, then eat them like Popsicles. You can also turn them into healthful Nutty Buddies. Simply dip the frozen bananas in melted vegan chocolate, roll them in crushed peanuts, and return them to the freezer until the chocolate hardens.

Whipped Cream Alternatives

There are a few fairly decent vegan whipped cream options on the market. Surprisingly, some that seem "safe" may not be, and others that appear to contain dairy may actually be vegan. Read package labels closely to be certain of what you are buying. For a homemade alternative, try Tofu Whipped Topping (page 232), or skip the whipped cream altogether and try a creamy dessert sauce, such as Very Vanilla Maple Cream Sauce (page 232).

Alternatives to eggs

Eggs are used as an ingredient in many types of dishes. They also are considered a food in and of themselves. There are many vegan recipes that easily replicate the taste, color, and texture of eggs, and I have included quite a few in this book. Instead of scrambled eggs, try Scrambled Tofu (page 65). Want fancy omelets or crêpes? Make Eggless Omelets (page 59), Okonomiyaki (page 142), or Stuffed Omelets (page 146). Missing egg salad? Try Missing Egg Salad (page 92). Looking for a low-fat, inexpensive mayonnaise? Whip up Deli Dressing (page 208). Craving quiche? Indulge in Classic Quiche (page 140).

While nearly every conventional egg-based recipe can be transformed to be vegan, some recipes, particularly those that are heavily dependent on eggs or that require light and frothy beaten egg whites (such as angel food cakes and meringue) don't translate very well. Therefore, I have not included recipes for these items in this book.

Eggs serve a variety of purposes in cooking: they are used as binders and thickeners in casseroles, and as binders and leavening agents in baked goods. There are a number of egg-replacement products on the market today, but

Flaxseed Goop Egg Replacer

A simple egg replacer can be made by blending 1 tablespoon finely ground flaxseeds with 3 tablespoons water until frothy and viscous. If time permits, let this mixture rest in the refrigerator for 1 hour or longer before using. Covered tightly and stored in the refrigerator, Flaxseed Goop will keep for up to 3 days. **Note:** Ground flaxseeds are perishable and should be stored in the freezer to prevent rancidity. When stored in a tightly sealed container or a heavy-duty zipper-lock plastic bag, ground flaxseeds will keep for several months in the freezer. They do not need to be defrosted before using, as the ground seeds remain soft and powdery even when frozen.

Vegan Options to Bind or Thicken Cooked Foods

These are good choices to use instead of eggs when preparing veggie burgers, bean and grain loaves, or casseroles.

- arrowroot starch
- breadcrumbs
- cornstarch
- cracker meal
- flour (any kind will work, including gluten-free flours)
- instant potato flakes
- kuzu starch
- mashed potatoes
- matzo meal
- nut butters (such as almond and cashew butters)
- oatmeal, cooked
- peanut butter
- porridge
- potato starch
- rolled oats
- seed butters (such as tahini)
- soft tofu blended with flour (use the ratio of 1 tablespoon flour to 1/4 cup tofu)
- sweet potatoes, cooked and mashed
- tomato paste
- white sauce (made with nondairy milk)
- winter squash, cooked and mashed

many of these still contain eggs! These products are geared toward health-conscious consumers who are seeking to reduce the amount of cholesterol in their diets. Since the cholesterol in eggs is contained in the yolk, and because the mucilaginous white of the egg is what is required for leavening and binding, these "egg replacers" typically consist of egg whites and colorants.

A popular, totally egg-free egg replacer is marketed by Ener-G Foods and is sold in natural food stores and many supermarkets. This commercial egg replacer consists of a variety of vegetable starches and is available in powdered form. It must be beaten with a liquid prior to using. I recommend it for use in baked goods only.

From my experience, most cakes, cookies, baked goods, pancakes, and similar foods that do not require a great deal of leavening and only call for one egg can easily be made without the egg. Just be sure to add two or three additional tablespoons of liquid to the batter.

If you feel you need something to stand in for the egg in a recipe, first determine the attribute you are seeking: binding and thickening (for casseroles, loaves, and burgers) or lightening and raising (for baked goods).

Vegan Options to Bind and Lighten Baked Goods

Each suggestion is equivalent to one egg.

- 1 teaspoon Ener-G Egg Replacer beaten with 2 tablespoons water
- 2 tablespoons flour + 1½ teaspoons vegetable oil + ½ teaspoon baking powder beaten with 2 tablespoons water
- 1 tablespoon cornstarch + 1 tablespoon instant soymilk powder beaten with 2 tablespoons water
- ¼ cup soft tofu blended with the liquid called for in the recipe
- ¼ cup mashed banana or applesauce + ½ teaspoon baking powder
- 1 heaping tablespoon soy flour or chickpea flour beaten with 1 tablespoon water
- 1 tablespoon finely ground flaxseeds blended with 3 tablespoons water until frothy and viscous (see Flaxseed Goop Egg Replacer, page 17)

The lists on page 18 and above offer a variety of ingredients and mixtures to use in recipes in place of eggs. Some of these alternatives, such as nut butter or tomato paste, may affect the flavor, color, or texture of your finished product. Let the type of recipe you are preparing and the outcome you desire guide your selection and the quantity you need.

Bleu

Bleu had a rough start in life. He was refused by his mother shortly after birth, and the sheep farmer who "owned" him was unwilling to provide him with the special care he needed to survive. But at Farm Sanctuary, Bleu was given a second chance at life. He was so tiny when he arrived that he was able to curl up inside his food bowl. And believe it or not, that's where he slept the first few nights he was at the sanctuary. Soon Bleu was too big to sleep in his food bowl, though, and caregivers knew he needed to be around other sheep. When they first introduced him to another orphaned lamb, Persia, he was so excited he almost wiggled out of his skin. The two became fast friends and have been inseparable ever since.

Alternatives to protein-centered meals

People who have been vegetarians for any length of time soon become familiar with the single most-often-asked question by non-vegetarians: Where do you get your protein? (Probably the single most-often-asked question of vegans is: Where do you get your calcium? The simple answer to that question is the same place the cows get theirs: from plant foods. In fact, many foods, including most beans and seeds, are very rich in calcium, and some vegetables, such as many dark leafy greens, have as much calcium as dairy products, and sometimes more.) The truth is that protein is an integral part of virtually all foods, including vegetables and grains. In addition, protein deficiencies are extremely rare, not only in North America but in most countries around the globe. People who are starving experience total malnutrition, not just a lack of protein. Moreover, too much protein, particularly animal protein, can overtax our bodies and have potentially detrimental side effects.

Nevertheless, most people living in North America are accustomed to a meat-centered, high-protein diet as a way of life. The idea of switching to a meatless diet conjures up the image of a huge void, triggering an irrational terror that might as well be called Fear of the Empty Plate Syndrome. Vegetarians have long known that there are many exciting cuisines that do not resemble the conventional meat meal. We have learned from other cultures that a diet that doesn't revolve around animal protein is more healthful and is also among the most common diets worldwide.

Modern North American eating styles evolved from the erroneous belief that animal-based foods must form the foundation of a meal. While we now know this isn't true, it is nevertheless a comfortable standard we've become accustomed to. To ease the transition from a meat-centered diet to a more healthful and humane way of eating, I have developed many recipes that parallel this familiar pattern and replicate old favorites. Nevertheless, feel free to use the recipes in any type of meal design that suits your needs and tastes, whether it's the typical meat-potatoes-and-vegetable pattern or something entirely different.

The vegan diet lends itself naturally to creativity and experimentation. Longtime vegetarians are usually familiar with various approaches to meal planning, in addition to the conventional protein-centered meal. The beauty of vegan cuisine is its adaptability to varying styles, schedules, tastes, and levels of cooking ability. If you would like to experiment with some fresh ways of eating and planning meals, try a few of the following ideas.

Salad Meals

Raw vegetable meals are refreshing and can keep us feeling light and energized. For a heartier and more substantial meal, raw salads can be tossed or topped with cooked vegetables, potatoes, grains, pasta, beans, tofu, sautéed tempeh, vegan cold cuts, and raw or toasted nuts or seeds. Salad entrées may be served warm or chilled; hot or warm items served on top of chilled salad greens is a pleasing contrast. A dressing is optional, or it may be served on the side or passed at the table. Salad greens and fixings also make terrific sandwich fillings that are surprisingly hearty and satisfying.

Soup Meals

A hearty bean, grain, or vegetable soup makes a satisfying main course, especially when complemented by whole grain bread or crackers and perhaps a leafy green salad. Cold soups or thin soups make excellent summer fare, whereas thicker soups and stews are ideal for colder weather. Explore the soup recipes on pages 116–130.

Pasta Meals

Cook any pasta you prefer, and toss it with a vegan cream sauce, nut-based sauce, tomato sauce, vegetable-based sauce, or just a little olive oil and perhaps a splash of balsamic or umeboshi vinegar. To round out the meal, add steamed, sautéed, or grilled vegetables, grated raw vegetables, fresh herbs, cooked beans, tofu or tempeh, vegan burger crumbles, sliced vegan hot dogs or sausages, ground or chopped nuts or seeds, sprouts, or vegan Parmesan.

Baked Potato Meals

Baked potatoes smothered with steamed or sautéed vegetables, a creamy gravy, tomato sauce, soy sour cream, hummus, chopped onions, black olives, salsa, vegan pesto, nutritional yeast flakes, or whatever topping strikes your fancy are an easy, fun, and filling entrée any time of the year. Be sure to select baking potatoes, such as russet, Idaho, or Oregon-type potatoes.

Perfect Baked Potatoes

Preheat the oven to 375 degrees F. Scrub the potatoes thoroughly with a stiff brush under cold running water. Dry them well. Using a standard table fork, poke 8–12 deep holes all over each potato so moisture can escape during cooking. If desired, place the potatoes in a bowl and coat them lightly with vegetable oil. Then sprinkle them with kosher salt. The oil and salt are optional but do make for a better-tasting baked potato. Place the potatoes directly on the rack in the middle of the oven. If using the oil and salt, place a baking sheet on the lower rack to catch any drippings. Bake for 1 to 1½ hours (or longer, if necessary), or until the skin feels crisp but the flesh beneath feels soft. To serve, create a dotted line from end to end with the tines of a fork, then crack the potato open by squeezing the ends toward each other. The potato will pop right open. Be careful, as it will release some steam. Use oven mitts when handling hot potatoes so you don't burn your fingers.

Grain Meals

Prepare grain meals just like pasta meals, but substitute the grain of your choice, such as rice (brown, basmati, or jasmine), wild rice, bulgur, whole wheat couscous, quinoa, millet, or polenta (cooked corn grits).

Vegetable Meals

Prepare three to six vegetables using your favorite method (steam, stir-fry, bake, broil, or grill). For a more substantial meal, include a potato, grain, pasta, or winter squash, and add cooked beans and/or serve a whole grain bread. Another option is to use a medley of roasted vegetables as a sandwich filling. Vegetable meals are delicious and interesting, with an abundance of visual appeal. For an array of year-round delights, select vegetables that are plentiful and in season where you live.

instead of

You can't sell the cow and have the milk too.

use

You can't sell the orchard and have the apples too.

Ingredients that may be new to you

Agar: Also known as agar-agar, this extract of red algae is used as a thickener, jelling agent, and stabilizer in foods. It is available in flakes, bars, or powder. If you need to substitute powder for flakes, use $\frac{1}{2}$ to 1 teaspoon of powder for every tablespoon of flakes. Agar is sold in natural food stores (look in the macrobiotic section) and in Asian grocery stores (where it often is less expensive). Also check the online retailers listed in Mail Order Sources (page 235). If you can only find agar in bars (which is sometimes the case in Asian grocery stores), simply grind up a portion of the bar in a food processor until it is the consistency of flakes. For the best results, allow agar flakes to "bloom" in cold or cool water for 10–15 minutes before boiling. This will ensure that the flakes are fully dissolved. Stored in an airtight container at room temperature, agar will keep indefinitely.

Agave syrup: Agave (pronounced uh-GAH-vay) syrup, also known as agave nectar, is a relatively recent sweetener. The agave plant has long been cultivated in the hilly, semi-arid soil of Mexico. Its fleshy leaves cover the pineapple-shaped heart of the plant, which contains a sweet sticky juice. The fermented juice is used to make tequila. Agave syrup has a mild, neutral flavor. Light-colored agave syrup is somewhat bland; the darker syrup has a slightly richer flavor. Either one is an ideal replacement for honey in beverages or recipes. Agave syrup can also replace rice syrup measure for measure. Try agave syrup in hot tea or as a topping for oatmeal or pancakes. Stored in a sealed container at room temperature, agave syrup will keep indefinitely.

Almond butter: Almond butter is made from the sweet almond variety and is sold in jars in most natural food stores. Whether raw or roasted, almond butter is mildly sweet and a delicious alternative to peanut butter as a sandwich spread. It can also be used as a base for creamy soups, sauces, and dips. Because almond butter contains no additives or stabilizers, the oil and solids sometimes separate in the jar; they can easily be stirred together shortly before using. Most almond butter is made without preservatives and should be kept refrigerated to prevent rancidity. If stored in a tightly sealed jar in the refrigerator, almond butter will keep for up to three months.

Arrowroot: Arrowroot is a white, powdery thickening agent that is ground more finely than flour. It is often preferable to cornstarch because it provides a clear finish rather than a cloudy paste. Arrowroot is extracted from rhizomes (roots in the same botanical family as ginger) and was traditionally used by Native Americans to heal arrow wounds, hence the name. Arrowroot is less refined than cornstarch and thickens at lower temperatures than either flour or cornstarch. It must first be combined with a cool liquid or water before using. Replace cornstarch with arrowroot measure for measure in recipes. Look for it at your natural food store. Stored at room temperature in an airtight, moisture-proof container or heavy-duty zipper-lock plastic bag, arrowroot will keep indefinitely.

Baking powder, aluminum-free: Most commercial brands of double-acting baking powder contain sodium aluminum sulfate, which may be harmful to your health. Natural food stores and some supermarkets carry baking powders that do not contain aluminum salts. Two common brands are Rumford and Featherweight. Store baking powder at room temperature. Most tins will have an expiration date stamped on them.

Balsamic vinegar: Balsamic vinegar is a dark brown vinegar with an exquisite, delicate, sweet-and-sour flavor. It is made from sweet Trebbiano grapes and acquires its dark color and pungency from being aged in wooden barrels for a minimum of ten years. Originally produced only in Modena, Italy, balsamic vinegar is now made in many places, chiefly in California. There is also a white balsamic vinegar (pale gold in color), which has a sharper twist to it than most darker balsamic varieties and works well when a light-colored dressing is desired. Balsamic vinegar is available in supermarkets, Italian markets, gourmet shops, and natural food stores. Store tightly sealed in a cool, dark place (do not refrigerate). It will keep indefinitely.

Brown rice vinegar: This vinegar, distilled from rice, has less of a sharp tang than cider vinegar and just a hint of sweetness. The Japanese use it in making rice for sushi, in dipping sauces, and to create many pickled dishes. It is also good for marinating tofu (with soy sauce and ginger) and in grain and bean salads. Widely used in Asian dishes, rice vinegar is popular because its light color does not significantly alter the appearance of the food. It is available in natural food stores and some supermarkets. Store tightly sealed in a cool, dark place (do not refrigerate). It will keep indefinitely.

Chickpea flour: This versatile, delicious, gluten-free flour is also known as *besan, gram flour, cici flour, chana flour*, and *garbanzo bean flour.* It is tan in color because it is made from dried (uncooked) chickpeas. Chickpea flour is commonly used in Indian, Italian, and some Middle Eastern cuisines. Look for it in Indian markets and natural food stores. For the longest shelf life, store it in an airtight container in the freezer. It will keep for up to five months.

Couscous: A staple of North African and several Mediterranean cuisines, couscous is semolina that is either granular (the texture of uncooked corn grits) or round, about the size of small beads (also known as Israeli couscous). Most natural food stores, Middle Eastern markets, and large supermarkets sell precooked couscous. Granular couscous literally cooks in seconds, and giant pearl couscous cooks in about 12 minutes.

Frozen juice concentrate: Frozen juice concentrates make handy sweeteners. Because they are concentrated and do not contain added sugar, they can help reduce the amount of sugar in a recipe while adding a boost of flavor and nutrition. Use calcium-fortified juice concentrates to add more calcium to your food. Unless the juice concentrate is solidly frozen, there is usually no need to defrost it before using it. Simply spoon out the amount you need, cover the container (a small piece of plastic wrap kept in place with a rubber band works well), and return it to the freezer.

Kuzu; kudzu starch: This thickener is made from the tuber of the kudzu plant, the obnoxious vine that was imported from Japan a number of years ago and is now growing out of control over most of the South. It is used as a thickening agent, similar to cornstarch, arrowroot, and potato starch. In Japan, kuzu is commonly used in soups, jelled foods, deep-fried foods, grains, and confections. It comes in small chunks. To measure, crush the chunks into a powder. To thicken a hot liquid, mix the powder with an equal amount of cold water, then stir the mixture into the hot liquid and simmer for a few minutes until the sauce is thickened. Look for kuzu in the macrobiotic section of your natural food store. Stored at room temperature in an airtight, moisture-proof container or heavy-duty zipper-lock plastic bag, kuzu will keep indefinitely.

Liquid smoke: Also called liquid hickory smoke, this handy flavoring is used to replicate the smoky taste of ham, bacon, or other smoked meats. Look for brands that contain only water, vinegar, and natural hickory smoke (some brands may also contain brown sugar and caramel coloring). Just a few drops are usually sufficient to effectively flavor most dishes. Liquid smoke is available in supermarkets. Store it at room temperature. It will keep indefinitely.

Millet: Millet is a staple grain for nearly one-third of the world's population, especially in Asia and Africa. In the United States, however, it is used mostly for birdseed. Millet is rich in protein and comes in several varieties. Its bland flavor makes it a good background grain for highly seasoned dishes. It can be made into a pilaf, similar to rice, or cooked with plenty of water and used to make a hot cereal similar to polenta. Look for millet in your natural food store.

Miso: Miso is a salty, savory bean paste that has been a mainstay of Japanese cooking for hundreds of years. Miso is made by mixing cooked soybeans (or sometimes other beans, such as chickpeas or adzuki beans), salt, a grain (usually barley or rice), and a starter (fermenting agent) called *koji*. There are many varieties of miso. They are classified by color (white, red, brown, and yellow), flavor (sweet or salty), and ingredients (usually depending on the type of grain used). Darker miso, which is usually red or brown, tends to be more salty. White miso tends to have a slightly sweeter flavor. Yellow miso is light yellowish in color and is not as sweet as white miso. Light miso (white and yellow) are usually made from rice and soybeans. For the recipes in this book that call for miso, white, yellow, and chickpea miso are recommended.

Miso can be smooth or chunky. Some Western companies produce a pasteurized miso that contains preservatives. Traditionally produced miso is unpasteurized and is aged for many months. It contains active enzymes that make it easy to digest; it also has a better flavor and is widely available.

Miso is most often sold in natural food stores and in Asian markets, but it is increasingly available in large supermarkets. Although some food co-ops sell miso in bulk, it is usually available in plastic tubs or glass jars in the refrigerated section of the store. Miso should be stored in the refrigerator, where it will keep for six to twelve months or longer (check the "use by" or expiration date on the container). The film of white mold that sometimes forms along the top is harmless and can either be scraped off or stirred right into the miso.

Nori flakes, green (aonori): Made from a different variety of sea vegetable than the type of nori used for sushi, this product has a blue-green tint and a distinctive fragrance. It's a flavorful condiment, both subtly sweet and salty. The bright green flakes are delicious on grains, noodles, vegetables, tofu, and salads. It is also traditionally sprinkled on okonomiyaki (see recipe on page 142). Stored in a sealed container at room temperature, green nori flakes will keep indefinitely.

Nutritional yeast: This is an inert yeast, which means it has no leavening capabilities (it cannot make bread rise) because it is toasted at high temperatures and deactivated. Nutritional yeast is used as a nutrition booster and flavor enhancer in recipes. Most people find it has a delicious cheesy taste.

The type of nutritional yeast I recommend is called Vegetarian Support Formula. You can usually find it in the bulk bins or on the supplement shelf at your natural food store in a bright yellow tin packaged by Kal (look for the domestic nutritional yeast by Kal, not the imported one). Also check Mail Order Sources (page 235) for online retailers.

Vegetarian Support Formula is a primary grown yeast, which means it is grown as a food crop and is not the by-product of any other industry. (Brewer's yeast is a by-product of beer making, and torula yeast is a by-product of the paper industry.) In addition to its wonderful flavor, Vegetarian Support Formula nutritional yeast is rich in B vitamins, including vitamin B_{12}, and many other vital nutrients. Store nutritional yeast at room temperature in an airtight container or jar, away from moisture, direct light, and heat. Do not store nutritional yeast in the refrigerator or freezer, as it will become gummy. It will keep indefinitely, and the nutrient profile will remain stable for at least one year from purchase.

Vegetarian Support Formula nutritional yeast comes in large flakes, mini flakes, and powder. **The recipes in this book call only for the large flakes.** If you cannot find the large flakes, substitute the following amounts for every 2 tablespoons of nutritional yeast called for in a recipe: for mini flakes, use 1½ tablespoons; for powder, use 1 heaping tablespoon. *It is important to reduce the amount of nutritional yeast according to the size of the flakes, because the more powdery it is, the more compressed and concentrated it will be; thus the flavor will be more intense and overpowering.*

Quinoa: Quinoa (pronounced KEEN-wah) was a staple of the ancient Incas, who called it "the mother grain." It is still an important food in South American cuisine. Quinoa contains more protein than any other grain, is higher in unsaturated fats and lower in carbohydrates than most grains, and provides a rich and balanced source of vital nutrients. Quinoa looks like a tiny, ivory-colored bead. It is prepared like rice, but cooks in half the time. As it cooks, it expands to about four times its original volume. Cooked quinoa is similar in appearance to couscous, and its light, delicate flavor makes it a good alternative to rice in main dishes, salads, soups, and side dishes. Look for quinoa in your natural food store and some supermarkets.

Rice syrup: This is a thick, mild sweetener made from sprouted rice. It resembles maple syrup, but it is not as sweet and has a lighter color and more delicate flavor.

Seitan: Seitan is a chewy, protein-rich food made from hard winter wheat. It resembles meat in texture and taste. Loosely translated, the Japanese word *seitan* means "is protein." Seitan is called *kofu* in China. In North America, it is commonly referred to as "wheat meat."

Seitan (pronounced say-tan) is made by making a dough out of wheat flour and water, and kneading it to develop the protein (called *gluten*) while rinsing away the starch and bran. After this process, only the gluten remains. It is then simmered in water or vegetable broth that has been seasoned with soy sauce to produce a chewy, firm, meatlike food. The longer the gluten simmers, the firmer it becomes. Seitan can then be sliced and added to sautéed or stir-fried dishes, diced and stirred into stews, soups, or casseroles, or ground and formed into roasts.

Prepared seitan chunks are sold refrigerated or frozen at natural food stores; they are sometimes packaged in a marinade or light broth. Vital wheat gluten, also called instant gluten flour, is also available. Vital wheat gluten is wheat flour that has had the starch and bran already removed, leaving only the powdered wheat gluten. Homemade seitan made from vital wheat gluten is less expensive than packaged seitan and is much faster and easier to prepare than seitan made from scratch. Do not use any other flour to make the seitan recipes in this book. ("High-gluten flour" is not the same as vital wheat gluten; it is simply regular wheat flour with a bit more gluten added to give bread a higher rise. It cannot be used for making seitan!)

You can make seitan from vital wheat gluten using the Basic Simmered Seitan recipe on pages 48–49. Also try Ground Seitan (page 50), Pot Roast (page 156), and Barbecue-Style Braised Short "Ribs" (page 154), which provide even more unique and delicious ways to use vital wheat gluten.

Prepared seitan can be stored in the refrigerator for up to one week, or in the freezer for up to six months. People who are allergic to wheat or wheat gluten should avoid seitan. See Mail Order Sources (page 235) for online retailers that sell vital wheat gluten, if you cannot find it locally.

Sesame oil, toasted: Toasted sesame oil is a dark, aromatic oil made from toasted sesame seeds. It is prized for its tempting, delicious flavor and is used primarily as a seasoning. Toasted sesame oil is available in natural food stores, Asian grocery stores, and some supermarkets.

Soy sauce: What many people think of as soy sauce is little more than hydrolyzed vegetable protein, sugar, and caramel coloring. However, excellent naturally fermented Chinese and Japanese soy sauce is readily available in natural food stores and most supermarkets. Check the labels closely and make sure the product contains only soybeans, salt, water, and possibly wheat. Good-quality soy sauces with reduced sodium are also available and are highly recommended. Naturally fermented soy sauce will be labeled as *shoyu* or *tamari*. If you have a sensitivity to yeasted or fermented foods, look for Bragg Liquid Aminos, a rich, beefy-tasting soy product that has not been fermented.

Tahini: Tahini is a smooth, creamy, tan-colored paste made by finely grinding hulled raw or roasted sesame seeds. It is an essential ingredient in many Middle Eastern recipes and adds a wonderful texture and nutty flavor to spreads, sauces, and dressings. Tahini may be very thick, like peanut butter, or thin and slightly runny depending on the brand. As with all unrefined nut and seed butters, store tahini in the refrigerator to keep it from becoming rancid and to keep the oil and solids from separating. However, if the oil does separate out, simply stir it back in. Tahini is available in many supermarkets, Middle Eastern grocery stores, natural food stores, and from online retailers (see Mail Order Sources, page 235).

Tempeh: This high-protein meat alternative hails originally from Indonesia. To make tempeh (pronounced tem-pay), whole soybeans are mixed with grains, usually rice or millet, and then incubated with a starter, which begins the fermentation process.

Because tempeh is perishable, it is usually sold in the refrigerated or frozen food section of natural food stores and Asian markets. Frozen tempeh can be kept for about three months. Once it is defrosted, it must be refrigerated and used within seven to ten days. Because tempeh is a fermented product, a light layer of mold can sometimes form on the outside. This mold is harmless and edible.

Tempeh contains a live, active culture, so it must always be consumed cooked (otherwise the culture will remain active in your stomach and make you sick). Because of its chewy texture and mild nutty flavor, reminiscent of mushrooms, tempeh makes a good meat replacement in many dishes. Tempeh is especially tasty sautéed in oil or cooked on the grill. There are many delicious ways to prepare tempeh. It can be steamed and then marinated in barbecue sauce or lemon marinade and grilled until brown; cut into chunks, sautéed, and added to chili or spaghetti sauce; and stir-fried with vegetables and a stir-fry sauce. Shredded tempeh can be used to make a "chicken" salad or tunalike spread for sandwiches. Try Fowl Play Tempeh Salad (page 93), Tempeh Tuna Spread (page 94), Messy Mikes (page 98), Barbecued Tempeh (page 100), Tempeh Tacos (page 112), Chuckwagon Stew (page 129), and Sweet-and-Sour Tempeh (page 133).

Tofu: Tofu is a delicate, mild, high-protein curd cheese made from soymilk. Chinese names for tofu that indicate its high status translate as "meat without bones" and "meat from the fields." To make tofu, a curdling agent is added

Regular Tofu

Regular tofu (also known as Chinese tofu or water-packed tofu) is made by pressing the curds very assertively in order to remove as much of the liquid as possible. The result is a firm but slightly grainy tofu that adds texture and "chew" to recipes. You can easily recognize regular tofu because it is always packed in water. Regular tofu is widely available in natural food stores and in most supermarkets, usually in vacuum-sealed tubs or packages containing a ten-ounce to one-pound portion. In natural food stores it is commonly found in the refrigerator case, often near the dairy foods. In supermarkets it is usually found in the produce section. The packages should be stamped with a freshness or expiration date. Regular tofu is also available in bulk in Asian markets and natural food co-ops.

Once a package of tofu is opened, the unused portion of tofu should be stored submerged in water in a clean, covered container in the refrigerator. Rinse the tofu and replace the old water with fresh water daily. Stored this way, tofu will keep for about five days in the refrigerator.

Regular tofu should be rinsed and patted dry before using. If your tofu begins to smell a little sour before you are able to use it, you can freshen it by simmering it in water for 10 minutes. Tofu freshened in this fashion will become slightly firmer and plumper. If you are going to use the tofu uncooked or "raw" (such as in a tofu salad or blended dressing), you may want to simmer it in water to cover for 10 minutes. This will destroy any harmful bacteria that may have accumulated in transit or during storage. Simmering is especially important for tofu sold in bulk or from places where its handling or storage are questionable.

to soymilk and the curds that result are then pressed into blocks. Tofu that is coagulated with calcium salts provides an excellent source of calcium.

There are two basic types of tofu: regular and silken. Depending on the manufacturer, both kinds of tofu may come in only one firmness or may be available in a range of firmnesses from soft, to firm, to extra firm. Because tofu has a mild flavor and a porous texture, it readily absorbs the flavors of other ingredients. This makes tofu a perfect addition to a wide variety of both savory and sweet dishes.

Flavored tofu is also available. It may be infused with herbs and spices to produce a Mediterranean or curry flavor. Sometimes it is baked or steamed with a sauce for a savory product that doesn't require any other preparation. Reduced-fat tofu is also available.

TSP (textured soy protein): Textured soy protein (TSP) is a fibrous, dehydrated meat alternative that is usually made by a process that isolates the proteins from soy flour. TSP is often an ingredient in prepared meat alternatives, such as vegetarian hot dogs, burgers, chicken-style patties and nuggets, cold cuts, burger crumbles, and sausage-style links. It is also a primary ingredient in many packaged mixes for vegetarian burgers and chili. Textured soy protein is a good substitute for ground beef in dishes such as tacos, chili, and stews.

TSP is usually sold as a dry (dehydrated) product that must be rehydrated before it can be used in recipes. It is available in natural food stores and some well-stocked supermarkets; it can also be purchased through online retailers (see Mail Order Sources, page 235). Use only organic TSP, since nonorganic soy is typically genetically modified. Once rehydrated, TSP granules can be used as a substitute for ground beef in recipes such as chili, spaghetti sauce, and tacos. TSP is also available in chunks that can be used to replace meat in stews and soups. The chunks are sometimes flavored to taste like beef, sausage, or chicken. Depending on the type, TSP may contain salt, flavorings, and other additives, so be sure to read the labels carefully before purchasing, if you have any concerns. Stored in an airtight container at room temperature, dehydrated textured soy protein will keep for at least six months.

To rehydrate TSP granules, add ¾ cup boiling water to 1 cup TSP granules and let stand for 10 minutes, or until the water is absorbed. Rehydrated TSP should be kept refrigerated and used within five days.

Umeboshi plums: These sour, pickled plums are actually Japanese green apricots. Pickled in a salt brine and red shiso leaves for a minimum of one year, they have a slightly fruity, salty taste. Umeboshi plums are traditionally served as a savory condiment with various dishes, including grains. In macrobiotics, they are reputed to aid in the cure of a wide array of ailments—from stomachaches to migraines. The best-quality umeboshi plums are the most expensive, but they are typically used in small amounts, so one jar will last a long time. Stored in a tightly covered container in the refrigerator, umeboshi plums will keep for about six months.

Umeboshi plum paste: This tangy, salty, concentrated condiment and seasoning is a purée made from umeboshi plums. Use it sparingly, as it is quite

Silken Tofu

For silken tofu (also known as Japanese tofu), the curds are not pressed at all. Instead, they are permitted to rest with the whey, which results in a creamy, custardlike product. This smooth consistency makes silken tofu ideal for using in sauces, creamy dressings and soups, custards, and puddings.

Mori-Nu brand silken tofu (the one I recommend) is commonly found in aseptic cartons on your grocer's shelf. Aseptically packed tofu is shelf stable and does not need to be refrigerated until it is opened. The carton will be stamped with an expiration date. Once the carton is opened, the tofu should be refrigerated and used within three to four days.

Freezing Tofu

Some cooks like to freeze regular tofu to make it chewier or extend its shelf life (freezing silken tofu is not recommended). Simply place the whole package—water and all—into the freezer until it is frozen solid. Alternatively, open the package, drain off the liquid, and squeeze out the excess moisture. To make it easier to defrost, cut the block into ½-pound or ¼-pound portions. (This is especially handy for small households.) Then wrap each portion tightly with plastic wrap, or place the tofu pieces in individual airtight, freezer-safe containers.

Frozen tofu will keep in the freezer for three to five months. As it freezes, the tofu will change color from white to caramel. Defrost frozen tofu in the refrigerator, or place it in a heatproof bowl and pour boiling water over it. Let the tofu rest in the hot water until it is completely defrosted, turning it over occasionally. If necessary, drain the water when it has cooled, then cover the tofu again with boiling water. Once it is fully defrosted, pour off the liquid and firmly squeeze out the excess moisture. Defrosted frozen tofu will be firmer, spongier, and have a slightly chewier texture. It can be marinated and then baked, sautéed, or grilled. It can also be shredded or crumbled and added to chili, tacos, or spaghetti sauce to create a meaty texture.

salty. When stored for long periods, salt crystals may rise to the surface and form a white crust. Simply scrape off any white areas (they are not harmful), and stir the remaining paste well. Stored in a tightly covered container in the refrigerator, umeboshi plum paste will keep for six to twelve months.

Umeboshi vinegar: Umeboshi vinegar is a pink brine with a deep, fruity aroma and a fruity sour flavor. It is a by-product produced when umeboshi (Japanese pickled plums) is made. Technically, it is not classified as a vinegar because it contains salt, but it is a good substitute for vinegar and salt in any recipe. It has a light, acetic tang that lends itself well to salad dressings and adds delicious flavor to steamed vegetables. Store it tightly sealed in a cool, dark place (do not refrigerate). It will keep indefinitely.

Vegetable broth, light and dark: Vegetable broth adds an extra flavor dimension to recipes and makes dishes taste more complex and sophisticated than when water alone is used. It is easy to make homemade vegetable broth. Simply save your vegetable scraps and peelings, carrot tops, and parsley and spinach stems, and store them in a covered container in the refrigerator or freezer. When you are ready to make broth, simply put the scraps in a large, heavy pot and cover them with water (approximately 2 parts water to 1 part vegetables) and bring to a boil. Lower the heat, cover, and simmer for about 1 hour. Strain well. Use immediately or store in a covered container in the refrigerator or freezer. The broth can also be frozen in ice cube trays for easy retrieval. Another handy way to make quick vegetable broth is by saving the water from steamed vegetables, potatoes, pasta, home-cooked beans, or the simmering broth from homemade seitan.

Light vegetable broth is usually made with vegetables and sometimes nutritional yeast. It is delicate, flavorful, and versatile, and is often intended as a vegetarian version of chicken broth. Dark vegetable broth is usually made with soy sauce, yeast extract, and/or a mushroom base, and vegetables. It has a rich "beefy" flavor (without the beef, of course).

There are several high-quality light vegetable broths, bouillon powders, and bouillon cubes on the market. Three good brands are Rapunzel (cubes and powder), Imagine Foods (prepared broth in aseptic cartons), and Superior Touch Better Than Bouillon No Chicken Base (concentrated paste). Dark vegetable broth is a little harder to find. Superior Touch brand Better Than Bouillon Vegetable Base, No Beef Base, and Mushroom Base products are vegan and make a superb dark vegetable broth. These are concentrated pastes, not powders, cubes, or liquids. Look for all of these products at your natural food store, gourmet store, supermarket, or online retailer.

Pressing Tofu

Firm regular tofu is at its best when it is pressed. Although pressing is purely optional, it does significantly improve the texture of regular tofu. This simple method removes excess moisture, leaving the tofu firmer and much denser. (This step is unnecessary for flavored and smoked tofu, as they have already been pressed during processing.) Pressed tofu is suitable for any of the recipes in this book calling for regular tofu (pressing is not recommended for silken tofu). Pressing is a particularly choice treatment for tofu that will be marinated. Although it is an additional step that takes a bit of extra time, it requires very little effort. Here's how to do it:

1. Cut a ½-pound block (8 ounces) into 2 slabs, or a 1-pound block into 3 or 4 slabs, slicing it either horizontally or vertically depending on how you will be using it. If desired, wrap each slab separately in a clean tea towel or thick paper towels. Lay the slabs flat, in a single layer, between two plates. The best place to do this is in your kitchen sink.

2. Place a heavy weight on the top plate. I like to use a jar of dried beans or the base of a blender, but almost any small, relatively heavy object will do. The idea is to apply firm pressure to the tofu without crushing it. The sides of the tofu should be bulging slightly but not cracking.

3. Let the tofu rest for 30–60 minutes. Drain off and discard the liquid that accumulates, and pat the tofu dry with a clean tea towel or paper towels. Do not press the tofu longer than 60 minutes.

4. Use immediately, or cover and refrigerate for up to two days.

How to Use Tofu

Since tofu has been used for centuries in Asian countries, it is a common ingredient in a variety of Asian dishes. But its increasing popularity in Western countries has given rise to many new uses for this versatile food. Here are a few ways to enjoy tofu with an international flair:

- Add chunks of soft tofu (regular or silken) to miso soup for a traditional Japanese delicacy.
- Stir-fry chunks of firm regular tofu with vegetables, soy sauce, and garlic for Chinese-inspired cuisine.
- Add chunks of firm tofu to a curry-seasoned sauce for the flavors of India or Thailand.
- Marinate tofu in soy sauce and fresh ginger, and then stir-fry it with garlic, onions, and hot peppers for a Korean-style dish.

Here are some more delicious ways to prepare tofu:

- Add chunks of firm regular tofu to vegetable soups or stews. Allow it to simmer for at least 30 minutes so the tofu can absorb the other flavors in the dish.
- Blend regular tofu with cooked spinach, ground nuts or ground sesame seeds, and salt, and use the mixture to stuff lasagne layers or pasta shells (see Baked Stuffed Shells, page 151, and Unstuffed Shells, page 153).

- Mash regular tofu with vegan mayonnaise and chopped celery for an egg-free egg-salad-like sandwich spread. For a yellow color, add a pinch of ground turmeric. Or try Missing Egg Salad (page 92).
- Scramble coarsely mashed regular tofu with onions, mushrooms, herbs, and a large sprinkle of nutritional yeast for a delicious breakfast scramble. Or try Scrambled Tofu (page 65).
- Purée silken or regular tofu with peanut butter or almond butter to make a fluffy sandwich spread.
- Blend soft regular or silken tofu with apple juice and bananas to make a breakfast smoothie.
- Blend firm silken tofu with a small amount of freshly squeezed lemon juice and chopped chives and use it to top a baked potato. Or try Sour Dressing (page 209).
- Purée silken tofu with herbs and cooked carrots or spinach; then thin it with plain soymilk or vegetable broth to make a creamy soup.
- Purée firm silken tofu with melted chocolate chips for a luscious creamy pie filling. Or try Rich Chocolate Pudding or Pie Filling (page 212).

If you cannot find a good-quality dark vegetable broth and are in a quandary, you can make a fast, effortless version. Simply combine a small amount of reduced-sodium soy sauce, Bragg Liquid Aminos (a rich, beefy-tasting soy product that has not been fermented), or dark miso with water. This will not have the deep, complex flavors of true vegetable broth, but it will work in a pinch.

Some recipes specify dark or light vegetable broth. When just "vegetable broth" is listed in a recipe, you can use whichever one you prefer or happen to have on hand. *Important: If your vegetable broth contains salt, be sure to reduce the amount of salt in the recipe accordingly!*

Vital wheat gluten: Vital wheat gluten, also called instant gluten flour, is the pure protein (gluten) part of the wheat kernel obtained from wheat flour that has had the starch and bran removed. Do *not* substitute any other flour. Vital wheat gluten is used to make seitan, also known as wheat meat, a protein-rich meat alternative that has been a popular food in Asian countries for thousands of years.

Made in the traditional fashion, seitan is time-consuming and labor intensive to prepare, but with vital wheat gluten, which needs only to be mixed with seasonings and a liquid, you can prepare seitan quickly and easily at home. (High-gluten flour is regular wheat flour with extra gluten added to make breads rise higher; is it *not* the same as vital wheat gluten or instant gluten flour, and *cannot* be used to make seitan.) Stored in an airtight container at room temperature, vital wheat gluten will keep indefinitely. You can find vital wheat gluten at natural food stores. Also check the online retailers in Mail Order Sources (page 235).

Zest: Zest is the perfumy outer portion of the colored peel of citrus fruits (it does not include the bitter white pith on the underside of the peel). The aromatic oils in citrus zest add a bright, tart flavor to raw, cooked, sweet, or savory food. Remove the zest with a special citrus zester, available in supermarkets, cookware shops, and department stores.

Lily

Against all odds, Lily escaped the slaughterhouse—twice! First, she managed to fall off a hog truck as it barreled down the freeway on its way to a pork processing plant. She lived with the family who rescued her for a time. Then, some months later, after being surrendered into the care of a local farmer, she was almost sent to slaughter again. This time, she was saved by a compassionate woman who heard of her plight. At Farm Sanctuary, Lily's safety is, at last, guaranteed. Her future is bright, with long days of napping in the sun, wading in the cool pond, and carousing with friends to look forward to.

Buying conventional or organic produce

Organically grown food (that is, food produced without the use of chemically formulated fertilizers, growth stimulants, antibiotics, or pesticides) is not only good for the environment and the animals, it's also good for our own health. For those of us on a budget, however, buying organic produce, which often is priced much higher than conventionally grown foods, is not always practical. When that is the case, we need to be selective with our purchases. If possible, buy produce directly from local farmers at farmers' markets, as they typically use minimal chemicals. The following lists are based on the findings of the United States Department of Agriculture (USDA) Pesticide Data Program. For more information about pesticide use, health hazards, and current research, visit Food News at www.foodnews.org.

Highest in Pesticides (the dirty dozen)

These twelve popular fresh fruits and vegetables are consistently the most contaminated with pesticides. Always buy these organic.

- Apples
- Bell peppers
- Celery
- Cherries
- Grapes (imported)
- Nectarines
- Peaches
- Pears
- Potatoes
- Red raspberries
- Spinach
- Strawberries

instead of

Eating crow.

use

Eating humble pie.

Lowest in Pesticides (consistently clean)

These twelve popular fresh fruits and vegetables consistently have the lowest levels of pesticides. Buy these either conventional or organic.

- Asparagus
- Avocados
- Bananas
- Broccoli
- Cauliflower
- Corn (sweet)
- Kiwifruit
- Mangoes
- Onions
- Papaya
- Peas (sweet)
- Pineapples

Genetically Engineered Foods

For information about organics, genetically modified foods, and biotechnology, visit the Organic Consumers Association at www.organicconsumers.org. The following genetically engineered crops are allowed in the U.S. food supply. To avoid genetically engineered organisms in your food, always buy these organic.

- Canola (canola oil)
- Chicory (radicchio)
- Corn (sweet corn, popcorn, cornstarch, corn oil)
- Cotton (cottonseed oil)
- Cucumber
- Flax (flaxseeds)
- Papaya
- Potato
- Soy
- Squash
- Sugarbeet
- Tomato
- Watermelon
- Zucchini

instead of

You can lead a horse to water but you can't make him drink.

use

You can sow fertile seeds but you can't make them sprout.

Getting started

Tips on Blending

Several of the milks, soups, sauces, uncheeses, and other recipes in this book will require blending. This must be done in several small batches, depending on the capacity of your blender container, so be sure to take this into consideration when processing. Don't overfill your blender jar! This is important because mixtures temporarily expand with air during processing, and without sufficient space, the contents of the blender jar will not be able to move freely and could possibly overflow.

Keep in mind that hot liquids, such as soups and sauces, release a surprising amount of steam when puréed. This can force the lid of the blender jar to pop off or propel a spray of hot mixture out from under the lid rim. As a standard precautionary measure, fill the blender container no more than halfway when blending hot nut or rice milks, puréeing soups, or processing other hot liquids, and use a kitchen towel to hold the lid (or the insert in the center of the lid) slightly ajar to allow some of the steam to escape.

To purée or blend soup in batches, transfer a small portion of the mixture to a blender. Process until the mixture is completely smooth. Pour the blended mixture into a large bowl, and process the remaining soup in the same manner, adding the blended mixture to the bowl after each batch has been processed. To purée soup safely, you may need to blend it in two, three, or four batches. When all the soup has been puréed, transfer the blended mixture back to the soup pot, and proceed with the recipe as directed.

For soups and sauces that do not need to be completely smooth, an immersion blender is an acceptable alternative. Just be sure to use suitable cookware (immersion blenders may scratch and damage nonstick or enameled cookware), and follow the manufacturer's instructions.

My favorite blender is a Vita-Mix. This high-performance, top-of-the-line equipment is among the most-used tools in my kitchen. It is expensive, but it will last a lifetime. It has much more torque and horsepower than standard blenders for home use, which means there is far less stopping and stirring needed. In addition, it can perform some tasks that are generally done in a food processor, and it can do certain jobs that neither blenders nor food processors can do (such as make nut butter or blend whole fruits and vegetables into juice). The large container also means that most of the recipes in this book that would usually require blending in several batches can be done in a Vita-Mix in a single batch. For more information on the Vita-Mix, visit www.vitamix.com.

Reducing Fat and Oil

If you want to reduce the amount of fat in recipes, you can do one of the following:

- Omit the oil used to sauté and stir-fry food. Instead, use nonalcoholic wine, vegetable broth, apple juice, herbal tea, or water.

- Cut in half or omit the oil used in savory dishes. It often isn't needed, and most dishes taste just as delicious with less fat.

- Replace a large portion or all of the oil in baked goods with home-made or store-bought fruit purée (prune purée is ideal), commercial fruit-based fat replacer (available in natural food stores and some supermarkets), mashed bananas, or applesauce (which is easy, inexpensive, and convenient).

- The easiest way to create a low-fat or no-fat sauce or salad dressing is simply to leave out the oil and substitute an equal amount of vegetable broth or water. The result will be a thinner sauce or dressing, but the flavor should be intact. You can also use my quick and simple Oil Replacer (page 40), which makes wonderful fat-free salad dressings. Simply replace all or part of the oil in a conventional sauce or dressing with Oil Replacer.

- Dressings and sauces that incorporate nuts, seeds, nut or seed butters, olives, or avocado require these ingredients to achieve a particular taste and consistency. Nevertheless, these ingredients may be reduced by one-quarter to one-half and replaced with an equal amount of silken tofu (regular or fat-reduced "lite") without dramatically affecting the recipe's outcome. Keep in mind that silken tofu will produce a creamier sauce or dressing with a lighter color and taste. It also requires blending in order to obtain a smooth consistency.

Oil Replacer

makes about 1 cup

This light, starch-based mixture is the ideal substitute for part or all of the oil called for in salad dressings and sauces. Be sure to start with cold water to prevent the starch from clumping. Note: Oil Replacer cannot be used instead of oil for sautéing or frying.

1 cup cold water

4 teaspoons arrowroot, kuzu, or cornstarch

Place the water and starch in a small saucepan, and whisk until the starch is well dissolved. Bring to a simmer over medium heat. Cook, stirring almost constantly, until the mixture is clear and slightly thickened (it should be about the consistency of oil). Cool completely. Stored in a covered container in the refrigerator, Oil Replacer will keep for about 1 week.

Properly Heating a Skillet

When cooking pancakes or French toast, scrambling tofu, or sautéing vegetables, it is important to make sure your skillet is properly heated after adding oil and before adding other ingredients. To test if the skillet is properly heated, moisten your fingertips with water and flick a few droplets into the pan. If the droplets sputter and steam, the skillet is ready. If the droplets skitter rapidly across the bottom, the skillet is extremely hot and the heat may be turned up too high.

Keeping Pancakes and French Toast Warm

It's wonderful to have everyone sit at the table and enjoy a hot meal together, but that's not always possible when foods such as crêpes, eggless omelets, pancakes, or French toast need to be cooked in batches. If you keep the completed batches warm while the final batch cooks, you'll be able to join everyone and relax.

To keep these foods warm, preheat the oven to 250 degrees F. Place the cooked items on a nonstick baking sheet, a regular baking sheet lined with parchment paper (for the easiest cleanup), or a baking sheet that has been misted with nonstick cooking spray. Place in the oven for 30–40 minutes (much longer than that and the food will start to dry out).

Wheat Flour 101

Some people find vegan baking to be a little bit challenging, especially when baked goods call for whole grain flours. In order to be successful, it's important to first understand different flours and their properties.

Whole wheat flour contains the bran (the fibrous outer layer) and the germ (the part that sprouts) of the whole wheat berry. Because it is naturally more complete, whole wheat flour has a higher overall nutritional profile, as well as more fiber and healthful fats, than white flours, which have had both the bran and germ removed. Whole wheat flour should be stored in the refrigerator or freezer to prevent rancidity of the delicate oils found in the germ. The texture of whole wheat flour can range from soft and powdery to coarse, depending on the amount of bolting (sifting) it receives at the mill. Bolting removes some of the coarse bran, making the flour finer.

Bleached white flour not only has had the bran and germ removed, taking with them essential vitamins and nutrients, it has been "whitened." White flour can be bleached naturally as it ages, or it can be bleached chemically. Potassium bromate, a chemical used as an oxidizing agent and also used to enhance baking characteristics, has been added regularly to some white flours for many years. Potassium bromate has been banned in Europe, Japan, and Canada. In California, flours containing this chemical must carry a label warning of its potential as a carcinogen. Unbleached white flour has also had the natural bran and germ removed, but it has not undergone a bleaching process. This flour retains more of the natural warm, golden color of wheat than does snowy-white bleached flour.

All-purpose flours (whole wheat, unbleached white, and bleached) are a blend of high-gluten hard wheat and low-gluten soft wheat and may be used, as the name implies, for all purposes, from thickening sauces and soups to making pastries and yeast bread. Depending on the recipe, however, some baked goods made with all-purpose flour may provide less-than-satisfactory results.

Pastry flour (white and whole wheat) is made from soft winter wheat, which has a higher starch and lower gluten content. Pastry flour produces the finest, most tender pie crusts and pastries, biscuits, muffins, and scones. Whole wheat pastry flour is more nutritious than white flour, but it can make some baked goods seem heavy and crumbly. Also, since most conventional pastry recipes call for white flour, when you substitute whole wheat pastry flour you may discover that you need to adjust the quantity of liquid used (this is because the bran in whole wheat flour causes it to absorb more moisture). Many people who are accustomed to a diet of refined and/or processed food but who want to adopt a more wholesome way of eating find that using a mixture of half unbleached white flour (pastry or all-purpose) and half whole wheat pastry flour makes their pastries and non-yeasted baked goods lighter and more palatable than if they used whole wheat flour alone.

White whole wheat flour is milled from a special strain of hard white winter wheat, a relatively new and very exciting variety. It does not have the strong flavor and dark color of traditional whole wheat flour, but since it includes the entire wheat berry, it contains the fiber-rich bran and mineral-rich germ. Substitute white whole wheat flour for all-purpose or pastry flour in your cookie, muffin, cake, brownie, pancake, and quick bread recipes, or try it in yeasted whole wheat bread for a lighter-colored, milder-tasting loaf.

Bread flour (white or whole wheat) is made from high-protein hard red spring wheat. The extra gluten (protein) in this flour means that yeast breads will rise more strongly and vigorously. Do not substitute pastry flour for bread flour in yeast bread recipes. Conversely, do not substitute bread flour for all-purpose or pastry flour in non-yeasted baked goods.

Be aware that different flours will contain varying amounts of moisture depending on the type of flour, its age, and how it has been stored. Therefore, you may need to adjust the amount of liquid needed in your recipes. If no particular flour is stipulated in a recipe, any kind may be used. Otherwise, for the best results, always use the flour that is specified.

Making Perfect Vegan Quick Breads and Muffins

Making vegan muffins and quick breads is as much a science as an art. It can be especially tricky when using whole grain flours because these flours tend to create a coarser, more crumbly texture. Conventional recipes that use eggs, butter, and cow's milk ensure a delicate crumb. Without these ingredients, muffins and quick breads may seem more dense, heavy, or gummy, especially if they are low in fat. Here are some tips to keep your whole grain baked goods light, tender, and delicious.

- Always preheat the oven and prepare the muffin tin before you mix the batter.
- Stir the batter just enough to combine the ingredients. Overbeating can make muffins heavy or tough.
- Work quickly; baking powder will loose its effectiveness if it is allowed to sit in a batter for too long.

- Make sure your baking powder is fresh. Most tins will have an expiration date stamped on them. Old or expired baking powder will lose its punch and will no longer be able to leaven baked goods properly. To test the freshness of your baking powder, put 1 teaspoon in half a glass of hot water. If the baking powder is fresh, it will actively bubble in the water.

- Distribute the batter equally among the muffin cups so all the muffins will turn out to be approximately the same size.

- Always bake muffins and quick breads on the center rack of the oven.

- For the best results, do not open the oven to peek at baked goods until the end of the recommended baking time.

- Egg-free, dairy-free, low-fat muffins and quick breads will be slightly gummy when very hot. For the best results, allow your baked goods to cool thoroughly before serving them.

- Muffins and quick breads will keep for 2 to 3 days at room temperature. Cool them thoroughly before wrapping or storing them.

- If refrigerated, low-fat vegan muffins will become gummy, especially on the top surface. After storing them for 2 to 3 days at room temperature, it is best to freeze any leftovers.

- Vegan muffins and quick breads freeze well. They will stay fresh for about 3 months in the freezer.

- To warm leftover quick breads or muffins, slice the bread or cut the muffins in half horizontally. Toast them (muffins should be split-side up) in a toaster oven or broiler (watch closely so they don't burn!), or heat for a few seconds in a microwave oven.

Ormsby

Rescued from abuse and neglect at the hands of a Wisconsin farmer, Ormsby was underweight and suffering from foot infections when he arrived at Farm Sanctuary. The friendly faces and warm affection he found at the sanctuary surprised him, because he had never been treated with kindness before. He loved the way his caregivers talked to him, though, and he wasn't about to complain. Soon his feet started feeling better and he began to relax more. Grateful for his freedom, Ormsby now spends his days roaming the green pastures of the sanctuary and basking in the afternoon sun, knowing that he is loved.

Punching Up the Flavor

If you like a lot of flavor in your food without going to a lot of effort, add one of these robust seasonings to turn up the taste a few notches. Each one adds a different but potent kick—sharp, hot/pungent, salty, or intense—so you may want to use only one at a time, or start with one and add others with caution.

- Bottled hot sauce
- Capers
- Cayenne
- Chili sauce
- Chipotle chili powder
- Chutney
- Cocktail sauce
- Crushed red pepper flakes
- Fresh herbs
- Garlic, roasted
- Gingerroot, peeled and grated
- Hoisin sauce
- Horseradish
- Horseradish mustard
- Hot chili oil
- Hot chili paste
- Hot curry paste
- Hot paprika
- Hot pepper sesame oil
- Lemon pepper
- Oil-cured kalamata olives
- Olive tapenade
- Pickled ginger
- Salsa
- Smoked paprika
- Smoked tofu
- Spicy mustard
- Sriracha sauce
- Sun-dried tomatoes, packed in oil
- Thai curry paste, red or green
- Umeboshi vinegar
- Wasabi paste
- Worcestershire sauce, anchovy free

Homemade veggie meats

What is the word "meat" doing in a vegan cookbook? While some vegans and vegetarians may scoff at the notion of meat "substitutes," the fact is that many of us grew up eating meat and still crave those old familiar flavors. Centering meals around a hunk of protein is a time-honored custom in North America, and one that makes meal planning fairly easy. We're comfortable with the "meat, starch, and vegetable" format, and if a similar vegan version makes it easier for people to follow a plant-based diet, there's surely no harm in it, and actually quite a bit of good.

We live in a meat-centered culture and are surrounded by meat eaters daily. Most vegans have grown up eating meat or live among meat eaters, so meat in all its forms is customary and familiar, even though we now find it disturbing. Animal flesh is a central feature of most holiday and social gatherings, and healthful or not, many of us learned to fashion our meals around animal products. It is reasonable that people accustomed to this way of eating would want a painless replacement for meat when they become vegan. Having a cruelty-free alternative to meat can make vegan meal planning a snap; it also can ease the transition to an animal-free diet.

Nevertheless, mock meats are not solely for new vegans; long-time vegans and even nonvegetarians enjoy them as well. For meat eaters who have no intention of ever making the leap to vegetarianism, these foods are an excellent way to help them cut back their meat consumption. Tasty analogs are ideal for meat-loving family members and friends, as they are foods we can delight in and share. They are perfect for warm weather cookouts when nearly everyone wants something to grill; they are also terrific for office parties, picnics, and other gatherings and celebrations. When co-workers, friends, or relatives are eating burgers, we can indulge in a veggie version and not feel left out. When people are eating foods that are comparable, even if they are not identical, there is a feeling of unity and camaraderie. Because these foods can be heated quickly, they are convenient for hectic lifestyles and people on the go. Students, teens, and busy parents find them a godsend when appetites are raging and time is in short supply.

For the most part, processed meat products don't resemble animal body parts. By the time raw meat reaches consumers, most of it is visually sanitized. Various cuts also may be formed into patties, loaves, roasts, links, and other assorted shapes. We identify hamburger with "meat," even though it actually doesn't resemble anything specific. Consequently, we associate veggie burgers with hamburgers because they have a similar appearance (and sometimes a comparable texture and flavor), but neither looks like an animal's limb. (There is no known body part called "burger.")

Another interesting detail about meat is that it hardly ever is eaten plain. Meat eaters generally douse it with tenderizers, gravies, sauces, herbs, spices, breading, and a variety of condiments. At the very least, it almost always is served with salt and pepper. Meat without these seasonings and treatments is usually bland and relatively unappealing, especially to the Western palate. When people say they crave meat, what they really long for are the flavor enhancements, the chewy texture, or a sense of fullness and satisfaction. All of these are easily replicated with pure plant foods in the form of mock meats.

The vast majority of vegans and vegetarians don't make their dietary choices because they dislike meat. While they may find animal products objectionable for myriad reasons, by and large this has more to do with how meat is produced, or its effect on human health or the environment, rather than an aversion to its flavor. No one should be ashamed about having enjoyed the taste of meat prior to becoming vegan. Generally, those of us who ate meat at some point in our lives liked it, and our taste preferences aren't going to vanish overnight simply because we choose to change our diet. Although we might feel that meat is repugnant on an ethical, spiritual, philosophical, or intellectual level, our palates have memory. We cannot erase a personal history of once having enjoyed the taste of meat, and our emotional attachment to it may endure.

There is no reason for vegans to avoid plant-based foods that simulate meat or other animal products. For many vegans, meat analogs fill a void. They are also handy, practical, comforting, and satisfying. Plant-based mock meats may be reminiscent of animal products, but the critical point is that they *aren't* meat.

instead of

Kill not the goose who lays the golden eggs.

use

Don't fell the tree that yields the sweetest fruit.

Pearl

Pearl was rescued from the cheerless confines of an auction house by a woman who could not bear to ignore the little goat's suffering. Blind, sickly, and emaciated, Pearl had been abandoned at the auction house weeks earlier, forced to fend for herself. Pearl weighed only ten pounds when she was rescued; yet, despite her small size, she had been placed in a pen crowded with more than twenty large sheep and goats. In these close quarters, Pearl was continually knocked down by the other animals as she struggled for space of her own. After falling, she was frequently kicked and trampled or pressed tightly against the rough wood of her pen. At the time of her rescue, Pearl was severely emaciated and suffering from anemia. She was also diagnosed with several infections including pneumonia, chlamydia, and conjunctivitis. Now the recipient of constant medical care and tireless affection at Farm Sanctuary's New York Shelter, Pearl has made a remarkable recovery. This courageous little girl has already gained over seventeen pounds and has recovered most of her sight. She loves to munch on alfalfa hay and sweet feed. She runs and bucks with her friend Zoop on their excursions out into their pasture, and sighs contentedly when she settles into her warm straw at night. Pearl has left her dark past behind. She is now living life to the fullest in a place where she is loved, comforted, and understood.

The popularity of meat alternatives is evidenced by the extensive array of options available at natural food stores and many mainstream supermarkets. Manufacturers have heeded our call and have made it easy to choose a cruelty-free diet. Some of these products can be a bit pricey or a little high in sodium or fat, so you might want to try your hand at homemade versions. It isn't difficult or time-consuming to make your own healthful veggie meats at home—it's actually fun! So whether you go with packaged products or homemade alternatives, there is something for everyone to enjoy.

instead of

Better to give the wool than the whole sheep.

use

Better to give the berries than the whole bush.

Basic Simmered Seitan

PER SERVING

Makes 6 servings (3 chunks; approx. 2 servings per chunk)

calories: 119
protein: 27 g
fat: 1 g
carbohydrate: 8 g
fiber: 1 g

*I*f you do not have access to commercially prepared seitan, want to save a little money, or if you simply prefer to fix as many foods as possible from scratch, this is the easiest, tastiest, fastest, and least-expensive way to make seitan at home. The chickpea flour makes a very tender seitan that can be sliced easily and thinly. If you cannot locate chickpea flour or prefer not to use it, you can substitute an equal amount of additional vital wheat gluten; the seitan will just have a chewier and slightly spongier texture.

DRY INGREDIENTS

1¼ cups vital wheat gluten

¼ cup chickpea flour or additional vital wheat gluten

¼ cup nutritional yeast flakes

½ teaspoon garlic powder

½ teaspoon onion powder

LIQUID INGREDIENTS

1 cup vegetable broth or water

3 tablespoons reduced-sodium soy sauce

1 tablespoon extra-virgin olive oil (optional)

SIMMERING BROTH

10 cups cold vegetable broth or water

½ cup reduced-sodium soy sauce

For the dry ingredients: Place the vital wheat gluten, chickpea flour, nutritional yeast flakes, garlic powder, and onion powder in a large bowl. Stir with a dry whisk until well combined.

For the liquid ingredients: Combine the broth, soy sauce, and optional oil in a small bowl. Pour into the dry ingredients and mix well. If there is still flour around the edges, add a small amount of additional water (1–2 tablespoons only!). You should now have a large, firm, spongy mass of gluten in the bowl. (After gluten is cooked it is called seitan.)

Knead the gluten directly in the bowl for about 30 seconds only, just to blend. (Do not add any more flour. Kneading any longer than this will make the seitan fluffy, spongy, and breadlike, rather than dense, chewy, and meat-like!) Using a very sharp knife, slice the gluten into 3 relatively equal pieces and set aside.

For the simmering broth: Combine the cold broth and soy sauce in a very large pot. Add the gluten pieces, and bring to a gentle boil. Lower the heat, and simmer partially covered (tilt the lid so there is room for steam to escape) for 1 hour. Maintain the heat so the liquid barely simmers, and turn the gluten over several times during cooking. (Boiling the gluten will make a rubbery or breadlike seitan, so be sure to keep the liquid at a low simmer.)

Remove from the heat, uncover, and let the seitan cool in the broth. When it is cool, transfer to storage containers and add enough of the simmering broth to keep the seitan immersed. Covered tightly, Basic Simmered Seitan will keep for 10 days in the refrigerator, or up to 6 months in the freezer.

Saving Seitan

Seitan keeps well in the refrigerator or freezer, so it is well worth having plenty on hand to use in other recipes from this book. To extend the life of fresh or defrosted seitan indefinitely, boil it in its soy sauce broth for 10 minutes twice a week.

Seitan may be used as an alternative for chicken, beef, or veal in standard meat-based recipes. However, seitan is already cooked—no further cooking is required except to infuse the seitan with additional flavors—so conventional recipes may need to be adapted to take this into account.

---

instead of

You can catch more flies with honey than with vinegar.

use

You can catch more smiles with nice than with nasty.

Ground Seitan

calories: 120
protein: 30 g
fat: 1 g
carbohydrate: 7 g
fiber: 1 g

*I*nstead of simmering the seitan, this recipe calls for baking it. Afterward, the seitan is ground and ready to be used in any standard recipe to replace cooked ground beef. Add it to spaghetti sauce, lasagne, chili, stew, or any other favorite recipe. It is very easy to make, and much less expensive than store-bought vegetarian "ground round" or burger crumbles. Try the variations for even more flavor enticements and versatility. Crumble sausage-style ground seitan on top of pizza, or brown the ground seitan in a little vegetable oil and add it to salads, soups, or sauces. You can also substitute it for ground sausage or pork in most conventional recipes. Italian-style ground seitan makes a terrific pizza topping, and Mexican-style ground seitan is a taste-tempting addition to chili.

DRY INGREDIENTS

1½ cups vital wheat gluten

2 tablespoons nutritional yeast flakes

½ teaspoon garlic powder

¼ teaspoon onion powder

LIQUID INGREDIENTS

½ cup vegetable broth or water

½ cup tomato juice

2 tablespoons reduced-sodium soy sauce

1 tablespoon extra-virgin olive oil (optional)

Preheat the oven to 350 degrees F. Mist a baking sheet with nonstick cooking spray or line it with parchment paper (for the easiest cleanup).

For the dry ingredients: Combine the vital wheat gluten, nutritional yeast flakes, garlic powder, and onion powder in a medium bowl, and stir with a dry whisk.

For the liquid ingredients: Combine the broth, tomato juice, soy sauce, and optional oil in a small bowl, and stir with a whisk. Pour into the dry ingredients, and stir with a wooden spoon to mix thoroughly. If there is still flour around the edges, add a small amount of additional water (1–2 tablespoons only). You should now have a large, firm, spongy mass of gluten in the bowl.

Knead the gluten directly in the bowl for about 30 seconds only, just to blend. (Do not add any more flour. Kneading any longer than this will make the gluten fluffy, spongy, and breadlike, rather than dense, chewy, and meat-like!) Let rest for 5 minutes. (This will make it easier to handle.)

Stretch and flatten the gluten into a slab about one-half inch thick. The gluten will be very springy and elastic, so just try to get it as close to one-half inch thick as you can. Place the gluten on the prepared baking sheet and bake for 15 minutes. Remove from the oven and prick the gluten all over with a fork. Return it to the oven and continue baking for 10–15 minutes longer.

Remove the seitan from the oven and invert a large bowl over it. (After gluten is cooked it is called seitan.) If necessary, fold the seitan or push it together to fit it all under the bowl. Let the seitan rest and steam under the bowl until it is cool enough to handle, about 30 minutes. (The inverted bowl will keep the seitan from drying out and forming a hard crust.)

Tear the seitan into chunks, and grind it in batches in a food processor until it is the consistency of ground beef. Let it cool completely; then transfer it to storage containers in 2-cup portions, and store it in the refrigerator or freezer. Stored in a covered container, Ground Seitan will keep for about 1 week in the refrigerator, and for at least 4 months in the freezer. Thaw frozen Ground Seitan in the refrigerator before using.

VARIATIONS

- **Sausage-Style Ground Seitan:** Add 2 teaspoons dried sage, 1 teaspoon ground fennel, 1 teaspoon dried marjoram, 1 teaspoon ground cumin, ½ teaspoon dry mustard, ¼ teaspoon ground black pepper, and ¼ teaspoon cayenne (optional, for "hot" sausage) to the dry ingredients. Increase the vegetable broth to 1 cup in the liquid ingredients and omit the tomato juice.

- **Italian-Style Ground Seitan:** Increase the garlic powder to 2 teaspoons, and add 2 teaspoons dried basil, 1 teaspoon dried oregano, ½ teaspoon dried marjoram, ½ teaspoon ground fennel, and ¼ teaspoon ground black pepper to the dry ingredients.

- **Mexican-Style Ground Seitan:** Increase the garlic powder to 1 teaspoon, and add 1 to 2 tablespoons chili powder, ¼ teaspoon ground black pepper, and ¼ teaspoon cayenne to the dry ingredients.

instead of

Don't look a gift horse in the mouth.

use

Don't look for bugs in a flower bouquet.

Tofu Bacon

PER SERVING

calories: 94
protein: 7 g
fat: 6 g
carbohydrate: 6 g
fiber: 1 g

Slicing the tofu paper thin and browning it thoroughly are the keys to achieving a crisp and crunchy vegan bacon. You won't believe how delicious this is!

½ pound (8 ounces) firm regular tofu, rinsed and patted dry

3 tablespoons reduced-sodium soy sauce

1 tablespoon nutritional yeast flakes

1 tablespoon maple syrup

1 teaspoon vegetable oil

¼ to ½ teaspoon liquid smoke

Press the tofu, if time permits (see page 33). Slice it into 24–28 strips, about 1 inch wide, 3½ inches long, and ⅛ inch thick. Arrange the strips in a single layer on two large, flat plates and set aside.

Place the soy sauce, nutritional yeast flakes, maple syrup, oil, and liquid smoke in a measuring cup or small bowl, and stir with a whisk until well combined. Spoon this marinade equally over the tofu strips. Turn the strips carefully, dipping each one into the marinade that remains on the plate so that all the pieces are coated well on both sides. Cover tightly with plastic wrap, and let marinate in the refrigerator for at least 1 hour or up to 24 hours before browning. Covered tightly and stored in the refrigerator, Tofu Bacon, after browning, will keep for 5–7 days.

For Skillet-Browned Tofu Bacon: Pour a thin layer of vegetable oil into a large, heavy skillet, and place over medium-high heat. When the oil is hot, add several of the strips in a single layer. Cook until they are deep golden brown on both sides, turning them over several times. Transfer to a plate lined with a double thickness of paper towels to blot off any excess oil and keep the strips crisp. Cook the remaining strips in the same fashion, adding a little more oil to the skillet between each batch as needed.

For Oven-Browned Tofu Bacon: Preheat the oven to 400 degrees F. Mist a baking sheet with nonstick cooking spray or line it with parchment paper (for the easiest cleanup). Arrange the tofu strips on the prepared baking sheet in a single layer. Bake for 10–12 minutes. Carefully turn the strips over and bake 10–12 minutes longer. The strips will crisp further as they cool.

Beverages

Rice Milk

*T*his is a light, tasty, low-fat milk that is easy and inexpensive to make at home. It is an excellent milk for drinking, pouring on cereal, and using in baked goods. If you will be using the milk in savory dishes, omit the vanilla and reduce or omit the rice syrup.

  1 cup hot, very soft, well-cooked rice (any kind)

  3 cups almost-boiling water

  2 to 3 tablespoons rice syrup (optional)

  ½ teaspoon vanilla extract (optional)

  Tiny pinch of salt

Place the rice in a blender along with 1 cup of the hot water, the optional rice syrup, optional vanilla extract, and salt. Process on medium speed to make a smooth, thick cream. Add the remaining hot water, 1 cup at a time, and blend on high for several minutes until creamy. (Refer to Tips on Blending, page 38.)

Strain the rice milk through a cheesecloth-lined strainer or colander, or use a nut milk bag. Alternatively, place a very fine mesh strainer over a large measuring cup or bowl. Pour the contents of the blender through the strainer into the cup or bowl. Stir the rice milk to help it go through the strainer more easily, and mash the residual rice meal firmly to expel as much liquid as possible. Discard the rice meal.

Transfer the rice milk to a beverage storage container. Stored in the refrigerator, Rice Milk will keep for 3–5 days. Shake well before using it. Serve thoroughly chilled.

PER CUP *calories:* 73, protein: 2 g, fat: 2 g, carbohydrate: 15 g, fiber: 1 g

Basic Nut Milk

calories: 91
protein: 3 g
fat: 8 g
carbohydrate: 3 g
fiber: 2 g

N ut milk is an ideal replacement for cow's milk—it's rich tasting, smooth, creamy, sweet, and delicious. In addition to being used as a beverage, nut milk can be used just like dairy milk to make cream sauces, cream soups, milk shakes, and puddings. All the ladies of the Farm Sanctuary cow barn say "moo-chas gracias."

⅓ cup raw nuts (any kind)

3 cups almost-boiling water

2 tablespoons maple syrup, rice syrup, agave syrup,
    or other sweetener of your choice (optional)

½ to 1 teaspoon vanilla extract (optional)

Grind the nuts in an electric coffee grinder or spice mill. Cover the grinder to activate the blades, and grind the nuts to a fine powder or paste, about 20 seconds. (If you are using a Vita-Mix, this step is not needed. You can place the whole nuts directly in the blender.)

Tips for Making Nut Milk

• Make sure the nuts you purchase have not been roasted. Only raw (unroasted) nuts are suitable for making nut milk.

• Almost any raw nut can be used to make nut milk. Good nuts for Basic Nut Milk are cashews, whole or blanched almonds, walnuts, pecans, and pine nuts. Use a single type of nut or a combination.

• Walnuts and walnut milk in combination with certain foods may impart a purplish color. Recipes containing walnuts and walnut milk will still be healthful and delicious, despite this occasional change in hue.

• If you do not own an electric coffee grinder or spice mill, you can grind the nuts directly in your blender. However, grinding nuts in a blender requires a little more care and patience. Blend briefly, stir, and repeat until you have a fine grind. Be careful not to over-grind or you may end up with nut butter.

• The secret to achieving the smoothest result is to first grind the nuts or seeds to a fine powder in an electric coffee grinder or spice mill, and to strain the finished nut milk through cheesecloth, a special nut milk bag (available at natural food stores or through online retailers), or the finest wire mesh strainer you can find. As a general rule, the smaller the strainer the finer the mesh. I prefer to make nut milks in a Vita-Mix blender, as this high-powered machine pulverizes the nuts so finely that straining is usually not necessary.

• If you will be using nut milk in savory dishes, omit the vanilla and reduce or omit the sweetener.

Place the ground nuts in a blender along with ½ cup of the hot water, and the maple syrup and vanilla extract, if using. Process the mixture on medium speed to make a smooth, thick cream. Add the remaining hot water, and blend several minutes on high until creamy. (Refer to Tips on Blending, page 38.)

Strain the nut milk through a cheesecloth-lined strainer or colander, or use a nut milk bag. Alternatively, place a very fine mesh strainer over a large measuring cup or bowl. Pour the contents of the blender through the strainer into the cup or bowl. Stir the nut milk to help it go through the strainer more easily, and mash the residual nut meal firmly to expel as much liquid as possible. Discard the nut meal. (Straining is optional if you are using a Vita-Mix.)

Transfer the nut milk to a beverage storage container. Stored in the refrigerator, Basic Nut Milk will keep for 5–7 days. Shake well before using. Serve thoroughly chilled.

VARIATIONS

- For a thinner nut milk, increase the water to 3½ cups.
- For a richer, extra-creamy nut milk, reduce the water to 2½ cups, or increase the nuts to ½ cup.

Cool Fools

Makes 2 servings

PER SERVING

Thick and filling, this delicious whipped fruit drink makes a great breakfast or satisfying snack.

1 frozen banana (see page 56)

1 cup fruit juice of your choice

½ cup crumbled silken tofu (any firmness)

½ cup sliced fresh or frozen fruit or berries

calories: 168
protein: 8 g
fat: 2 g
carbohydrate: 32 g
fiber: 4 g

Break the banana into chunks and place it into a blender along with the remaining ingredients. Process several minutes until very smooth and creamy. Serve at once.

instead of

Neither fish nor fowl.

use

Neither greens nor grains.

Fruit S'moo-thie

PER SERVING

calories: 275
protein: 7 g
fat: 8 g
carbohydrate: 47 g
fiber: 6 g

A creamy, refreshing shake without any dairy products! This is my favorite smoothie recipe, and the Farm Sanctuary cows rave about it constantly (they even ask for it by name). It is exceptionally filling, so you might want to serve it as a meal rather than a snack.

1 frozen banana

½ to 1 cup ice

½ cup soymilk, rice milk, fruit juice, or water

½ cup sliced fresh or frozen fruit or berries

2 tablespoons raw nuts, or 1 tablespoon nut or seed butter (see notes)

2 tablespoons maple syrup, more or less to taste

½ teaspoon vanilla extract

¼ teaspoon ground cinnamon

⅛ teaspoon ground nutmeg

Break the banana into chunks and place it along with the remaining ingredients in a blender. Process until the mixture is very smooth and creamy. (The nuts and ice cubes will make quite a clatter, so don't be alarmed.) Serve at once.

NOTES

- Use any raw nut you prefer, such as cashews, almonds, pecans, walnuts, or pine nuts.
- Use any raw or roasted nut or seed butter that you prefer, such as peanut butter, cashew butter, almond butter, or tahini.

Freezing Bananas

To freeze a banana, peel it and place it on a dinner plate. Put it in the freezer for several hours or overnight until it is solidly frozen. Transfer to a heavy-duty zipper-lock plastic bag and return it to the freezer. If freezing more than one banana, wrap each one in plastic wrap to keep them from sticking together.

B

Bread and breakfast

Phenomenal French Toast

Makes 4 slices

*T*his French toast is warming and delicious. As a bonus, it is incredibly easy to make.

⅔ cup plain or vanilla soymilk or rice milk

4 teaspoons flour (any kind)

1½ teaspoons nutritional yeast flakes

Pinch of salt

4 slices whole grain bread

Combine the soymilk, flour, nutritional yeast flakes, and salt in a small bowl, and beat with a whisk to make a smooth, thin batter. Pour into a wide, shallow bowl.

Dip the bread slices, one at a time, into the batter, making sure that both sides are well saturated. Mist a large, heavy skillet (nonstick will work best) with nonstick cooking spray or coat it with a thin layer of vegetable oil. Place over medium-high heat. When hot, add the soaked bread slices in a single layer. If all four slices will not fit in the skillet comfortably, cook them in batches, adding a layer of oil between each batch (this is essential to prevent sticking, even if you are using a nonstick skillet). Cook until golden brown on both sides, turning once.

PER SLICE *calories:* 82, protein: 4 g, fat: 2 g, carbohydrate: 12 g, fiber: 3 g

Maple Walnut Granola

calories: 269
protein: 8 g
fat: 12 g
carbohydrate: 35 g
fiber: 5 g

Serve this crunchy, satisfying cereal with plenty of chopped fresh fruit or berries and your favorite nondairy milk. It far surpasses store-bought granola. This recipe makes a large quantity, but it will keep for a long time in the refrigerator, so there's no excuse to skip breakfast!

6 cups old-fashioned rolled oats

1 cup barley flour (see note)

1 cup coarsely chopped walnuts

1 cup raw sunflower seeds

½ teaspoon salt

1 cup maple syrup

½ cup frozen apple juice concentrate, thawed

¼ cup vegetable oil

2 teaspoons vanilla extract

1 cup seedless raisins or chopped dried fruit

Combine the oats, barley flour, walnuts, sunflower seeds, and salt in a large bowl. In a separate bowl, whisk together the maple syrup, juice concentrate, oil, and vanilla extract. Pour over the dry ingredients, and mix thoroughly until evenly moistened.

Preheat the oven to 325 degrees F. Divide the mixture between two large pans, spreading it out into a one-inch-thick layer. Bake 50–60 minutes, or until golden brown. Stir well every 15 minutes, spreading the mixture back to a one-inch-thick layer before returning it to the oven.

When the granola is finished baking, remove it from the oven and stir in the raisins while the granola is still hot. The steam from the hot cereal will help plump the raisins. Let cool completely. Stored in airtight containers, Maple Walnut Granola will keep for 2–3 months in the refrigerator.

NOTE

- Barley flour is available in natural food stores. Stored in an airtight container in the freezer, barley flour will keep for at least 4 months.

instead of
Pig out.

use
Stuff your face.

Eggless Omelets

Makes 4 omelets (2 to 4 servings)   **PER SERVING**

These tender, fluffy, egg-free omelets are terrific plain or topped with soy sour cream for breakfast. You can also serve them stuffed with fruit or savory vegetables and beans. They are surprisingly easy and quick to make.

calories: 176
protein: 9 g
fat: 4 g
carbohydrate: 28 g
fiber: 5 g

¾ cup flour (whole wheat, unbleached white, or a combination)

2 tablespoons nutritional yeast flakes

1 teaspoon baking powder

¼ teaspoon salt

Pinch of ground turmeric

Scant 1 cup plain soymilk or rice milk

½ teaspoon vegetable oil

Place the flour, nutritional yeast flakes, baking powder, salt, and turmeric in a medium bowl, and stir with a dry whisk until well combined. Pour in the soymilk and oil, stirring well with the whisk to make a smooth batter. Let rest for 5–10 minutes, then stir it again.

Oil a 9- or 10-inch skillet (nonstick will work best), or mist it with nonstick cooking spray, and place over medium-high heat. When hot, pour in ⅓ cup of the batter. Immediately tilt and rotate the skillet to distribute the batter evenly and create a 5- or 6-inch round. Cook until the top is completely dry, the bottom is deep golden brown, and the edges start to curl up slightly.

Carefully loosen the omelet with a metal spatula and gently turn it over. Cook the second side until it also is deep golden and flecked with brown. Slide the finished omelet out of the skillet onto a dinner plate. Cook the remaining omelets in the same fashion.

Adjust the heat as necessary during cooking, and always add a layer of vegetable oil to the skillet before cooking each omelet. (This is essential in order to prevent the omelets from sticking, even when using a nonstick pan.) Stack the cooked omelets, one on top of the other, on the dinner plate.

To serve, fold the omelets in half (with the most attractive side out), or stuff the omelets with your favorite filling prior to folding them.

"Buttermilk" Biscuits

PER BISCUIT

calories: 179
protein: 5 g
fat: 5 g
carbohydrate: 28 g
fiber: 3 g

Makes about 10 biscuits

A Southern tradition and a country staple, these highly acclaimed scratch biscuits are exceptionally easy to make. Try them topped with your favorite sweet or savory spread or hot gravy.

⅔ cup plain soymilk or rice milk

2 teaspoons freshly squeezed lemon juice

2 cups whole wheat pastry flour

2 teaspoons baking powder

½ teaspoon salt

3 tablespoons vegetable oil

1 tablespoon frozen apple juice concentrate or other liquid sweetener of your choice

Preheat the oven to 400 degrees F. Pour the soymilk into a small glass measuring cup and stir in the lemon juice. Let it rest at room temperature for 10 minutes to sour.

Combine the flour, baking powder, and salt in a medium bowl, and stir with a dry whisk to combine. Place the oil and juice concentrate in a small measuring cup, and beat with a fork until well combined. Pour into the flour mixture, and cut it in with a pastry blender or fork until the mixture resembles fine crumbs.

Using a fork, stir in just enough of the soured soymilk so the dough leaves the sides of the bowl and can be formed into a ball. (Too much soymilk will make the dough sticky; not enough soymilk will make the biscuits dry.) Place the dough on a lightly floured surface, and knead it very gently 10–15 times (this will take 20–30 seconds). Then smooth it into a ball.

Roll or pat the dough into a ½-inch-thick circle. Cut the dough with a floured 2½-inch biscuit cutter. Place the biscuits on a baking sheet as soon as they are cut, arranging them about one inch apart for crusty sides, or touching for soft sides.

Bake on the center rack of the oven for 10–12 minutes, or until golden brown. Immediately transfer to a cooling rack. Serve hot or warm.

VARIATIONS

- **Cornmeal Biscuits:** Replace ½ cup of the flour with ½ cup yellow cornmeal. Sprinkle a little cornmeal over the biscuits before baking them, if desired.

■ **Drop Biscuits:** Increase the soymilk to approximately ¾ cup (more or less as needed), using just enough to make a very thick batter. Instead of using a fork, stir the batter with a wooden spoon. Mist the baking sheet with nonstick cooking spray or line it with parchment paper (for the easiest cleanup), and drop the dough onto it by large rounded spoonfuls to make 10 biscuits.

Applejacks

Makes 8 small pancakes (about 2 servings)

*D*evon, one of Farm Sanctuary's vocal roosters, takes the morning off when these moist and hefty pancakes are on the menu. He knows that the aroma alone is a terrific wake-up call.

PER SERVING

calories: 241
protein: 9 g
fat: 2 g
carbohydrate: 45 g
fiber: 7 g

¾ cup whole wheat pastry flour

1 teaspoon baking powder

½ teaspoon ground cinnamon

½ cup vanilla soymilk or rice milk

1 Granny Smith apple, peeled and grated (about ¾ cup, lightly packed)

3 tablespoons seedless raisins (optional)

Place the flour, baking powder, and cinnamon in a medium bowl, and stir with a dry whisk until well combined. Pour in the soymilk and stir with a wooden spoon to mix well. Stir in the grated apple and optional raisins.

Mist a large, heavy skillet (nonstick will work best) with nonstick cooking spray or coat it with a thin layer of vegetable oil. Place over medium-high heat. When hot, spoon in the batter using 2 level tablespoonfuls for each pancake. Spread out each pancake using the back of a spoon. You will need to cook the pancakes in several batches, depending on the size of your skillet. Add a layer of oil between each batch (this is essential to prevent sticking, even if you are using a nonstick skillet). Cook until golden brown on both sides, turning once.

instead of

Pigheaded or bullheaded.

use

Hardheaded or stiff-necked.

Muffins That Taste Like Donuts

PER MUFFIN

calories: 155
protein: 4 g
fat: 3 g
carbohydrate: 28 g
fiber: 3 g

Makes 12 muffins

Moist and sweet, these muffins are sure to satisfy any craving for powdered donuts, with just a mere fraction of the fat and calories donuts typically contain.

TOPPING

¼ cup granulated sugar

1 teaspoon ground cinnamon

DRY INGREDIENTS

2 cups whole wheat pastry flour

¼ cup granulated sugar

2 teaspoons baking powder

1 teaspoon baking soda

½ teaspoon ground nutmeg

¼ teaspoon ground cinnamon

WET INGREDIENTS

1 cup applesauce

½ cup plain or vanilla soymilk or rice milk

2 tablespoons maple syrup

2 tablespoons vegetable oil

1 tablespoon freshly squeezed lemon juice

Preheat the oven to 350 degrees F. Mist a 12-cup standard muffin tin with nonstick cooking spray.

For the topping: Combine the sugar and cinnamon in a small bowl and set aside.

For the dry ingredients: Place the flour, sugar, baking powder, baking soda, nutmeg, and cinnamon in a medium bowl, and stir with a dry whisk until well combined.

For the wet ingredients: Place the applesauce, milk, maple syrup, oil, and lemon juice in a small bowl, and stir until well combined. Pour into the dry ingredients, and mix well with a wooden spoon.

Immediately spoon the batter equally into the prepared muffin cups. Sprinkle the surface evenly with the reserved topping mixture. Bake for

20–25 minutes, or until a toothpick inserted into the center of a muffin comes out clean.

Remove from the oven and allow to rest for 3–5 minutes in the pan. Gently loosen the muffins (carefully run a very thin table knife around the edges) and transfer them to a wire rack to cool, taking care not to shake off the topping. Serve warm or at room temperature.

Banana Flapjacks

Makes 8 to 10 pancakes (about 2 servings)

PER SERVING

Serve these country-style pancakes with maple syrup or your favorite toppings, and start your day with a smile.

calories: 270

protein: 10 g

fat: 2 g

carbohydrate: 52 g

fiber: 8 g

¾ cup whole wheat pastry flour

1 teaspoon baking powder

1 small ripe banana

½ cup vanilla soymilk or rice milk

Place the flour and baking powder in a medium bowl, and stir with a dry whisk until well combined.

Place the banana in a separate bowl, and mash it well using a fork or your hands. Measure out ⅓ cup (set aside any additional banana to eat separately or use in another recipe) and return it to the bowl. Stir in the milk. Pour into the dry ingredients and stir until well combined.

Mist a large, heavy skillet (nonstick will work best) with nonstick cooking spray, or coat it with a thin layer of vegetable oil. Place over medium-high heat. When hot, spoon in the batter using 2 level tablespoonfuls for each pancake. You will need to cook the pancakes in several batches depending on the size of your skillet. Add a layer of oil between each batch (this is essential to prevent sticking, even if you are using a nonstick skillet). Cook until golden brown on both sides, turning once.

instead of

Separate the sheep from the goats.

use

Separate the wheat from the oats.

Yankee Corn Muffins

calories: 124
protein: 4 g
fat: 4 g
carbohydrate: 18 g
fiber: 2 g

*W*ith just a hint of sweetness, these highly adaptable muffins are a great breakfast treat. If you add a few savory seasonings, however, you can easily transform them into a very special dinner or soup accompaniment.

DRY INGREDIENTS

1 cup whole wheat pastry flour

⅔ cup yellow cornmeal

2 teaspoons baking powder

1 teaspoon baking soda

½ teaspoon salt

WET INGREDIENTS

½ pound (8 ounces) firm regular tofu, patted dry and crumbled, or 1 cup crumbled firm silken tofu

½ cup frozen apple juice concentrate

½ cup water

2 tablespoons vegetable oil

Preheat the oven to 350 degrees F. Mist a 12-cup standard muffin tin with nonstick cooking spray.

For the dry ingredients: Place the flour, cornmeal, baking powder, baking soda, and salt in a large bowl, and stir with a dry whisk until well combined.

For the wet ingredients: Place the tofu, juice concentrate, water, and oil in a blender, and process until smooth and creamy. Pour into the dry ingredients, and mix with a wooden spoon just until the dry ingredients are moistened. The batter will be stiff.

Immediately spoon the batter equally into the prepared muffin cups. Bake for 20–25 minutes, or until a toothpick inserted into the center of a muffin comes out clean.

Remove from the oven and let the muffins rest in the tin for 5 minutes. Gently loosen the muffins (carefully run a very thin table knife around the edges) and turn them on their sides in the muffin cups. Cover with a clean tea towel and let the muffins rest for 5 minutes. (This will keep them from developing a hard crust.) Transfer the muffins to a cooling rack. Serve warm or at room temperature.

VARIATIONS

- **Maple Corn Muffins:** Replace the juice concentrate with an equal amount of maple syrup.

- **Orange Corn Muffins:** Replace the apple juice concentrate with an equal amount of frozen orange juice concentrate.

- **Blueberry Corn Muffins:** Fold 1 cup fresh blueberries, rinsed and patted dry, into the batter.

- **Spicy Corn Muffins:** Stir ½ cup sliced green onions, ¼ cup chopped green chiles, and 1 teaspoon ground cumin into the batter.

- **Smoky Corn Muffins:** Stir ¼ to ½ cup vegan bacon bits into the batter.

- **Extra-Corny Muffins:** Stir 1 cup whole corn kernels into the batter. Use fresh, thawed frozen, or drained canned corn.

Scrambled Tofu

Makes 2 servings | **PER SERVING**

This union of tofu and vegetables makes a tasty and appealing morning meal. For a very special brunch, serve it with sliced tomatoes, Tofu Bacon (page 52), and whole grain toast or Pecan Sticky Buns (page 68).

calories: 156
protein: 14 g
fat: 8 g
carbohydrate: 6 g
fiber: 2 g

1 teaspoon vegetable oil

¼ cup grated carrots

¼ cup minced green onions

⅛ teaspoon ground turmeric

½ pound (8 ounces) firm regular tofu, rinsed, patted dry, and crumbled

1 to 2 teaspoons nutritional yeast flakes

Salt or seasoned salt

Ground black pepper

1 to 2 tablespoons minced fresh parsley (optional)

Pour the oil into a medium skillet, and place over medium-high heat. When hot, add the carrots, green onions, and turmeric, and cook and stir for 2 minutes. Add the tofu, nutritional yeast flakes, and salt and pepper to taste. Mix well, and continue to cook and stir over medium heat for 5 minutes, or until hot. Stir in the parsley, if using, and mix well. Serve hot.

Flaxjacks

calories: 265
protein: 10 g
fat: 8 g
carbohydrate: 38 g
fiber: 6 g

These tender pancakes are great for leisurely mornings when you don't need to rush. They are light and fluffy and utterly fabulous. Try them topped with applesauce, fruit-sweetened jam, or pure maple syrup for a very special treat. If you like, add sliced strawberries, blueberries, or, if you are feeling particularly decadent, chocolate chips.

1 cup whole wheat pastry flour

2 teaspoons baking powder

Pinch of salt

1 tablespoon whole flaxseeds

¼ cup water

¾ cup plain soymilk or rice milk

1 tablespoon vegetable oil, plus additional for cooking

1 tablespoon granulated sugar

½ teaspoon vanilla extract

Combine the flour, baking powder, and salt in a medium bowl. Place the flaxseeds in a dry blender and grind them into a very fine powder. Add the water and blend until a gummy mixture is achieved, about 30 seconds. Add the soymilk, oil, sugar, and vanilla extract to the flaxseed mixture in the blender, and process until frothy and well blended. Pour into the flour mixture and stir just until everything is evenly moistened.

Mist a large, heavy skillet (nonstick will work best) with nonstick cooking spray or coat it with a thin layer of vegetable oil. Place over medium-high heat. When hot, spoon in the batter using about 2 level tablespoonfuls for each pancake. You will need to cook the pancakes in several batches, depending on the size of your skillet. Add a layer of oil between each batch (this is essential to prevent sticking, even if you are using a nonstick skillet). Cook for 2–3 minutes, or until bubbles pop through the top of the pancakes and the bottoms are golden brown. Turn over and continue cooking until golden and cooked through, about 1 minute longer.

instead of

Don't let the cat out of the bag.

use

Don't let the nut out of the shell.

Orange-Pecan Muffins

A hint of orange adds a delicate taste, while buttery pecans lend a burst of flavorful texture. These muffins are fabulous spread with Orange Butter (page 87).

calories: 207
protein: 6 g
fat: 7 g
carbohydrate: 30 g
fiber: 3 g

DRY INGREDIENTS

2 cups whole wheat pastry flour

2 teaspoons baking powder

1 teaspoon baking soda

WET INGREDIENTS

½ pound (8 ounces) firm regular tofu, patted dry and crumbled, or 1 cup crumbled firm silken tofu

½ cup frozen orange juice concentrate

½ cup maple syrup

2 tablespoons vegetable oil

½ cup coarsely chopped raw or toasted pecans

Preheat the oven to 350 degrees F. Mist a 12-cup standard muffin tin with nonstick cooking spray.

For the dry ingredients: Place the flour, baking powder, and baking soda in a large bowl, and stir with a dry whisk until well combined.

For the wet ingredients: Place the tofu, juice concentrate, maple syrup, and oil in a blender, and process until smooth and creamy. Pour into the dry ingredients, and mix with a wooden spoon until evenly moistened. The batter will be very stiff and dry-looking; this is normal. Stir in the chopped pecans.

Immediately spoon the batter equally into the prepared muffin cups. Bake for 20–25 minutes, or until a toothpick inserted into the center of a muffin comes out clean.

Remove from the oven and let the muffins rest in the tin for 5 minutes. Gently loosen the muffins (carefully run a very thin table knife around the edges) and turn them on their sides in the muffin cups. Cover with a clean tea towel and let the muffins rest for 5 minutes. (This will keep them from developing a hard crust.) Transfer the muffins to a cooling rack. Serve warm or at room temperature.

Pecan Sticky Buns

calories: 266
protein: 7 g
fat: 8 g
carbohydrate: 42 g
fiber: 5 g

*W*ho could possibly resist sweet, gooey sticky buns dripping with maple syrup and pecans? Dive into heavenly goodness with this luscious but wholesome version.

⅔ cup plain or vanilla soymilk or rice milk

¼ cup frozen apple juice concentrate (do not thaw)

1 tablespoon plus 1 teaspoon vegetable oil

1½ teaspoons active dry yeast

¼ teaspoon salt

2½ cups whole wheat flour, more or less as needed
    (at room temperature)

½ cup maple syrup

½ cup coarsely chopped pecans or walnuts

2 tablespoons granulated sugar

1 teaspoon ground cinnamon

1 teaspoon vegetable oil

Pour the soymilk into a small saucepan and scald it over medium-high heat. Remove from the heat and pour into a large bowl. Stir in the juice concentrate. The mixture should now be lukewarm (105–115 degrees F).

Stir in the 1 tablespoon oil, yeast, and salt. Gradually beat in 2 cups of the flour (more or less as needed) with a wooden spoon, adding only ½ cup at a time, until the mixture forms a soft but pliable dough.

Turn the dough out onto a floured board, and knead it for about 5 minutes, or until it is smooth and elastic. Alternatively, knead the dough directly in the mixing bowl. It is necessary to work in the additional ½ cup of flour (more or less as needed) in order to knead the dough properly and achieve a smooth, elastic consistency.

Scalding Liquids

To "scald" means to heat a liquid to a temperature just below boiling. Place the liquid in a saucepan over medium-high heat. It will be scalded when tiny bubbles just begin to appear around the edge of the liquid.

A Warm Place for Dough to Rise

One of the best warm places (about 85–100 degrees F) to let dough rise is in a gas oven with a pilot light (do not turn the oven on), or in an electric oven heated at 200 degrees F for 1–2 minutes *only* and then turned off. Place the covered bowl of bread dough in the oven *after* you have turned off the heat.

Lightly oil a large, clean bowl and place the dough in it. Turn the dough around so that it is lightly oiled all over. Cover the bowl with a clean, damp tea towel, and let the dough rise in a warm place for 30–60 minutes, or until doubled in size.

Mist an 8-inch square glass baking pan or a 9-inch round cake pan with nonstick cooking spray. Pour the maple syrup into the pan, and spread it around so it evenly covers the bottom. Sprinkle the nuts evenly over the maple syrup. Set aside.

Combine the sugar and cinnamon in a small bowl. Stir well and set aside.

Punch the dough straight down into the center with your fist. Then punch it in about 8 places. Turn the dough out onto a board or flat surface and knead it for 1–2 minutes.

Flour the board lightly and roll the dough out into a rectangle, approximately 8 x 15 inches. Using your fingers, spread the 1 teaspoon of oil over the dough. Sprinkle the cinnamon-sugar mixture evenly over the oil, to within one-half inch of the edge. Roll the dough into a log, starting with one of the shorter sides. Pinch the end seam closed with lightly water-dampened fingers.

Slice the log into 9 equal slices for the square pan, or 10 equal slices for the round pan, and place the pieces swirl-side up over the nuts and maple syrup in the prepared pan. Arrange the buns so they are not touching. Cover the buns with a clean, damp cloth or tea towel, and let them rest for 10 minutes. Preheat the oven to 350 degrees F while the buns are resting.

Bake for 20–22 minutes, or until the buns are lightly golden brown. Place a large plate or serving platter over the buns. Hold the plate and baking pan together using an oven mitt or pot holder in each hand, and carefully turn them over in unison. Let the baking pan cover the buns for 1–2 minutes before lifting it off straight up. This will allow the maple syrup and nuts to adhere to the buns. Serve warm or at room temperature.

Sour Cream Streusel Coffee Cake

calories: 210
protein: 5 g
fat: 8 g
carbohydrate: 30 g
fiber: 4 g

*N*o eggs, no milk, no butter—just pure, sweet indulgence. This heirloom family recipe is a superb cake to serve for a leisurely Sunday morning breakfast or for a special brunch or social gathering.

STREUSEL

½ cup granulated sugar

½ cup finely chopped walnuts, pecans, or almonds

½ teaspoon ground cinnamon

WET INGREDIENTS

1 cup applesauce

½ cup Sour Dressing (page 209) or soy sour cream

⅓ cup maple syrup

2 tablespoons vegetable oil

1 teaspoon vanilla extract

DRY INGREDIENTS

2 cups whole wheat pastry flour

1 teaspoon baking powder

1 teaspoon baking soda

½ teaspoon salt

¼ teaspoon ground nutmeg

Preheat the oven to 350 degrees F. Mist an 8-inch square glass baking pan with nonstick cooking spray and set aside.

For the streusel: Combine the sugar, walnuts, and cinnamon in a small bowl, and stir well. Set aside.

For the wet ingredients: Combine the applesauce, Sour Dressing, maple syrup, oil, and vanilla extract in a large bowl, and stir until well blended.

For the dry ingredients: Place the flour, baking powder, baking soda, salt, and nutmeg in a medium bowl, and stir well with a dry whisk. Gradually stir the dry ingredients into the wet ingredients, sprinkling in about one-third of the dry ingredients at a time. Beat well with a wooden spoon after each addition. The batter will be very thick.

Spread half of the batter evenly into the prepared pan. Sprinkle half of the reserved streusel evenly over the batter. Spread the remaining batter evenly over the streusel. The easiest way to do this is to place dollops of the batter on top of the streusel, and smooth it out carefully with a rubber spatula. Then sprinkle the remaining half of the streusel evenly over the top of the batter. Pat the streusel down very lightly with the palm of your hand.

Bake for 40 minutes, or until a toothpick inserted in the center comes out clean. Place the pan on a wire rack to cool for at least 15–20 minutes before serving. Serve warm or at room temperature. Cover the leftover cake tightly with plastic wrap. Sour Cream Streusel Coffee Cake will keep for 2 days at room temperature or 5 days in the refrigerator. Packed into a heavy-duty zipper-lock plastic bag, Sour Cream Streusel Coffee Cake will keep for up to 3 months in the freezer.

Simon

Found as a baby, alone and wandering the streets of Brooklyn, Simon was rescued and taken to Farm Sanctuary's New York Shelter, emaciated (weighing only seven pounds) and extremely sick. He was so ill at first that he needed special care. Simon had to be separated from the other animals in the shelter hospital so he could get the attention he needed. He greatly missed socializing with others and would often cry while in the hospital. One day, however, a special friend entered Simon's life.

Dan arrived a week after Simon. He was starting work at Farm Sanctuary's Education Center as a summer tour guide. He lived in the shelter house, with a room right above Simon's. Unable to bear Simon's mournful, lonely cries, Dan often came down from his room, laptop in hand, and watched DVDs with Simon sitting in his lap. After snuggling with Dan, Simon stopped crying, and the healing really began. Simon especially loved to listen to Dan play the saxophone in the evening. His affinity for music, friendship with Dan, and the tender loving care he received from the Farm Sanctuary staff all helped Simon in his healing process. He is now happy and healthy and lives with the other goats in the goat barn, where he is free to frolic and play.

Banana Tea Loaf

Makes 1 loaf (10 to 12 servings)

calories: 191
protein: 5 g
fat: 6 g
carbohydrate: 31 g
fiber: 5 g

*T*his dense, flavorful bread is sweetened only with a little fruit juice concentrate and the rich, natural sweetness of ripe bananas. This is a great way to use up bananas that are getting a tad too ripe.

DRY INGREDIENTS

2¼ cups whole wheat pastry flour

2 teaspoons baking powder

1 teaspoon baking soda

WET INGREDIENTS

1½ cups mashed ripe bananas (3 to 4 medium)

6 tablespoons frozen apple juice concentrate

2 tablespoons vegetable oil

2 teaspoons vanilla extract

⅓ cup chopped walnuts

⅓ cup seedless raisins or currants (optional)

Preheat the oven to 350 degrees F. Mist an 8½ x 4½-inch loaf pan with non-stick cooking spray and set aside.

For the dry ingredients: Place the flour, baking powder, and baking soda in a large bowl, and stir with a dry whisk.

For the wet ingredients: Combine the mashed bananas, juice concentrate, oil, and vanilla extract in a medium bowl, and stir well. Pour into the dry ingredients and stir to form a very thick batter. Stir in the walnuts and raisins, if using.

Spoon into the prepared loaf pan. Bake on the center rack of the oven for about 50 minutes, or until a toothpick inserted in the center comes out clean.

Let the bread cool in the pan on a cooling rack for 5 minutes. Turn out of the pan onto the cooling rack, and carefully turn the bread upright. Cool completely before slicing or storing. Wrap the cooled bread tightly. Banana Tea Loaf will keep for up to 3 days stored at room temperature, or up to 1 week stored in the refrigerator. Packed into a heavy-duty zipper-lock plastic bag, Banana Tea Loaf will keep for up to 2 months in the freezer.

Pumpkin Pecan Bread

This moist, dense bread can be enjoyed at breakfast or for snacks. It's fantastic!

calories: 251
protein: 4 g
fat: 11 g
carbohydrate: 35 g
fiber: 4 g

DRY INGREDIENTS

2 cups whole wheat pastry flour

2 teaspoons baking powder

1 teaspoon baking soda

½ teaspoon ground cinnamon

¼ teaspoon ground cloves

WET INGREDIENTS

1 can (15 ounces) unsweetened pumpkin (about 1¾ cups)

½ cup maple syrup

2 tablespoons vegetable oil

1 teaspoon vanilla extract

½ cup coarsely chopped pecans

½ cup golden raisins

Preheat the oven to 350 degrees F. Mist an 8½ x 4½-inch loaf pan with non-stick cooking spray and set aside.

For the dry ingredients: Place the flour, baking powder, baking soda, cinnamon, and cloves in a large bowl, and stir with a dry whisk.

For the wet ingredients: Place the pumpkin, maple syrup, oil, and vanilla extract in a medium bowl, and stir until well combined. Pour into the dry ingredients and stir until just evenly moistened. Stir in the pecans and raisins, and mix until evenly distributed.

Spoon into the prepared loaf pan. Bake on the center rack of the oven for 50–55 minutes, or until a toothpick inserted in the center comes out clean.

Let the bread cool in the pan on a cooling rack for 5 minutes. Turn out of the pan onto the cooling rack, and carefully turn the bread upright. Cool completely before slicing or storing. Wrap the cooled bread tightly. Pumpkin Pecan Bread will keep for up to 3 days stored at room temperature, or up to 1 week stored in the refrigerator. Packed into a heavy-duty zipper-lock plastic bag, Pumpkin Pecan Bread will keep for up to 2 months in the freezer.

Griddle Rounds

calories: 109
protein: 3 g
fat: 4 g
carbohydrate: 14 g
fiber: 3 g

*T*hese small, soft, and pliable yeast breads are baked in a griddle or skillet. Roll them around your favorite filling, or use them just like bread. They are as adaptable as a flour tortilla or chapati, just a little smaller and thicker, and their flavor is magnificent.

1 cup lukewarm water (105–115 degrees F)

1½ teaspoons active dry yeast

1½ teaspoons granulated sugar or other sweetener of your choice

¼ cup vegetable oil

¾ teaspoon salt

2½ cups whole wheat bread flour, more or less as needed (at room temperature)

Combine the lukewarm water, yeast, and sugar in a bowl, and let stand until foamy, about 5 minutes. Stir in the oil, salt, and just enough flour to make a soft dough. Turn out onto a floured board and knead until smooth and elastic. Form into a ball and place in an oiled bowl, turning the dough to coat it all over. Cover the bowl with a clean, damp tea towel, and let the dough rise in a warm spot (see page 69) until doubled, about 1 hour.

Punch the dough straight down into the center with your fist. Then punch it in about 8 places. Turn the dough out onto a board or flat surface. Slice it into quarters; then cut each quarter into 4 equal pieces. Keep the pieces covered with a damp tea towel (this will keep them from drying out). Working with one piece at a time, form into a ball, then roll into a 4-inch circle.

Place a dry or lightly oiled griddle or heavy skillet (nonstick works best) over medium-high heat. When hot, cook each round until lightly browned and slightly rippled with bubbles, about 40 seconds on each side. You can rapidly roll out the next rounds to be cooked while others are on the griddle.

Stack the cooked rounds, and wrap them in a clean, dry tea towel to keep them soft and warm. They are best served hot. Cooled and tightly covered, leftover Griddle Rounds will keep for 1 day at room temperature, or for 4 days in the refrigerator. Packed into heavy-duty zipper-lock plastic bags, Griddle Rounds will keep for up to 2 months in the freezer.

No-Knead Whole Wheat Herb Bread

Makes 1 loaf | **PER 1/16 LOAF**

This bread recipe is an old friend. I've made it for countless years and it still never fails to satisfy. The aroma as it bakes is intoxicating and always lifts my mood.

calories: 95

protein: 4 g

fat: 2 g

carbohydrate: 15 g

fiber: 3 g

- 1½ cups plain soymilk or rice milk
- 1½ tablespoons granulated sugar
- 1 teaspoon salt
- 1 tablespoon extra-virgin olive oil
- 1 tablespoon active dry yeast
- ½ cup warm water
- 2¼ cups whole wheat flour
- ½ small onion, minced
- 1 teaspoon dried rosemary, crushed
- ½ teaspoon dried dill weed

Mist a bread pan with nonstick cooking spray and set aside.

Pour the soymilk into a small saucepan and scald it over medium-high heat (see page 68). Add the sugar and salt and stir until they are dissolved. Add the olive oil and cool to lukewarm.

Dissolve the yeast in the warm water in a very large bowl. Add the lukewarm soymilk mixture, flour, onion, and herbs. Beat well with a large wooden spoon. Cover the bowl with a clean, damp tea towel, and let the soft dough rise in a warm place (see page 69) for about 1 hour, or until doubled in bulk.

Stir down the dough and beat it vigorously with the wooden spoon for a few minutes. Turn into the prepared pan and let it rest, uncovered, for 15–20 minutes. While the dough is resting, preheat the oven to 350 degrees F. Bake for 1 hour.

instead of

Running around like a chicken with its head cut off.

use

Running around in circles.

Date and Nut Bread

PER SERVING

calories: 267
protein: 5 g
fat: 7 g
carbohydrate: 48 g
fiber: 4 g

*D*uring the American "white-glove era" of the fifties, when ladies often lunched in charming tea rooms, a popular midday indulgence was a tea sandwich made from date and nut bread thickly spread with cream cheese. This delicious taste can be savored today by vegans, sans the white gloves, of course.

DRY INGREDIENTS

2 cups whole wheat pastry flour

2 teaspoons baking powder

1 teaspoon baking soda

WET INGREDIENTS

1 cup applesauce

½ cup plain or vanilla soymilk or rice milk

¼ cup maple syrup

2 tablespoons frozen orange juice concentrate

2 tablespoons vegetable oil

1 teaspoon vanilla extract

½ cup chopped dates

½ cup coarsely chopped walnuts

Preheat the oven to 350 degrees F. Mist an 8½ x 4½-inch loaf pan with non-stick cooking spray and set aside.

For the dry ingredients: Combine the flour, baking powder, and baking soda in a large bowl, and stir well with a dry whisk.

For the wet ingredients: Combine the applesauce, milk, maple syrup, juice concentrate, oil, and vanilla extract in a medium bowl, and stir until well combined. Pour into the dry ingredients and stir with a wooden spoon until just evenly moistened. Stir in the dates and walnuts, making sure they are evenly distributed.

Pour into the prepared loaf pan, and bake on the center rack of the oven for about 50 minutes, or until a toothpick inserted in the center comes out clean.

Let the bread cool in the pan on a cooling rack for 5 minutes. Turn out of the pan onto the cooling rack, and carefully turn the bread upright. Cool completely before slicing or storing. Wrap the cooled bread tightly. Date and Nut Bread will keep for up to 3 days stored at room temperature, or up to 1 week stored in the refrigerator. Packed into a heavy-duty zipper-lock plastic bag, Date and Nut Bread will keep for up to 2 months in the freezer.

VARIATIONS

- **Cranberry Nut Bread:** Replace the dates with ½ cup fresh or frozen cranberries. For the best results, coarsely chop the cranberries by pulsing them briefly in a food processor. Frozen cranberries should not be thawed before using.

- **Prune and Nut Bread:** Replace the dates with ½ cup chopped prunes.

Cornwall

Cornwall and sixteen other ducklings were rescued from a man who decided to close down his small farm. The man wanted to get rid of all of his animals, including his ducks, chickens, and llama. He said he only kept them for "fun" anyway, and he did not want to care for them anymore. Thankfully, a kind individual learned of the man's plans and intervened. Now Cornwall and her young duck friends are living happily at Farm Sanctuary's New York Shelter, where they are safe from the cruelty and apathy of the outside world and are valued just for being themselves. Cornwall spends every day now with the other rescued ducks and geese. She relaxes in the sun, swims in the pond, and sleeps in the comfort of the cozy, straw-filled duck and goose barn at night.

instead of

You can't get blood from a turnip.

use

You can't get water from a stone.

unCheeses

Tofu Ricotta

Makes about 2 cups

Use this versatile nondairy mixture in any traditional recipe that calls for creamy ricotta cheese. Omit the optional seasonings for use in sweeter fare and dessert recipes.

- 1 pound (16 ounces) firm regular tofu, rinsed and patted dry
- 3 tablespoons freshly squeezed lemon juice
- 2 teaspoons agave syrup or rice syrup
- 1 teaspoon dried basil (optional)
- ½ teaspoon salt
- ¼ teaspoon garlic powder (optional)

Crumble the tofu into a bowl and add the remaining ingredients. Mash and stir the mixture until it has a fine grainy texture similar to ricotta cheese. Chill several hours or overnight before serving to allow the flavors to blend. Stored in a covered container in the refrigerator, Tofu Ricotta will keep for up to 5 days.

PER ¼ CUP *calories: 66, protein: 7 g, fat: 3 g, carbohydrate: 3 g, fiber: 1 g*

Gee Whiz Spread

*J*ust like jarred American cheese or "velvetized" cheese products, you can use Gee Whiz Spread as a filling for sandwiches or a topping for crackers. Stir several spoonfuls into your favorite soups to make them cheesy-tasting, or add it to a nondairy white sauce for an instant cheez sauce. Thin a little Gee Whiz Spread with plain nondairy milk and warm it over low heat or in the microwave. Pour this luscious sauce over broccoli, cauliflower, macaroni, fettuccine, or potatoes. Slather Gee Whiz Spread on a bun and add your favorite veggie burger for an instant cheezburger. Gee Whiz Spread is a magical food. Make some soon, and watch it quickly disappear.

calories: 54
protein: 4 g
fat: 1 g
carbohydrate: 7 g
fiber: 2 g

1 can (15 or 16 ounces) white beans, rinsed and drained
  (about 1¾ cups)

½ cup roasted red peppers
  (skin and seeds removed) or pimiento pieces, drained

6 to 8 tablespoons nutritional yeast flakes

3 tablespoons freshly squeezed lemon juice

2 to 3 tablespoons tahini or cashew butter

½ teaspoon prepared yellow mustard

½ teaspoon salt

¼ teaspoon garlic powder

¼ teaspoon onion powder

Combine all the ingredients in a food processor, and process until completely smooth and evenly colored (this may take several minutes). Stop the processor and scrape down the sides of the work bowl as necessary. Chill thoroughly before serving. Stored in a tightly covered container, Gee Whiz Spread will keep for 5–7 days in the refrigerator, or up to 1 month in the freezer (defrost completely in the refrigerator before using).

VARIATIONS

- **Instant Cheez Sauce:** Combine 2 cups Gee Whiz Spread with 1 cup plain soymilk in a medium saucepan. Warm over medium-low heat, stirring often, until heated through.

- **Nippy Tomato Non-Queso Sauce:** Combine 1½ to 2 cups salsa with 1 cup Gee Whiz Spread. Serve at room temperature, or warm gently on low heat, stirring often, until heated through.

Classic White Uncheese

PER 2 TBSP

calories: 48
protein: 3 g
fat: 3 g
carbohydrate: 3 g
fiber: 2 g

Makes 1 block (1¼ cups; 10 ounces)

*U*se this versatile, all-purpose uncheese to lend a rich, dairy-free, cheesy flavor to any recipe. Shred it with a very gentle touch to use on pizza, slice it to use as a sandwich filling, or cube it and let it melt into dairy-free cream sauces, soups, or casseroles.

¼ pound (4 ounces) firm regular tofu, rinsed, patted dry, and crumbled

3 tablespoons nutritional yeast flakes

2 to 3 tablespoons tahini or cashew butter

2 tablespoons freshly squeezed lemon juice

1 to 2 tablespoons vegetable oil (optional)

1½ tablespoons light miso

1 teaspoon onion powder

¾ teaspoon salt

¼ teaspoon garlic powder

¾ cup water

3 tablespoons agar flakes

Lightly oil a 1¼-cup (10-ounce) heavy-plastic storage container (rectangular or round) with a lid, a miniature bread loaf pan, a small bowl with a rounded bottom, or other small container of your choice.

Place the tofu, nutritional yeast, tahini, lemon juice, optional oil, miso, onion powder, salt, and garlic powder in a blender. Set aside.

Place the water and agar flakes in a small saucepan and let rest for 5–10 minutes. Bring to a boil, reduce the heat, and simmer, stirring frequently, for 5–10 minutes, or until the agar is completely dissolved. Pour into the blender containing the other ingredients, and process until completely smooth. You will need to work quickly before the agar begins to set, but it is important to process the mixture very thoroughly. Stop the blender frequently to stir the mixture and scrape down the sides of the jar.

Pour the mixture into the prepared container. Use a rubber spatula to remove all of the blended mixture. Place the open container in the refrigerator to let the uncheese firm up. When it is firm and no longer warm to the touch, cover the container with the lid or plastic wrap. Let the uncheese chill for several hours or overnight before serving. Stored in a covered container in the refrigerator, Classic White Uncheese will keep for 5–7 days.

VARIATIONS

- **American-Style Cheez:** Blend in ¼ cup (2 ounces) drained pimiento pieces or roasted red peppers (skin and seeds removed), and process until no red flecks are visible. This will make a naturally orange-colored uncheese.

- **Pepper Jack Cheez:** Stir ¼ cup well-drained and finely chopped canned chiles, or ¼ to ½ teaspoon crushed red pepper flakes, into the blended mixture before pouring it into the mold.

- **Olive Cheez:** Stir ¼ cup sliced pimiento-stuffed green olives or black olives into the blended mixture before pouring it into the mold.

- **Dilled Cheez:** Stir 1 teaspoon dried dill weed into the blended mixture before pouring it into the mold.

- **Smoky Cheez:** Blend in a dash or more of liquid smoke, to taste.

Tips for Making the Best Block Uncheeses

- When simmering agar flakes, be sure the agar is dissolved completely before adding the mixture to the blender. To soften the agar, always let it soak in cool water for 5–10 minutes before bringing to a boil. This will help it "bloom" and dissolve more thoroughly.

- For richer-tasting block uncheeses, use plain soymilk instead of water and/or add a tablespoon or two of mild vegetable oil while blending.

- Any shape container (square, round, rectangular, or tube-shaped) will work with the block uncheeses as long as the sides are straight and do not slope inward. Inward-sloping sides will make it impossible to remove the uncheese as a block.

- For a larger block of cheese, double the recipe. Be sure to use a larger mold that can hold at least 2½ cups.

---

instead of

Pull the wool over one's eyes.

use

Pull the hat over one's eyes.

Crock Cheez

PER 2 TBSP

calories: 47
protein: 4 g
fat: 3 g
carbohydrate: 2 g
fiber: 1 g

Makes 1½ cups

This cheddar-style spread is sharp, tangy, and rich. It is reminiscent of the grainy, aged-cheddar spreads found in small brown pottery crocks in gourmet restaurants and specialty food shops. This recipe has brought in more rave reviews than almost any other recipe I've created.

½ pound (8 ounces) firm regular tofu, drained and crumbled

3 tablespoons nutritional yeast flakes

2 tablespoons tahini or cashew butter

2 tablespoons freshly squeezed lemon juice

1½ tablespoons light miso

1 teaspoon onion powder

¾ teaspoon salt

½ teaspoon paprika

¼ teaspoon garlic powder

¼ teaspoon dry mustard

Combine all the ingredients in a food processor, and process into a smooth paste, stopping to scrape down the sides of the work bowl as necessary. *Important: Chill several hours or overnight before serving to allow the flavors to blend.* Stored in a covered container in the refrigerator, Crock Cheez will keep for 5–7 days.

NOTE

- For a delicious cheddar-style sauce, thin Crock Cheez with a little plain soymilk or water until the desired consistency is obtained. Warm through over low heat. Serve over pasta, potatoes, grains, or vegetables.

instead of
The nearer the bone, the sweeter the flesh.

use
The nearer the stone, the sweeter the peach.

Melty White Cheez

*P*our this thick, luscious sauce over steamed vegetables, baked potatoes, macaroni (for instant macaroni and cheez), toast points, or
corn chips, or drizzle it over pizza or casseroles before or after baking.

calories: 127
protein: 7 g
fat: 5 g
carbohydrate: 14 g
fiber: 3 g

- 1½ cups plain soymilk or water
- ¼ cup nutritional yeast flakes
- ¼ cup flour (any kind)
- 2 tablespoons tahini or cashew butter
- 2 tablespoons arrowroot, kuzu, or cornstarch
- 2 teaspoons freshly squeezed lemon juice
- 1 teaspoon onion powder
- ¾ teaspoon salt
- ¼ teaspoon garlic powder

Combine all the ingredients in a blender, and process until completely smooth.
Transfer to a small saucepan. Cook over medium-high heat, stirring almost
constantly with a whisk, until very thick and smooth. Serve hot.

NOTE

- Stored in a covered container in the refrigerator, leftover Melty White
  Cheez will keep for about 5 days. It becomes very thick and firm when
  chilled, but it will turn "melty" again when gently reheated. A double
  boiler works well for reheating.

Cheese vs. Uncheese

Vegan uncheeses do not have the stretch that melted dairy cheeses have; this is because
dairy cheeses contain casein, a protein in cow's milk that gives them this characteristic
stretch. However, agar-based uncheeses will get soft and gooey when heated and will
brown nicely when broiled (so watch closely!). You can enhance their ability to melt by
adding extra oil to the recipe and covering sandwiches, casseroles, or soups when
heating them.

Creamy Cottage Cheez

calories: 115
protein: 5 g
fat: 9 g
carbohydrate: 3 g
fiber: 1 g

*I*nspired by Farm Sanctuary's bovine beauties, this delicious dairy-free creation has won moocho acclaim. This is an excellent replacement for dairy cottage cheese. Try it in scooped out melon halves or with other fresh fruit, as well as with your favorite savory foods. It also can be used to make stuffed "omelets." Just spoon it onto Eggless Omelets (page 59), gently fold the omelets in half over the filling, and top with a dollop of Sour Dressing (page 209).

1 pound (16 ounces) firm regular tofu, rinsed and patted dry

⅔ cup vegan mayonnaise

2 teaspoons onion powder (optional)

1 teaspoon garlic powder (optional)

1 teaspoon salt

1 teaspoon dried dill weed, ground dill seed, or ground caraway seed (optional)

Crumble the tofu into a bowl and add the remaining ingredients. Mash and stir the mixture until it has a texture similar to cottage cheese. Chill several hours or overnight before serving to allow the flavors to blend. Stored in a covered container in the refrigerator, Creamy Cottage Cheez will keep for up to 5 days.

NOTE

- Omit the onion powder, garlic powder, and dill weed if using Creamy Cottage Cheez with fruit or sweet dishes.

instead of

A bird in the hand is worth two in the bush.

use

A berry in the hand is worth two on the bush.

Parmezano Sprinkles

Sprinkle this delightful topping over pasta or pizza or wherever you would normally use Parmesan cheese. It is very easy to make if you have a food processor, and costs much less than commercial vegan Parmesan. This recipe is easily doubled, tripled, or quadrupled, which can be very convenient, especially if you use it often.

calories: 32
protein: 2 g
fat: 2 g
carbohydrate: 1 g
fiber: 1 g

½ cup whole or blanched raw almonds or white sesame seeds

2 tablespoons nutritional yeast flakes

1 to 2 teaspoons light or chickpea miso

Heaping ¼ teaspoon salt

Grind the almonds or sesame seeds to a fine powder in a food processor, electric coffee grinder, or spice mill. Transfer (if necessary) to a food processor and add the remaining ingredients. Pulse or process until the ingredients are evenly incorporated; the mixture should be crumbly, with a texture like coarse sand. Stored in an airtight container, Parmezano Sprinkles will keep for at least 1 month in the refrigerator, or 3 months in the freezer (thaw completely before using). Shake the container before serving to break up any lumps.

NOTE

- The almonds may be ground in a food processor using the S blade. You may find that sesame seeds are too small to be ground effectively in a food processor, or you may find they must be processed for a much longer time. If necessary, or if you prefer, grind them in an electric coffee grinder or spice mill and then transfer the powder to a food processor.

instead of

Slippery as an eel.

use

Slippery as oil.

Butters, dips, spreads, and pâtés

Onion Lovers' Chip Dip

Makes about 1½ cups

Break open the corn chips, potato chips, and pretzels—here's a thick, satisfying dip no self-respecting chip dipper can resist! Look for dried onion flakes in the spice aisle of your supermarket.

- 1 package (about 12 ounces) firm silken tofu, crumbled
- 3 tablespoons freshly squeezed lemon juice
- 2 tablespoons tahini or extra-virgin olive oil
- 2 teaspoons granulated sugar
- ½ teaspoon salt
- Dash of reduced-sodium soy sauce (optional)
- ¼ cup minced green onions
- 3 to 4 tablespoons dried onion flakes
- 1 teaspoon dried tarragon
- ½ teaspoon dried dill weed

Combine the tofu, lemon juice, tahini, sugar, salt, and optional soy sauce in a food processor, and process several minutes until very smooth and creamy. Add the green onions, onion flakes, tarragon, and dill weed and pulse until evenly distributed. Chill for at least 1 hour before serving to allow the flavors to blend. Stored in a covered container in the refrigerator, Onion Lovers' Chip Dip will keep for up to 5 days.

PER 2 TBSP *calories: 38, protein: 2 g, fat: 2 g, carbohydrate: 3 g, fiber: 1 g*

Carrot Butter

*I*f you enjoy having something rich and tasty to put on your bread, toast, or muffins, this naturally sweet and creamy spread will fit the bill. Similar in consistency to whipped butter, you can use it on baked potatoes, hot ears of corn, or anywhere you want to add a luscious buttery flavor—with no churning required!

calories: 15
protein: 1 g
fat: 1 g
carbohydrate: 2 g
fiber: 1 g

1 cup chopped carrots

1 cup water

1 tablespoon almond butter

1 teaspoon reduced-sodium soy sauce

Salt

Combine the carrots and water in a small saucepan and bring to a boil. Lower the heat, cover, and simmer for 15–20 minutes, or until the carrots are very tender. Drain, but reserve the cooking liquid.

Place the carrots, almond butter, soy sauce, and salt to taste in a food processor or blender. Process until completely smooth. Only if necessary, gradually add a very small amount of the cooking liquid to achieve a spreadable consistency. *Important: The butter should be very thick, smooth, and creamy, not watery.* Serve warm or chilled. Stored in a covered container in the refrigerator, Carrot Butter will keep for up to 1 week.

VARIATIONS

- **Cinnamon-Sugar Toast Spread:** Add ¼ teaspoon ground cinnamon and 1 teaspoon granulated sugar to 1 tablespoon Carrot Butter. Spread on 1 or 2 slices of hot toast or on biscuits or rolls.

- **Orange Butter:** Add 2 teaspoons frozen orange juice concentrate and 1 teaspoon sweetener of your choice to 2 tablespoons Carrot Butter. Use as a spread for sweet muffins or rolls.

- **Maple Butter:** Add 1 tablespoon maple syrup and a tiny pinch of ground nutmeg to 2 tablespoons Carrot Butter. Spread on sweet bread or rolls.

- **Garlic Bread Butter:** Add 1 teaspoon nutritional yeast flakes and ¼ teaspoon crushed garlic (or a scant ¼ teaspoon garlic powder) to 2 tablespoons Carrot Butter. Spread on 1 or 2 slices of plain or toasted Italian bread or 1 split Italian roll, plain or toasted.

Creamy Spinach Dip

Makes about 2 cups

PER 2 TBSP	
calories: 34	
protein: 3 g	
fat: 0 g	
carbohydrate: 6 g	
fiber: 2 g	

*T*his classic dip is a staple for every type of gathering. It is delicious served with veggies, crackers, corn chips, or your favorite breads for dipping. The recipe is easily doubled if you need to serve a crowd.

1 package (10 ounces) frozen chopped spinach, thawed

1 can (15 or 16 ounces) white beans, rinsed and drained (about 1¾ cups), or 1 package (about 12 ounces) firm silken tofu, crumbled

½ cup chopped fresh herbs (cilantro, basil, parsley, or dill weed)

3 to 4 tablespoons freshly squeezed lemon juice

1½ tablespoons extra-virgin olive oil (optional)

1½ teaspoons reduced-sodium soy sauce (optional)

½ teaspoon crushed garlic, or 2 green onions, sliced

Salt

Ground black pepper

Bottled hot sauce or cayenne

Place the thawed spinach in a colander and squeeze it with your hands to remove the excess liquid. It should be fairly dry. Place the spinach in a food processor along with the remaining ingredients, adding salt, pepper, and hot sauce to taste. Process until well combined. Chill for at least 1 hour before serving to allow the flavors to blend. Stored in a covered container in the refrigerator, Creamy Spinach Dip will keep for about 5 days.

NOTE

- For the beans, choose among Great Northern, cannellini, navy, or any other white bean you prefer.

instead of

Slippery as a greased pig.

use

Slippery as wet soap.

Lentil and Walnut Pâté

| Makes 4 cups | PER ¼ CUP |

*T*his luscious mock liver pâté is simply out of this world. Serve it in a rounded mound on lettuce leaves or with crackers or rye bread. Your guests won't believe this isn't chopped liver!

calories: 115
protein: 5 g
fat: 7 g
carbohydrate: 11 g
fiber: 4 g

4 cups water

1½ cups dried lentils, picked over and rinsed

2 tablespoons vegetable oil

2 large onions, chopped

1 cup finely chopped or ground walnuts

1 tablespoon reduced-sodium soy sauce (optional)

Salt

Ground black pepper

Combine the water and lentils in a large saucepan and bring to a boil. Lower the heat, cover, and simmer for 45 minutes. Uncover and continue to simmer, stirring often, until any remaining liquid has cooked off and the lentils are very tender.

While the lentils are cooking, heat the oil in a large skillet. When hot, add the onions and cook until very dark and caramelized, about 1 hour. Watch the onions closely and adjust the heat as necessary so they do not burn. Transfer to a food processor along with the lentils, walnuts, optional soy sauce, and salt and pepper to taste. Process into a smooth, thick paste. Chill thoroughly before serving. Stored in a covered container, Lentil and Walnut Pâté will keep for up to 1 week in the refrigerator, or up to 3 months in the freezer.

instead of

Many a pearl is still hidden in the oyster.

use

Many a potato is still buried beneath the snow.

Green Bean Pâté

calories: 45
protein: 2 g
fat: 3 g
carbohydrate: 4 g
fiber: 1 g

This beguiling vegetable pâté is temptation at its finest. It combines sophisticated allure with old-country flavor. It's a superb spread for crackers or petite rounds of party bread.

1½ cups cut green beans, fresh or thawed frozen

⅓ cup chopped walnuts

1 teaspoon vegetable oil

1 cup chopped onions

¼ cup crumbled firm silken tofu or regular tofu

1 tablespoon reduced-sodium soy sauce

⅛ teaspoon ground black pepper

Pinch of ground nutmeg

Steam the green beans until tender, about 10 minutes. Refresh under cold running water, drain well, and set aside.

Toast the walnuts in a dry skillet over medium-high heat, stirring almost constantly, for 5–7 minutes, or until golden and fragrant. Transfer to a food processor.

Heat the oil in the same skillet used to toast the walnuts. When hot, add the onions and cook and stir until tender and very well browned. This will take at least 15–20 minutes. Watch the onions closely and adjust the heat as necessary to prevent them from burning. Transfer to the food processor with the walnuts and add the reserved green beans, tofu, soy sauce, pepper, and nutmeg. Process into a smooth paste. Serve warm or thoroughly chilled. Stored in a covered container in the refrigerator, Green Bean Pâté will keep for 5–7 days.

instead of

There's more than one fish in the sea.

use

There's more than one leaf on the tree.

Southwestern Red Bean Spread

Makes about 1½ cups | PER ¼ CUP

This spread is similar to the Middle Eastern bean dip hummus, but it is made with pinto beans instead of chickpeas and incorporates the spicy flavors of the American Southwest. It makes a great dip for tortilla chips, a fantastic filling for rolled tortillas or chapatis, and a terrific base for tacos. For added flair, stir in some chunks of avocado, minced green onions, or sliced olives. Muy bueno! Or, as the Farm Sanctuary cows say: Moo-y bueno!

calories: 106
protein: 6 g
fat: 3 g
carbohydrate: 15 g
fiber: 5 g

1 can (15 or 16 ounces) pinto beans, rinsed and drained
    (about 1¾ cups)

2 tablespoons freshly squeezed lemon juice

2 tablespoons freshly squeezed lime juice

2 tablespoons tahini

¼ to ½ teaspoon crushed garlic

¼ teaspoon ground cumin

¼ teaspoon ground coriander

¼ teaspoon smoked paprika or chipotle chili powder

¼ cup chopped fresh cilantro, or 1 teaspoon dried oregano

¼ cup chopped fresh parsley or additional cilantro

Combine the beans, lemon juice, lime juice, tahini, garlic, cumin, coriander, and paprika in a food processor, and process until very smooth and well blended. Add the fresh cilantro and parsley, and pulse until the herbs are finely chopped and evenly distributed. Stored in a covered container in the refrigerator, Southwestern Red Bean Spread will keep for up to 1 week.

instead of

Stubborn as a mule.

use

Stubborn as a stain.

Missing Egg Salad

calories: 111
protein: 5 g
fat: 8 g
carbohydrate: 5 g
fiber: 1 g

*K*eep your heart healthy and the hens happy by using this tofu-based spread instead of egg salad. It's a cinch to prepare and makes a terrific sandwich filling or spread for crackers.

½ pound (8 ounces) firm regular tofu, rinsed and patted dry

¼ cup diced celery

¼ cup vegan mayonnaise

2 tablespoons minced fresh parsley (optional)

2 teaspoons well-drained pickle relish

½ teaspoon onion powder

⅛ teaspoon ground turmeric

Salt

Ground black pepper

Place the tofu in a medium bowl and mash it well with a fork. Add the celery, mayonnaise, optional parsley, pickle relish, onion powder, turmeric, and salt and pepper to taste. Stir until thoroughly combined. Chill for at least 1 hour before serving to allow the flavors to blend. Stored in a covered container in the refrigerator, Missing Egg Salad will keep for up to 1 week.

Marmalade

Rescued from a life of suffering and neglect, Marmalade and dozens of other birds were weak and ailing when they first arrived at Farm Sanctuary. Lucky to have survived exposure to freezing temperatures as well as a severe upper respiratory infection, Marmalade has thrived beyond anyone's expectations. With the help of a devoted caregiver who spent time acclimating Marmalade to sanctuary life, this timid yet curious hen has not only regained her health, she has learned about the joys of friendship. Anticipating her caregiver's daily visits and recognizing her pal or even the sound of her voice from a distance, Marmalade runs to greet her, following her friend everywhere and running to catch up if she becomes distracted by insects and falls behind.

Fowl Play Tempeh Salad Good!
(Vegan Chicken Salad)

| | Makes 4 servings | PER SERVING |

Everyone squawks for more of this chunky, chewy salad—it's great on crackers or in sandwiches. For an attractive luncheon, scoop the salad onto lettuce-lined plates, garnish it with a little paprika, and surround it with fresh tomato wedges.

calories: 251
protein: 11 g
fat: 20 g
carbohydrate: 11 g
fiber: 4 g

½ pound (8 ounces) tempeh, cut into ¼-inch cubes

1 cup diced celery or grated carrots

½ cup vegan mayonnaise

¼ cup thinly sliced green onions (optional)

3 to 4 tablespoons minced fresh parsley

¼ teaspoon poultry seasoning,
      or ½ to 1 teaspoon curry powder (optional)

Salt

Ground black pepper

Steam the tempeh for 20 minutes. Transfer to a medium bowl and add the celery, mayonnaise, optional green onions, parsley, optional poultry seasoning, and salt and pepper to taste. Mix gently but thoroughly. Serve warm or thoroughly chilled. Stored in a covered container in the refrigerator, Fowl Play Tempeh Salad will keep for up to 3 days.

instead of

It's a silly fish that is caught twice with the same bait.

use

It's a foolish man who stumbles twice on the same stone.

Tempeh Tuna Spread

calories: 228
protein: 12 g
fat: 17 g
carbohydrate: 10 g
fiber: 4 g

Not only tuna, but *all* sea life is protected when you choose this tempting tempeh spread.

½ pound (8 ounces) tempeh, cut into ¼-inch cubes

1½ tablespoons cold water

⅓ cup vegan mayonnaise

2 tablespoons minced red onions

2 tablespoons finely diced celery

2 tablespoons minced fresh parsley

2 teaspoons dried dill weed

2 teaspoons prepared yellow mustard

Salt

Steam the tempeh for 20 minutes. Transfer to a medium bowl. Immediately add the cold water and mash thoroughly using a fork or potato masher. Stir in the mayonnaise, onions, celery, parsley, dill weed, mustard, and salt to taste. Chill thoroughly before serving. Stored in a covered container in the refrigerator, Tempeh Tuna Spread will keep for up to 3 days.

Andromeda

Andromeda was rescued from a factory farm. Before coming to Farm Sanctuary, she lived in a cage and was never allowed to breathe fresh air or feel sunshine on her back. Now she spends her

days under the wide-open sky, free to come and go as she pleases and encouraged to run and play to her heart's content. Thrilled by the feeling of cool dust in her feathers, Andromeda loves to plop down into the dirt, flap her wings excitedly, and coat her body with dust until she is as brown as the paint on our barns. At night, she snuggles into warm, clean straw to sleep, preening herself and clucking softly to her companions before she drifts off.

Chickpea Tuna Salad

Spread this delicious salad on whole grain bread, or stuff it into whole wheat pita pockets along with lettuce and diced fresh tomatoes.

calories: 213

protein: 9 g

fat: 7 g

carbohydrate: 30 g

fiber: 8 g

1 can (15 or 16 ounces) chickpeas, rinsed and drained (about 1¾ cups)

½ cup finely diced celery

2 tablespoons freshly squeezed lemon juice

1 green onion, thinly sliced

2 tablespoons minced fresh parsley (optional)

1 tablespoon extra-virgin olive oil

2 teaspoons well-drained pickle relish

2 teaspoons brown mustard

¼ teaspoon paprika

Salt

Ground black pepper

Coarsely chop the beans in a food processor, or mash them well with a potato masher or fork. Stir in the celery, lemon juice, green onion, optional parsley, olive oil, pickle relish, mustard, paprika, and salt and pepper to taste. Mix well. Chill thoroughly before serving. Stored in a covered container in the refrigerator, Chickpea Tuna Salad will keep for up to 1 week.

instead of

One man's meat is another man's poison.

use

One man's treat is another man's trouble.

Boneless Chickenless Chicken Salad

PER ½ CUP

calories: 203
protein: 8 g
fat: 16 g
carbohydrate: 8 g
fiber: 1 g

Makes 4 cups

*T*his salad is a great pretender—it has all the ingredients that make a great "chicken" salad, but without the bird! Serve it on a bed of fresh crisp salad greens or as a hearty sandwich filling.

1 pound (16 ounces) extra-firm regular tofu, rinsed and patted dry

1 cup water

¼ cup reduced-sodium soy sauce

½ cup finely diced celery

½ cup finely diced green or red bell peppers

Thinly sliced green onions or grated onion (optional)

1 cup vegan mayonnaise

1½ to 2 teaspoons Dijon mustard

Preheat the oven to 400 degrees F. Oil a baking sheet, coat it with nonstick cooking spray, or line it with parchment paper (for the easiest cleanup).

Cut the tofu into ¼-inch-thick slices, and place it in two shallow dishes large enough to fit the tofu in a single layer. Combine the water and soy sauce and pour over the tofu. Let marinate at room temperature for 20–30 minutes.

Remove the tofu from the marinade, and place it on the prepared baking sheet. Bake for about 30 minutes, or until it is deep golden brown and the surface is dry. Cool.

Slice the tofu into very thin strips or shreds. Transfer to a bowl and add the celery, bell peppers, and optional green onions to taste. Combine the mayonnaise and mustard in a small bowl. Add just enough to the tofu mixture to moisten it to your liking. Toss gently until evenly coated. Chill thoroughly before serving. Stored in a covered container in the refrigerator, Boneless Chickenless Chicken Salad will keep for 5–7 days.

instead of

It's no use crying over spilled milk.

use

It's no use weeping over burnt toast.

Sandwiches

Welsh Rarebit

*W*elsh Rarebit is an open-faced sandwich typically consisting of a melted mixture of cheddar cheese, beer or milk, and seasonings. Here we replace the cheddar with a rich, cheesy-tasting nondairy sauce that retains all the elegance of this luxurious dish.

    4 slices whole grain toast
    4 to 8 slices vegan Canadian bacon or ham, cooked according to
        package directions
    2 ripe tomatoes, thickly sliced, or 2 cups steamed broccoli florets
    1¼ cups hot Tomato Rarebit (page 187)

Place the toast on four plates and top with the vegan Canadian bacon slices. Arrange the tomato slices or broccoli florets equally over the Canadian bacon. Spoon the hot Tomato Rarebit on top and serve at once with a knife and fork.

PER SANDWICH   *calories: 176*, protein: 8 g, fat: 4 g, carbohydrate: 22 g, fiber: 4 g

Messy Mikes

calories: 274
protein: 15 g
fat: 11 g
carbohydrate: 32 g
fiber: 7 g

Yummy!

This quick sandwich staple is the vegan version of beef-based Sloppy Joes. Both kids and grown-ups adore it.

1 tablespoon vegetable oil

1 medium onion, diced

½ pound (8 ounces) tempeh, crumbled

2 tablespoons reduced-sodium soy sauce

½ cup ketchup

1 teaspoon prepared yellow mustard

1 teaspoon apple cider vinegar

1 teaspoon granulated sugar or other sweetener of your choice

4 whole grain burger buns, split

Heat the oil in a medium saucepan. When hot, add the onion, tempeh, and soy sauce, and cook and stir for about 10 minutes, or until the onion is tender and lightly browned.

Add the ketchup, mustard, vinegar, and sugar, and mix well. Lower the heat and simmer uncovered for 10 minutes, stirring often. Spoon the hot mixture equally over the buns and serve at once.

VARIATIONS

- **Messy Mikes with TSP:** Replace the tempeh with 1 cup TSP granules or flakes (see page 30). Rehydrate the TSP with ⅞ cup boiling water, and let rest for 5 minutes. Proceed with the recipe as directed.

- **Messy Mikes with Burger Crumbles:** Replace the tempeh with one package (12 ounces) vegan burger crumbles. Omit the soy sauce. Add the burger crumbles to the browned onion along with the ketchup, mustard, vinegar, and sugar. Simmer for 10 minutes.

instead of

Casting pearls before swine.

use

Singing your song to a stone.

Sloppy Lennys

*T*his fast and simple hot sandwich filling is a pleasure to make and satisfying to eat. Rely on it whenever you want something soothing and delicious that doesn't take much work. Serve it in whole grain buns or ladled over toast points.

calories: 215
protein: 13 g
fat: 3 g
carbohydrate: 37 g
fiber: 12 g

1 tablespoon vegetable oil

1 onion, chopped

1 red or green bell pepper, chopped

¼ to ½ teaspoon crushed garlic

1½ teaspoons chili powder

1½ teaspoons dry mustard

½ teaspoon ground cumin

½ teaspoon ground turmeric

4 cups cooked lentils or beans (any kind), well drained

1 cup tomato sauce

1½ tablespoons light molasses, dark agave syrup, or rice syrup

2 teaspoons apple cider vinegar

Dash of bottled hot sauce

Pour the oil into a large skillet or pot, and place over medium-high heat. When hot, add the onion, bell pepper, and garlic, and cook and stir until the onion is soft. Add the chili powder, dry mustard, cumin, and turmeric, and stir to mix well. Add the lentils, tomato sauce, molasses, vinegar, and hot sauce to taste. Mix gently but thoroughly. Simmer over medium-low heat, stirring occasionally, for about 15 minutes, or until bubbly and hot.

NOTE

- To store leftovers, cool thoroughly. Stored in a covered container in the refrigerator, leftover Sloppy Lennys will keep for about 1 week. Leftovers may be reheated or served cold as a sandwich spread.

Barbecued Tempeh

PER SERVING

calories: 300
protein: 17 g
fat: 8 g
carbohydrate: 44 g
fiber: 9 g

This hot sandwich filling is so nutritious and simple to make that it is sure to become a standard item on your menu.

½ pound (8 ounces) tempeh

½ cup tomato paste (no salt added)

¼ cup minced onions

¼ cup minced green bell peppers

2 tablespoons apple cider vinegar

2 tablespoons dark molasses

2 tablespoons maple syrup

1 tablespoon reduced-sodium soy sauce

1 teaspoon dry mustard

½ teaspoon ground cinnamon

Dash of bottled hot sauce

4 whole grain burger buns, split

Preheat the oven to 375 degrees F. Lightly oil a casserole dish or mist it with nonstick cooking spray.

Cut the tempeh into ½-inch squares. Combine the tomato paste, onions, green bell peppers, vinegar, molasses, maple syrup, soy sauce, dry mustard, cinnamon, and hot sauce to taste in a medium bowl. Add the tempeh and stir to coat well. Transfer to the prepared casserole dish, cover, and bake for 35 minutes. Divide equally among the buns. Serve hot.

instead of

There's more than one way to skin a cat.

use

There's more than one way to peel a potato.

Gooey Grilled Cheez

*T*hese long-time sandwich favorites have all the goo and glory we love, but now they are healthful and dairy free. If you like, serve them with a dab of grainy mustard spread on top, or add a slice of tomato inside before grilling them.

⅔ cup water

¼ cup nutritional yeast flakes

2 tablespoons oat flour (see note) or other flour of your choice

2 tablespoons tahini

2 tablespoons freshly squeezed lemon juice

1½ tablespoons ketchup

2 teaspoons arrowroot, kuzu, or cornstarch

1 teaspoon onion powder

¼ teaspoon garlic powder

¼ teaspoon ground turmeric

¼ teaspoon dry mustard

¼ teaspoon salt

8 slices whole grain bread

Combine the water, nutritional yeast flakes, flour, tahini, lemon juice, ketchup, arrowroot, onion powder, garlic powder, turmeric, dry mustard, and salt in a medium saucepan, and whisk vigorously until the mixture is smooth. Bring to a boil, stirring constantly with the whisk. Reduce the heat to low and cook, stirring constantly, until the mixture is very thick and smooth. Remove from the heat. Place 4 of the bread slices on a flat surface. Cover one side of each slice evenly with the cooked mixture. Top with the remaining bread slices.

Grill in a large, heavy skillet coated with vegetable oil or nonhydrogenated vegan margarine. Brown each side well, carefully turning the sandwiches over once. Slice the sandwiches in half diagonally and serve at once.

NOTE

▪ If you do not have oat flour you can make it yourself from rolled oats. Just put ¾ cup rolled oats in a blender, and process for 1–2 minutes until finely ground. This will yield about ½ cup oat flour.

Tuna-Free Melt

PER SANDWICH

calories: 358
protein: 13 g
fat: 18 g
carbohydrate: 40 g
fiber: 9 g

Makes 4 sandwiches

*T*hese no-bake open-faced sandwich melts are exquisite.

4 slices whole grain bread, toasted

1 can (15 or 16 ounces) chickpeas, rinsed and drained (about 1¾ cups)

¼ cup minced celery

¼ cup minced onions

4 tablespoons vegan mayonnaise

1 tablespoon freshly squeezed lemon juice

½ teaspoon onion powder

¼ teaspoon garlic powder

¼ teaspoon paprika

1 ripe tomato, thinly sliced

1¼ cups hot Incredible Cashew Cheez Sauce (page 190)

Paprika and/or parsley, for garnish

Arrange the toast on individual serving plates. Place the beans in a bowl and mash them with a sturdy fork or potato masher. Stir in the celery, onions, mayonnaise, lemon juice, onion powder, garlic powder, and paprika, and mix well. Distribute the bean spread evenly over the toast, covering it completely to the edges, and top with the tomato slices. Spoon the hot sauce equally over the tomatoes. Garnish with paprika and/or parsley, if desired. Serve immediately with a knife and fork.

instead of

Don't count your chickens before they are hatched.

use

Don't count your bushels before they are reaped.

Pickle, Tahini, and Tomato Sandwiches (PLTs)

Makes 2 sandwiches | **PER SANDWICH**

*S*alty dill pickles combined with rich tahini and juicy tomatoes make a memorable sandwich that's even more satisfying than cheese. It's also more healthful and remarkably delicious.

calories: 217
protein: 8 g
fat: 10 g
carbohydrate: 25 g
fiber: 6 g

- 4 slices whole grain bread, toasted if desired
- 2 tablespoons tahini
- 2 reduced-sodium dill pickles, thinly sliced lengthwise
- 1 ripe tomato, thickly sliced
- 2 thin slices mild red onion (optional)
- Salt
- Ground black pepper
- 2 large leaves romaine or leaf lettuce, washed and patted dry

Spread one side of each slice of the bread with some of the tahini. Over 2 of the slices, layer the pickles, tomato, and optional onion. Sprinkle with salt and pepper to taste. Top with the lettuce leaves and remaining bread, tahini-side in. Slice the sandwiches in half diagonally and serve.

Studley

Studley was rescued from a goat dairy farm where he was being raised as a breeder goat. Viewed as a mere commodity, he would have continued to be used as a virtual breeding machine for his entire "productive" life. Once aging past his prime, Studley would then have been sent to slaughter, being of no use to the facility alive anymore. Thankfully, a Farm Sanctuary member stepped in and changed Studley's fate. He was rescued, along with his best goat friend, Rumi, and brought to safety at Farm Sanctuary. Studley now enjoys a life of leisure at our California Shelter. He is free to roam the rolling pastures, soak in a life full of peace, and frolic as he pleases with Rumi and his other friends in the goat herd.

Kale and Kraut Sandwiches

PER SANDWICH

Makes 4 sandwiches

calories: 316
protein: 13 g
fat: 14 g
carbohydrate: 40 g
fiber: 10 g

*H*umble kale and tangy sauerkraut reach exciting culinary heights when married in this simple but tempting sandwich. I make this sandwich regularly—it's one of my favorites. Kales makes a hearty, chewy, remarkably meaty sandwich filling.

1 cup sauerkraut, well drained

1½ pounds fresh kale

8 slices whole grain bread, toasted if desired

4 tablespoons tahini, as needed

4 tablespoons Dijon mustard, as needed

Place the sauerkraut in a strainer or colander in the sink and squeeze it with your hands until most of the moisture has been removed. Set aside.

Rinse the kale well, taking care to wash off any sand or grit. Remove the thick center ribs, and coarsely tear the leaves. You should have about 8 cups. Steam for 10–12 minutes, or until wilted and very tender. Cool until the kale can be easily handled. Place it in a colander in the sink and squeeze out as much moisture as possible using your hands. The kale should be fairly dry.

While the kale is steaming, spread one side of 4 of the bread slices equally with the tahini, using about 1 tablespoon per slice. Spread one side of the remaining 4 slices of bread with the mustard, using about 1 tablespoon per slice. Distribute the kale equally over the tahini or mustard. Distribute the sauerkraut over the kale. Top with the remaining bread slices, spread-side in. Slice the sandwiches in half diagonally and serve at once.

VARIATION

- **Grilled Kale and Kraut Sandwiches:** Prepare the sandwiches with untoasted bread. After they are assembled, grill the sandwiches in a hot skillet coated with a thin layer of vegetable oil or nonhydrogenated vegan margarine, browning them well on both sides.

Radical Reubens

Extravagantly delectable, this recipe re-creates the taste of real deli food, vegan style, right in your own kitchen. Don't forget to include the obligatory pickle spear on the side!

calories: 314
protein: 29 g
fat: 3 g
carbohydrate: 44 g
fiber: 8 g

1 cup sauerkraut, well drained

8 slices rye bread, toasted

¼ to ½ cup Gee Whiz Spread (page 79)

¼ cup vegan Thousand Island dressing (homemade or store-bought)

16 to 24 slices veggie salami or other veggie deli meat
    (one flavor or a variety)

Place the sauerkraut in a strainer or colander in the sink and squeeze it with your hands until most of the moisture has been removed. Set aside.

Spread one side of 4 of the slices of toast with the Gee Whiz Spread, using 1–2 tablespoons per slice. Spread one side of the 4 remaining slices of toast with the Thousand Island dressing, using 1 tablespoon per slice. Arrange 4–6 slices of the veggie salami over the Gee Whiz Spread. Divide the sauerkraut equally over the salami, using about ¼ cup for each. Top with the remaining slices of toast, dressing-side in. Slice the sandwiches in half diagonally and serve.

VARIATION

- **Grilled Reubens:** Prepare the sandwiches with untoasted bread. After the sandwiches are assembled, grill them in a hot skillet coated with a thin layer of vegetable oil or nonhydrogenated vegan margarine, browning them well on both sides.

instead of

He who treads on eggs must tread lightly.

use

He who treads on thin ice must tread lightly.

Delectable Devonshires

PER SANDWICH

Makes 4 sandwiches

calories: 256
protein: 17 g
fat: 14 g
carbohydrate: 19 g
fiber: 5 g

*I*n this luscious plant-based rendition, veggie mock meats replace the turkey and bacon found in traditional Devonshires. Then everything is smothered in a sensuous nondairy cheez sauce to complete this very special open-faced sandwich.

4 slices whole grain bread, toasted

8 slices veggie turkey

8 slices veggie Canadian bacon

1 large ripe tomato, cut into 4 thick slices

1¼ cups hot Incredible Cashew Cheez Sauce (page 190)
    or Cashew Pimiento Cheez Sauce (page 191)

Preheat the oven to 400 degrees F. Oil a shallow baking dish (large enough to fit four slices of bread side by side), or mist it with nonstick cooking spray. Arrange the toast in a single layer in the prepared baking dish. Layer 2 slices of veggie turkey, 2 slices of veggie Canadian bacon, and 1 slice of tomato over each piece of toast. Spoon the hot cheez sauce evenly over each sandwich. Bake until the sauce is bubbly and the tops are golden brown, about 15 minutes. Serve immediately with a knife and fork.

Mario

Mario was found on a "dead pile" at a dairy farm. Considered worthless because he was born male and was suffering from a broken leg, he was discarded like trash. At Farm Sanctuary, however, Mario is considered priceless. After a complicated surgery, ten days of intensive care in the hospital, and plenty of TLC, he made a full recovery and can now buck, and run, and wander the spacious green sanctuary pastures just like the rest of the herd. Still the youngest and most inexperienced in the group, Mario continues to look to his big brothers and sisters for lessons in being a bovine. By watching them, he has learned how to chase the hay trailer and beg caregivers for the biggest flakes to eat, how to identify the best spots for sunbathing, and when it's best to leave grumpy herd-mates (especially those with big horns) alone.

Better Burgers

*D*elicious, chewy, and satisfying—what more could we ask of a burger? Serve these on buns with all your favorite trimmings. Despite a lengthy list of seasonings, these burgers are a breeze to prepare.

calories: 158
protein: 14 g
fat: 3 g
carbohydrate: 19 g
fiber: 4 g

1 cup TSP flakes or granules (see page 30)

¼ cup rolled oats

½ teaspoon dried basil

½ teaspoon dried oregano

½ teaspoon dried parsley flakes

½ teaspoon garlic powder

½ teaspoon onion powder

¼ teaspoon dry mustard

¾ cup boiling water

2 tablespoons ketchup

2 tablespoons reduced-sodium soy sauce

1 rounded tablespoon smooth peanut butter

¼ cup flour (any kind)

1 tablespoon nutritional yeast flakes (optional)

Place the TSP, oats, basil, oregano, parsley, garlic powder, onion powder, and dry mustard in a medium bowl, and stir until evenly combined. In a small bowl, combine the boiling water, ketchup, and soy sauce, and stir until blended. Pour into the TSP mixture, and stir until well combined. Let rest for 5–10 minutes so the TSP and oats can absorb the liquid.

Add the peanut butter, and mix until it is well incorporated. Stir in the flour and optional nutritional yeast flakes, and mix thoroughly. Shape into 4 flat patties, about 4 inches in diameter. Place the patties on a sheet of waxed paper as soon as they are formed.

Coat a large, heavy skillet with a thin layer of vegetable oil and place over medium-high heat. When hot, add the patties. Lower the heat and brown the patties for 6–8 minutes on each side.

Easy Chickpea Oat Burgers

calories: 195
protein: 7 g
fat: 8 g
carbohydrate: 25 g
fiber: 5 g

*I*f you use canned chickpeas, these scrumptious burgers can be made lickety-split.

2 teaspoons vegetable oil

1½ cups chopped onions

2 cups quick-cooking rolled oats (not instant)

½ cup ground walnuts

1 cup cooked or canned chickpeas, rinsed and drained

¾ cup plain soymilk or rice milk

¾ teaspoon salt

½ teaspoon garlic powder

½ teaspoon onion powder

¼ teaspoon whole celery seeds

¼ teaspoon dried sage

Heat the oil in a large skillet. When hot, add the onions and cook and stir for about 15 minutes, or until very tender and golden brown. Watch closely and adjust the heat as necessary so the onions do not burn.

Combine the oats and walnuts in a large bowl. Place the chickpeas, soymilk, salt, garlic powder, onion powder, celery seeds, and sage in a blender, and process until very smooth and creamy. Pour into the oats and walnuts. Add the browned onions and mix well. The mixture will be fairly stiff. Allow to rest for 5–10 minutes so the oats can absorb the liquid.

Form into 8 thin, flat patties using about ⅓ cup per patty. Place on a sheet of waxed paper as soon as they are formed.

Coat a large skillet with a thin layer of vegetable oil and place over medium heat. When hot, add the burgers, lower the heat, and brown them for 5–7 minutes on each side, turning them over once.

instead of
Don't put the cart before the horse.

use
Don't slice the bread before it's baked.

Cornucopia Oat Burgers

Makes 8 burgers | **PER BURGER**

*T*hese simple, wholesome, extraordinarily tasty burgers are among my favorites.

calories: *233*
protein: 6 g
fat: 13 g
carbohydrate: 24 g
fiber: 3 g

4 teaspoons vegetable oil

1 cup chopped onions

1 cup rolled oats

1 cup fresh breadcrumbs

1 cup chopped walnuts

¼ cup flour (any kind)

1 teaspoon dried sage

½ teaspoon dried thyme

½ teaspoon salt

1⅓ cups boiling water

Pour the oil into a large, heavy skillet, and place over medium-high heat. When hot, add the onions and cook and stir for 15–20 minutes, or until tender and golden brown. Watch closely and adjust the heat as necessary so the onions do not burn.

Place the oats, breadcrumbs, walnuts, flour, sage, thyme, and salt in a medium bowl, and stir to combine. Pour in the boiling water and mix well. Stir in the browned onions. Let rest for 10 minutes, or until cool enough to handle comfortably. Form into 8 patties (lightly moistening your hands will help keep the mixture from sticking to them). Place the patties on a sheet of waxed paper as soon as they are made.

Add a layer of vegetable oil to a clean skillet (or use the same skillet used to brown the onions) and place over medium heat. When hot, add the patties and brown them well on both sides, turning once.

How to Make Fresh Breadcrumbs

Fresh breadcrumbs can be easily made by tearing fresh bread into small pieces and whirling them in a food processor. Packed into heavy-duty zipper-lock plastic bags, fresh breadcrumbs will keep for 1 week in the refrigerator or up to 6 months in the freezer.

Gyros

PER SERVING

calories: 365
protein: 30 g
fat: 10 g
carbohydrate: 47 g
fiber: 7 g

Makes 4 servings

*T*raditionally made with lamb, this Greek specialty is easily made vegan by employing thinly sliced seitan and using a tofu-based creamy cucumber sauce.

CUCUMBER SAUCE

1 cup crumbled firm silken tofu

1 cup chopped English cucumbers

1½ tablespoons extra-virgin olive oil

2 teaspoons freshly squeezed lemon juice

½ teaspoon salt

¼ teaspoon ground black pepper

SEASONED SEITAN

3 tablespoons reduced-sodium soy sauce

2 tablespoons water

2 teaspoons dried oregano

1 teaspoon dried rosemary, crushed, or ¼ teaspoon ground rosemary

1 teaspoon garlic powder

2 cups thinly sliced seitan

SANDWICH FIXINGS

4 pita breads

2 cups romaine lettuce, torn into bite-size pieces

2 small ripe tomatoes, chopped

Thinly sliced onions

For the sauce: Combine the tofu, cucumbers, olive oil, lemon juice, salt, and pepper in a food processor or blender, and process until well combined but still a bit chunky. Set aside.

For the seitan: Combine the soy sauce, water, oregano, rosemary, and garlic powder in a small bowl, and stir until well combined. Coat a large skillet with a layer of vegetable oil and place over medium-high heat. When hot, add the seitan strips in a single layer and brown them lightly on both sides, turning them over once or twice with a fork. Pour the soy sauce mixture over the seitan and bring to a boil, tossing the seitan gently. Cook for 1–2 minutes only and remove from the heat.

To assemble: Place the pita breads flat on individual plates and divide the seitan equally among them. Top with the lettuce, tomatoes, and onion slices. Spoon some of the Cucumber Sauce over each sandwich. To eat, fold the pita bread over and eat the sandwich burrito-style using your hands. Alternatively, pick up and eat the sandwich unfolded (flat), taco-style.

Vegan Lox and Bagels

Makes 4 servings

PER SERVING

calories: 257

protein: 7 g

fat: 10 g

carbohydrate: 36 g

fiber: 3 g

Vegan cream cheese and red bell pepper "lox" is a phenomenal combination. You can use jarred or canned roasted red bell peppers, which are very convenient, or you can roast your own following the directions on page 186. The "lox" in this recipe is so delicious that you may wish to double the recipe and use it as a condiment, garnish, or salad ingredient.

2 large roasted red bell peppers, skin and seeds removed

1 tablespoon extra-virgin olive oil

½ teaspoon crushed garlic (optional)

¼ to ½ cup vegan cream cheese (homemade or store-bought)

4 bagels, split and toasted

Green nori flakes or nori, dulse, or kelp granules (optional)

Drain the peppers and pat them dry. Cut them into thick strips and place them in a small bowl. Sprinkle with the olive oil and optional garlic, and toss gently. (This is the vegan lox.) If time permits, let the pepper strips marinate in the refrigerator for at least 30–60 minutes before serving. To serve, spread the vegan cream cheese on the toasted bagels and top with the vegan lox. Sprinkle with green nori flakes, if desired. Serve at once.

NOTE

- Green nori flakes and nori, dulse, and kelp granules are available in natural food stores. These mineral-rich sea vegetables will add a delicious taste of the sea to your vegan lox. Mitoku brand green nori flakes and Maine Coast Sea Vegetables brand Sea Seasonings are highly recommended.

Good!

Tempeh Tacos

Makes 4 to 8 servings (1 to 2 tacos per person)

calories: 127
protein: 7 g
fat: 5 g
carbohydrate: 16 g
fiber: 3 g

For a Tex-Mex treat, serve these south-of-the-border specialties with plenty of your favorite toppings.

½ pound (8 ounces) tempeh, grated or finely crumbled

2 tablespoons reduced-sodium soy sauce

2 teaspoons chili powder

1 teaspoon garlic powder

½ teaspoon ground cumin

½ teaspoon dried oregano

Dash of bottled hot sauce

2 teaspoons extra-virgin olive oil

½ cup chopped onions

8 soft corn tortillas or hard corn taco shells

Combine the tempeh, soy sauce, chili powder, garlic powder, cumin, oregano, and hot sauce in a medium bowl, and toss until thoroughly combined.

Heat the oil in a medium skillet. When hot, add the onions, lower the heat, and cook and stir for 10–15 minutes, or until tender. Add the tempeh mixture and brown it, stirring almost constantly, for 4–6 minutes.

If using soft tortillas, warm them by placing them one at a time in a dry skillet over medium heat for about 1 minute. Immediately remove the tortilla

Topping Options for Tacos or Bean Burritos

(select one or more)

- Avocado, cut into chunks
- Bell peppers (green or red), slivered or diced
- Carrot, shredded
- Cilantro
- Green onions, sliced
- Guacamole
- Lettuce, shredded

- Hot peppers, seeded and slivered or diced
- Olives (black or green), sliced
- Onions (red), slivered, sliced, or chopped
- Salsa
- Sour Dressing (page 209) or vegan sour cream
- Tomatoes, chopped

from the skillet and lay it on a flat surface. Warm the remaining soft tortillas in the same fashion. If using hard taco shells, warm them briefly in the oven or microwave.

Divide the hot tempeh mixture among the warm tortillas or taco shells. Add your favorite toppings (see page 112) or place bowls of several different toppings on the table so everyone can choose their favorites. Gently fold the soft tortillas, enclosing the filling. To eat, pick up the tacos carefully with your hands.

Bean Burritos Good! Easy!

Makes 4 to 8 servings (1 to 2 burritos per person) | PER BURRITO

Burritos are always fun to construct, and they make a quick and satisfying lunch or dinner that both children and adults enjoy.

calories: 210
protein: 8 g
fat: 4 g
carbohydrate: 34 g
fiber: 6 g

2 cans (15 or 16 ounces each) pinto beans, rinsed and drained (about 3 cups)
1 cup tomato sauce
¼ cup chopped green chiles (fresh or drained canned) or red or green bell peppers
2 teaspoons chili powder
½ teaspoon ground cumin
½ teaspoon garlic powder
½ teaspoon dried oregano
Dash of bottled hot sauce
8 flour tortillas

Combine the beans, tomato sauce, chiles, chili powder, cumin, garlic powder, oregano, and hot sauce in a medium saucepan and bring to a boil. Lower the heat and simmer uncovered for 5 minutes, stirring occasionally. Remove from the heat and mash the beans slightly with a fork, potato masher, or the back of a wooden spoon. Keep warm.

Warm the tortillas by placing them one at a time in a dry skillet over medium heat for about 1 minute. Immediately remove the tortilla from the skillet and lay it on a flat surface. Warm the remaining tortillas in the same fashion.

Place each tortilla on a plate. Spoon a portion of the bean mixture onto each tortilla, placing it in a strip along one side, slightly off-center. Add your favorite toppings (see page 112) and roll the tortillas around the filling. To eat, carefully pick up the burritos with your hands, or use a knife and fork.

Fajitas

PER SERVING

calories: 317
protein: 16 g
fat: 15 g
carbohydrate: 34 g
fiber: 5 g

*T*hese vegetarian fajitas (pronounced fah-HEE-tuhs) contain marinated tempeh or seitan that is browned and coupled with sautéed vegetables and fresh salad greens. Then everything is rolled burrito-style in warm flour tortillas. A little guacamole or a spoonful of spicy salsa would make a delicious garnish.

FAJITA MARINADE

¼ cup red wine vinegar

¼ cup orange juice

2 tablespoons reduced-sodium soy sauce

2 teaspoons dried oregano

½ teaspoon ground cumin

Dash of bottled hot sauce

½ pound (8 ounces) tempeh or seitan, cut into 2½ x ¼-inch strips

VEGETABLE FILLING AND TORTILLAS

4 teaspoons vegetable oil

1 onion, cut into 8 wedges and separated

1 red or green bell pepper, cut into 2 x ½-inch strips

4 flour tortillas

OPTIONAL TOPPINGS

Diced ripe tomatoes

Sliced green onions

Shredded lettuce

For the marinade: Combine the vinegar, orange juice, soy sauce, oregano, cumin, and hot sauce in a small glass measuring cup or bowl. Stir until well combined.

Place the tempeh or seitan strips in a medium ceramic or glass bowl, and pour the marinade over them. Toss very gently so the strips don't break apart, making sure each piece is well coated with the marinade. Cover the bowl and set aside. Marinate at room temperature for 10–20 minutes.

For the filling: Drain the tempeh or seitan strips. Heat 2 teaspoons of the oil in a large, heavy skillet. When hot, add the tempeh or seitan in a single layer. Cook for about 5 minutes, or until the bottom side is golden brown. Carefully turn the strips over and brown the other side for about 3 minutes. Remove from the skillet and set aside.

Add the remaining oil to the skillet, and place it over medium-high heat. When hot, add the onion and bell pepper and cook and stir for 5–8 minutes, or until tender to your liking.

For the tortillas: Warm the tortillas by placing them one at a time in a dry skillet over medium heat for about 1 minute. Immediately remove the tortilla from the skillet and lay it on a flat surface. Warm the remaining tortillas in the same fashion.

To assemble: Spoon equal amounts of the tempeh and the vegetable filling onto each tortilla, placing them in a strip slightly off-center. Top with the optional toppings of your choice. Roll up each tortilla to enclose the filling. To eat, pick up the fajitas carefully with your hands, or use a knife and fork.

Kari

Kari was rescued off of a livestock truck found abandoned on a Washington DC street. It had been very hot and crowded on the truck, so Kari was relieved when rescuers arrived to get her out. When Kari first walked into the pig barn at Farm Sanctuary, she must have known she was in a special place. At the sanctuary, she is treated with the love and affection she deserves, and she is allowed to live the way she wants to live. Usually, she spends her days lying side by side with her best friend, Gretchen, or wading in the pond, and she always amuses the staff and volunteers with her speaking skills. As soon as anyone enters the pig barn, she starts grunting happily, "Huh, huh, huh," and her belly shakes and her ears perk up. She is living the perfect life for a pig and she knows it. Her grunts are her way of showing her joy and gratitude.

instead of

Ants in your pants.

use

Pepper in your pants.

Soups, chowders, and stews

French Onion Soup

Makes about 1½ quarts

You won't believe how easy it is to prepare this delectable classic. Simple and succulent.

1 tablespoon vegetable oil

2 large onions, thinly sliced or chopped

1 to 2 teaspoons crushed garlic

¼ cup flour (any kind)

4 cups water

¼ cup reduced-sodium soy sauce

4 to 6 slices French bread, or 1 to 1½ cups croutons

Pour the oil into a large pot and place over medium-high heat. Add the onions and garlic, lower the heat, and cook and stir for 5 minutes. Stir in the flour, mixing it in well. Gradually stir in the water and soy sauce, taking care to avoid lumps, and bring to a boil. Lower the heat, cover, and gently simmer for 20 minutes, or until the onions are very tender. Just before serving, place 1 slice of French bread or about ¼ cup of croutons in the bottom of each soup bowl. Ladle some of the soup on top and serve at once.

PER CUP   *calories: 134,* protein: 5 g, fat: 3 g, carbohydrate: 22 g, fiber: 2 g

Hungarian Mushroom Soup

Makes about 1 quart | **PER CUP**

Enjoy this timeless medley of Old World flavors—it's always the farmhands' choice.

calories: 113
protein: 6 g
fat: 4 g
carbohydrate: 15 g
fiber: 3 g

2 teaspoons vegetable oil

1 large onion, chopped

2 cups vegetable broth or water

2 cups sliced mushrooms

1 tablespoon dried dill weed, plus more as needed

1 tablespoon Hungarian paprika, plus more as needed

1 tablespoon reduced-sodium soy sauce

¼ cup flour (any kind)

1 cup plain soymilk or rice milk

½ teaspoon salt, or ¼ teaspoon if broth is salted

Ground black pepper

Heat the oil in a large pot. Add the onion, lower the heat, and cook and stir until soft, about 10 minutes. Stir in ½ cup of the broth, the mushrooms, dill weed, paprika, and soy sauce, and mix well. Cover and simmer gently for 15 minutes.

Place the flour in a small bowl. Gradually whisk in the soymilk, making sure the mixture has no lumps. Stir into the simmering mushroom mixture, and cook, stirring constantly, until thickened.

Stir in the remaining broth, salt, and pepper to taste. If desired, stir in additional dill weed or paprika to taste. Heat through, but do not boil.

instead of

An oath and an egg are soon broken.

use

A promise and a plate are soon broken.

Sadie's Vitality Broth

PER SERVING

calories: 222
protein: 10 g
fat: 1 g
carbohydrate: 42 g
fiber: 6 g

Makes 4 to 6 servings

No ruffled feathers go into this nutritious, soothing, simple soup. It's the perfect broth and noodle soup any time you please, and the ideal alternative to chicken noodle soup.

6 cups water

1 can (15 or 16 ounces) chickpeas, rinsed and drained (about 1¾ cups)

¼ cup nutritional yeast flakes

1 to 2 tablespoons minced fresh parsley, or 1 to 2 teaspoons dried

1 teaspoon salt

1 teaspoon onion powder

½ teaspoon garlic powder

½ teaspoon paprika

½ teaspoon ground coriander

⅛ teaspoon ground turmeric

¾ cup orzo (a rice-shaped pasta) or other small pasta

Combine the water, chickpeas, nutritional yeast flakes, parsley, salt, onion powder, garlic powder, paprika, coriander, and turmeric in a large saucepan and bring to a boil. Add the pasta and stir well. Lower the heat slightly and simmer, stirring occasionally, until the pasta is tender, about 20 minutes. Serve hot.

Astoria

Astoria was rescued from a "free range" egg production facility where, in truth, the hens were not given much freedom at all. When she first emerged from her carrier at Farm Sanctuary, her steps were awkward and slow, because she had been caged for so long. But soon, Astoria learned to walk and run comfortably, and now nothing can slow her down! Each day, she spends hours scampering about wildly with her friends, stretching and flapping her wings, and making expeditions into the tall green grass behind the chicken barn. She especially enjoys the warmth of the California sunshine and can often be seen soaking up some rays on a summer afternoon.

Cheez Please Soup

C reamy cheddar cheese soup was a childhood favorite, so I was compelled to create a dairy-free version that was as velvety and rich-tasting as the one I fondly remember.

calories: 178
protein: 15 g
fat: 4 g
carbohydrate: 23 g
fiber: 6 g

1 large potato, peeled and diced

1 large onion, coarsely chopped

1 large carrot, coarsely chopped

1 cup vegetable broth or water

1 package (about 12 ounces) firm silken tofu, crumbled

1 cup plain soymilk, vegetable broth, or water

½ to 1 cup nutritional yeast flakes

2 tablespoons freshly squeezed lemon juice

2 tablespoons extra-virgin olive oil (optional)

1¼ teaspoons salt, or ½ teaspoon if broth is salted

1 teaspoon onion powder

¼ teaspoon garlic powder

1½ to 2 cups bite-size broccoli or cauliflower florets, steamed until tender (optional)

Combine the potato, onion, carrot, and vegetable broth in a large pot and bring to a boil. Lower the heat, cover, and simmer, stirring once or twice, until the vegetables are tender.

Combine the tofu, soymilk, nutritional yeast flakes, lemon juice, optional oil, salt, onion powder, and garlic powder in a large bowl. Mix well and stir into the cooked vegetables.

Purée the soup in batches in a blender. Process until completely smooth (this will take a few minutes per batch). Pour the blended batches into a clean, large bowl. When all the soup has been blended, return it to the pot and add the optional broccoli. Warm over low heat until hot. Adjust the seasonings, if necessary.

VARIATION

- **Cheezy Vegetable Soup:** Add 1 package (10 ounces) mixed frozen vegetables, cooked according to the package directions and drained well.

Butternutty Chowder

calories: 218
protein: 9 g
fat: 11 g
carbohydrate: 23 g
fiber: 5 g

This nourishing soup is surprisingly easy to prepare, and it's a complete one-pot meal!

1 large butternut squash

8 cups light vegetable broth

½ cup long-grain brown or white rice

2 cups finely chopped or shredded green cabbage

½ to 1 cup smooth peanut butter

½ to 1 cup chopped fresh cilantro or parsley

Soy sauce

Salt

Bottled hot sauce or cayenne

Slice the squash in half lengthwise from top to bottom. Scoop out the seeds and pulp and discard them. Slice the squash horizontally into ½-inch-thick half circles. Using a paring knife, slice away the thick rind. Cut the squash into bite-size chunks and place them in a large pot. Add the vegetable broth, rice, and cabbage, and bring to a boil. Lower the heat, cover, and simmer for 1 hour, or until the rice is well cooked and the squash is very tender and starting to disintegrate.

Shortly before serving, remove from the heat, stir in the peanut butter, and mix until it is well incorporated. Stir in the cilantro, and season with soy sauce, salt, and hot sauce to taste. If the soup is too thick, thin it with a little vegetable broth, water, or plain soymilk.

instead of

Never put all your eggs in one basket.

use

Never put all your berries in one bowl.

Potato, Tomato, and Cheez Chowder

*T*his chowder is thick and satisfying—perfect for lunch or dinner on a chilly day.

calories: 209
protein: 9 g
fat: 6 g
carbohydrate: 34 g
fiber: 7 g

2 cups diced potatoes (thin-skinned or peeled)

1 large onion, chopped

½ cup diced celery

6 cups light vegetable broth or water

2 cups plain soymilk or rice milk

½ cup flour (any kind)

½ cup tahini

½ cup nutritional yeast flakes

½ cup pimiento pieces, drained, or roasted red peppers
    (skin and seeds removed)

2 tablespoons freshly squeezed lemon juice

2 teaspoons onion powder

2 teaspoons salt, or ½ to 1 teaspoon if broth is salted

½ teaspoon crushed garlic

½ teaspoon dry mustard

¼ cup minced flat-leaf parsley, or 4 teaspoons dried parsley flakes

1 can (16 ounces) chopped tomatoes, with juice (no salt added)

Combine the potatoes, onion, celery, and vegetable broth in a large, heavy pot and bring to a boil. Lower the heat, cover, and simmer for 15 minutes, or until the vegetables are tender. Combine the soymilk, flour, tahini, nutritional yeast flakes, pimientos, lemon juice, onion powder, salt, garlic, and dry mustard in a blender, and process until completely smooth. Pour into the pot with the potatoes, and simmer over medium heat, stirring often, for 15–20 minutes, or until smooth and thickened. Stir in the parsley and tomatoes, and heat through but do not boil. Serve hot.

Lima Bean Soup

Makes about 1½ quarts

PER CUP

calories: 211
protein: 10 g
fat: 4 g
carbohydrate: 35 g
fiber: 8 g

This is a thick, creamy, stick-to-your-ribs soup. It's so rich and delectable, no one will believe it's low in fat and doesn't contain any dairy products!

2 packages (10 ounces each) frozen large lima beans (about 4 cups)

2 cups vegetable broth

1 tablespoon vegetable oil

1 onion, chopped

1 cup finely chopped carrots

½ teaspoon crushed garlic

2 tablespoons flour (any kind)

1 teaspoon dried thyme, crushed

1 teaspoon salt, or ¼ to ½ teaspoon if broth is salted

Ground black pepper

1 cup plain soymilk or rice milk

Place the lima beans in a large pot, and cover them completely with water. Bring to a boil, lower the heat, cover, and simmer gently for 10–12 minutes, or until tender. Drain well. Transfer half the beans to a blender, add 1 cup of the vegetable broth, and process until creamy and completely smooth. Process the remaining beans and broth in the same fashion. Set aside.

Pour the oil into a large pot and place over medium-high heat. When hot, stir in the onion, carrots, and garlic. Cover the pot and lower the heat. Cook, stirring occasionally, for 10–15 minutes, or until the vegetables are tender. Stir in the flour, thyme, salt, and pepper to taste, and mix well. Gradually stir in the soymilk (taking care to avoid lumps) and cook, stirring almost constantly, until the mixture thickens slightly. Stir in the blended beans and warm through on medium-low heat. Serve hot.

NOTE

- Keep a close eye on the lima beans as they cook. Lima beans create a lot of foam that can be forced out from under the lid of the pot. To keep foam to a minimum, stir the lima beans often, lift the lid occasionally, cook the lima beans with the lid slightly ajar, and/or add a teaspoon of vegetable oil to the cooking water.

Bread and Tomato Soup

calories: 116

*A*lthough most North Americans have never heard of bread soup, it is a popular staple throughout Europe, with various regions having their own special versions. Slightly stale bread is ideal to use, and this recipe probably came about as a great way to use it up. Use the best-tasting bread you can find, as it will add a gorgeous flavor to your soup. It's also worth the effort to look for extra-juicy, red ripe organic tomatoes to infuse your soup with outstanding taste and a rich texture.

protein: 3 g

fat: 4 g

carbohydrate: 18 g

fiber: 3 g

1 tablespoon extra-virgin olive oil

1 small onion, diced

½ teaspoon crushed garlic

4 ripe tomatoes, coarsely chopped

2 tablespoons tomato paste (no salt added)

Pinch of crushed red pepper flakes

2½ cups light vegetable broth or water

1½ cups bread cubes, firmly packed

¼ cup torn fresh basil, or 1 teaspoon dried

Salt

Ground black pepper

Pour the oil into a large, heavy pot, and place over medium-high heat. When hot, add the onion and garlic, lower the heat, and cook and stir for 15 minutes, or until the onion is tender and golden brown. Add the tomatoes, tomato paste, and red pepper flakes, and stir until the tomato paste is well incorporated. Raise the heat to bring the mixture to a simmer, then simmer uncovered for 20 minutes, stirring occasionally. Adjust the heat as necessary to keep the tomatoes from scorching.

After 20 minutes, add the vegetable broth, bread cubes, and basil. Bring to a boil, lower the heat, and simmer uncovered for 10–15 minutes, stirring occasionally and mashing the bread into the soup with the back of a wooden spoon. Take care that the bread doesn't scorch on the bottom of the pot. Season with salt and pepper to taste. Serve hot, warm, or chilled.

Elegant Broccoli Bisque

PER CUP

calories: 128
protein: 6 g
fat: 4 g
carbohydrate: 18 g
fiber: 2 g

Makes about 7 cups

*T*he enchanting flavor of this creamy soup makes it exquisite company fare, but the simplicity of the ingredients and directions make it perfect for everyday meals as well.

4 cups broccoli (or 2 cups broccoli and 2 cups cauliflower),
   cut into small florets

2 cups light vegetable broth or water

2 potatoes, peeled and cut into chunks

1 cup chopped onions

2 teaspoons dried tarragon

2 cups plain soymilk or rice milk

2 tablespoons almond butter

1 tablespoon Dijon mustard

Salt

Ground black pepper

Combine the broccoli, broth, potatoes, onions, and tarragon in a large, heavy pot. Bring to a boil, lower the heat, cover, and simmer 10–12 minutes, or until the vegetables are very tender.

Process the soup in batches in a blender, adding a portion of the milk, almond butter, and mustard to each batch. Rinse out the pot and return the blended mixture to it. Season with salt and pepper to taste. Place over medium-low heat, stirring often, until heated through. Serve hot.

instead of

Sauce for the goose is sauce for the gander.

use

Sauce for the peach is sauce for the plum.

Stewed Winter Vegetables

his is the vegan answer to chicken soup! It's soothing, healing, and satisfying. The flavor is sweet and mild, and the texture is thick and juicy. Serve it with plenty of whole grain bread to dip into the delicious broth.

calories: 154
protein: 4 g
fat: 1 g
carbohydrate: 36 g
fiber: 5 g

6 to 8 cups peeled and cut root vegetables (such as winter squash, yams, rutabaga, turnips, parsnips, potatoes, and/or carrots), in large chunks

1 large onion, cut into wedges

6 to 8 garlic cloves (whole, halved, sliced, or coarsely chopped)

Vegetable broth or water, as needed

2 cups torn or chopped greens (such as kale, collard greens, turnip greens, or mustard greens)

1 to 2 tablespoons extra-virgin olive oil (optional)

Salt

Place the root vegetables, onion, and garlic in a large, heavy pot. Add enough vegetable broth to more than cover the vegetables. Bring to a boil, lower the heat, cover, and simmer for 30 minutes. Stir in the greens, cover, and continue to simmer for 10–15 minutes longer, or until the vegetables are very tender and starting to break apart. Stir in the optional olive oil and season with salt to taste.

How to Prevent Peeled Yams from Turning Brown

To prevent yams from discoloring after they have been peeled and cut, place them in a bowl of water to which a little lemon juice has been added. Just before using, place the yams in a colander and thoroughly rinse off the lemon water before proceeding with the recipe.

Stick-to-Your-Ribs Chili

Makes about 1 quart

calories: 219
protein: 10 g
fat: 3 g
carbohydrate: 41 g
fiber: 13 g

*N*othing satisfies quite like a steaming hot bowl of red. The bulgur in this recipe adds a hearty, chewy quality that complements the soft, rich texture of the beans.

2 teaspoons vegetable oil

1 cup minced onions

½ cup minced celery

½ to 1 teaspoon crushed garlic

2 ripe tomatoes, peeled, seeded, and coarsely chopped

1 can (15 or 16 ounces) red, pink, or black beans, rinsed and drained (about 1¾ cups)

1 can (8 ounces) tomato sauce

1 cup water

⅓ cup bulgur

2 tablespoons tomato paste (no salt added)

1 tablespoon chili powder

1 tablespoon granulated sugar or other sweetener of your choice

½ teaspoon dried oregano

¼ teaspoon ground black pepper

¼ teaspoon ground cumin

⅛ teaspoon ground allspice or cinnamon

Pinch of cayenne

Salt

How to Peel and Seed a Tomato

- **To peel a tomato:** Cut a small cross on the bottom of the tomato using a sharp knife. Turn the tomato over and cut out the core. Immerse the tomato in a pot of boiling water for 10–15 seconds. Remove it from the pot using a slotted spoon, and place it in a bowl of cold water. Let it rest for 1 minute, then remove it from the cold water and peel off the skin using your fingers; it should peel away easily.

- **To seed a tomato:** Cut the tomato in half crosswise, and gently squeeze out the seeds or scoop them out using your fingers or a small spoon.

Pour the oil into a large, heavy pot, and place over medium-high heat. When hot, add the onions, celery, and garlic. Lower the heat and simmer, stirring occasionally, for 10–15 minutes, or until the onions are tender. Add the tomatoes, beans, tomato sauce, water, bulgur, tomato paste, chili powder, sugar, oregano, pepper, cumin, allspice, and cayenne, and stir until well combined. Bring to a boil, lower the heat, cover, and simmer for 20 minutes, stirring occasionally. Season with salt to taste. Serve hot.

Creamy Potato Kale Soup

Makes about 7 cups | **PER CUP**

*P*otatoes and kale are a match made in culinary heaven. You'll be surprised how thick and rich-tasting this nutritious soup is, even without any dairy products.

calories: 134
protein: 5 g
fat: 1 g
carbohydrate: 27 g
fiber: 3 g

4 cups chopped or torn kale leaves, firmly packed

4 cups diced peeled potatoes

3 cups light vegetable broth or water

1 cup chopped onions

1 teaspoon crushed garlic

1½ cups plain soymilk or rice milk

1 tablespoon extra-virgin olive oil (optional)

Salt

Ground black pepper

Combine the kale, potatoes, broth, onions, and garlic in a large pot and bring to a boil. Lower the heat, cover, and simmer, stirring occasionally, for 30 minutes, or until the kale is very tender.

Purée the soup in batches in a blender, adding a portion of the soymilk to each batch. Rinse out the pot and return the blended mixture to it. Season with the optional olive oil and salt and pepper to taste. Place over medium-low heat, stirring often, until heated through. Serve hot.

Farmhouse Stew

PER SERVING

Makes 4 servings

calories: 356
protein: 24 g
fat: 8 g
carbohydrate: 54 g
fiber: 8 g

Enjoy great old-fashioned beef stew flavor with a new-fangled twist—no beef!

4 cups diced potatoes (thin-skinned or peeled)

4 large carrots, peeled, sliced in half lengthwise, and cut into 1-inch chunks

2 celery stalks, finely chopped

2 cups dark vegetable broth or water

2 bay leaves

2 teaspoons vegetable oil

1 cup chopped onions

2 cups sliced mushrooms

2 tablespoons flour (any kind)

2 tablespoons tahini

½ cup water

3 tablespoons reduced-sodium soy sauce

2 cups seitan chunks

Salt

Ground black pepper

Combine the potatoes, carrots, celery, vegetable broth, and bay leaves in a large, heavy pot, and bring to a boil. Lower the heat, cover, and simmer, stirring occasionally, for about 20 minutes, or until the vegetables are tender.

While the vegetables are simmering, pour the oil into a large skillet, and place over medium-high heat. When hot, add the onions and cook and stir for 8 minutes, or until almost tender. Add the mushrooms and continue to cook, stirring often, for 4–6 minutes, or until the mushrooms are tender. Remove from the heat. Stir in the flour and mix well. Stir in the tahini and mix well. Gradually stir in the ½ cup water and soy sauce, and mix vigorously until the sauce is completely smooth (except for the onions and mushrooms). Stir into the cooked vegetables and broth and mix well.

Add the seitan chunks and bring the stew to a boil, stirring almost constantly. Lower the heat and simmer, stirring often, for 3–5 minutes, just until the sauce thickens. Remove the bay leaves, and season with salt and pepper to taste. Serve hot.

Chuckwagon Stew

*P*lenty of herbs and seasonings make a sensational broth for this stew. Bread for dipping into the delicious gravy is absolutely essential. Come and get it!

calories: 260
protein: 15 g
fat: 7 g
carbohydrate: 39 g
fiber: 7 g

3 cups dark vegetable broth or water

½ pound (8 ounces) tempeh, cut into ½-inch cubes

2 potatoes, peeled and cut into bite-size chunks

2 onions, cut into wedges

4 carrots, peeled and sliced

½ cup ketchup

¼ cup reduced-sodium soy sauce

2 teaspoons extra-virgin olive oil (optional)

1 teaspoon garlic powder

1 teaspoon dried tarragon

¼ teaspoon ground black pepper

Salt

¼ cup flour (any kind)

⅓ cup cold water

1 to 2 tablespoons chopped fresh parsley, for garnish

Combine the vegetable broth, tempeh, potatoes, onions, carrots, ketchup, soy sauce, optional oil, garlic powder, tarragon, and pepper in a large, heavy pot, and bring to a boil. Lower the heat, cover, and simmer gently, stirring occasionally, for 30 minutes, or until the vegetables are very tender. Season with salt to taste.

Place the flour in a small bowl or measuring cup. Gradually stir in the water, beating vigorously with a fork until the mixture is smooth. Stir this mixture into the stew, stirring constantly until the gravy is thickened and bubbly. Ladle into soup bowls, and garnish with the parsley.

VARIATIONS

- **Chuckwagon Stew with Beans:** Replace the tempeh with 1 can (15 or 16 ounces) of your favorite beans, rinsed and drained (about 1¾ cups).

- **Chuckwagon Stew with Seitan:** Replace the tempeh with 1 to 2 cups seitan chunks.

Lentil and Eggplant Goulash

calories: 213
protein: 13 g
fat: 1 g
carbohydrate: 42 g
fiber: 14 g

Serve this flavorful Hungarian stew over rice or pasta, or in bowls as a thick stew. Although it takes a while to cook, it takes very little effort to make. Garnish it with a dollop of Sour Dressing (page 209) or vegan sour cream, if you like, and a generous sprinkling of Hungarian paprika.

½ cup vegetable broth

1 large onion, cut in half and thinly sliced

3 medium carrots, peeled and diced

1½ cups dried lentils

¼ cup chopped flat-leaf parsley

2 tablespoons herbal seasoning blend (see note)

½ to 1 teaspoon crushed garlic

1 teaspoon dried oregano

1 teaspoon dried basil

2½ cups water or vegetable broth

1 medium eggplant, peeled and cubed

1 can (6 ounces) tomato paste (no salt added)

¼ cup red wine vinegar

¼ teaspoon ground cinnamon

Salt

Ground black pepper

Heat ¼ cup of the vegetable broth in a large soup pot. Add the onion, and cook and stir until it is limp. Stir in the carrots, lentils, parsley, herbal seasoning, garlic, oregano, and basil. Mix well. Add the water and bring to a boil. Lower the heat, cover, and simmer for 1 hour.

While the lentils are cooking, heat the remaining ¼ cup vegetable broth in a large skillet or saucepan (nonstick will work best). Add the eggplant, and cook and stir until soft. If necessary, add more broth or water to keep the eggplant from sticking. When the lentils have simmered for 1 hour, add the eggplant, tomato paste, vinegar, cinnamon, and salt and pepper to taste. Simmer for 1 hour longer. Add additional water or broth as necessary to achieve the desired consistency.

NOTE

■ Although any herbal blend will work well in this recipe, Gayelord Hauser brand Spike all-purpose seasoning is highly recommended.

Main dishes

Noodles and Greens

*T*his recipe is so incredibly delicious that nobody will give two hoots about how healthful it is. It's a weekly staple in my home, especially on days when schedules are hectic and no one feels like cooking. Look for the firmest, most flavorful smoked tofu you can find. Extra-firm smoked tofu will shred more easily, and one with a deep, intensely smoked flavor will really make the flavors pop and the dish come alive. A food processor fitted with a shredding disc will make fast work of preparing the tofu.

    1 bunch (about 1 pound) collard greens (see page 132)

    7 to 8 ounces long, flat noodles (such as udon, linguine, or fettuccine)

    1 carrot, peeled and shredded (optional)

    2 tablespoons extra-virgin olive oil

    2 tablespoons reduced-sodium soy sauce

    1 tablespoon umeboshi vinegar

    6 to 8 ounces extra-firm smoked tofu, shredded

Fill a large pot with water and bring to a boil. Clean the collard leaves and lay them flat on a cutting board. Working with one leaf at a time, slice out the stem lengthwise and discard it (once the stem is cut out, the leaves will be in two pieces). Pile the leaves so the outside curves are facing the same direction (in order to do this, the first leaf will face up, the next leaf will face down, the next leaf will face up, and so forth). Take a stack of four leaves and roll them

PER SERVING   *calories: 325*, protein: 16 g, fat: 10 g, carbohydrate: 47 g, fiber: 7 g

tightly like a cigar. Using a sharp knife, slice the roll crosswise very thinly. This will make fine, spaghetti-like strands when the slices are unraveled. Stack, roll, and slice the remaining leaves in the same fashion. Transfer the sliced collard greens to the pot of boiling water, cover, and lower the heat. Simmer for about 20 minutes, or until the greens are tender to your liking.

Add the noodles to the pot with the greens. Simmer uncovered, stirring occasionally, until the noodles are tender. Drain the noodles and greens well and return them to the pot. Add the optional shredded carrot, oil, soy sauce, and vinegar, and toss until the noodles and greens are evenly coated. Taste and add more oil, soy sauce, or vinegar, if necessary.

Divide the noodles and greens among four serving bowls. Top each portion with one-quarter of the shredded smoked tofu.

NOTE

- The collard greens may be chopped or torn instead of thinly sliced. Slice out and discard the stems before chopping the leaves.

VARIATIONS

- **Noodles and Kale:** Replace the collard greens with 1 pound chopped or finely torn kale.
- **Noodles, Greens, and Olives:** Instead of the smoked tofu, use ½ cup pitted oil-cured kalamata olives, coarsely chopped.

Buying, Storing, and Cleaning Collard Greens

Collard greens are a dark green leafy vegetable with a flavor similar to cabbage and kale. They are a staple in Southern cuisine. Collards grow as large oval leaves on long stalks. Although collards can be found fresh or frozen, they are typically available fresh year-round. Fresh collards are usually sold as a loose bunch of leaves. Look for leaves that are on the small side, since these will be more tender. Avoid leaves that are yellowed or withered or that have insect holes. Wrap collards in a damp paper towel and store them in a perforated plastic bag in the refrigerator; they will keep for up to one week. Clean collard leaves thoroughly before cooking them by dunking each leaf into a bowl of fresh water several times; then rinse the leaves under running water.

Sweet-and-Sour Tempeh

Makes 4 servings

PER SERVING

calories: 292
protein: 13 g
fat: 13 g
carbohydrate: 37 g
fiber: 6 g

This notable entrée always receives rave reviews. Serve it with your favorite cooked grain, steamed greens, and a salad.

2 tablespoons extra-virgin olive oil

½ pound (8 ounces) tempeh, cut into cubes

1 cup grated carrots

1 red bell pepper, sliced into strips

1 green bell pepper, sliced into strips

½ teaspoon crushed garlic

2 cups canned pineapple chunks, packed in juice

¼ cup apple cider vinegar

¼ cup water

2 tablespoons reduced-sodium soy sauce

1 tablespoon granulated sugar

1 tablespoon cornstarch

1 teaspoon ground ginger

2 green onions, thinly sliced, for garnish (optional)

Pour the oil into a large, heavy skillet, and place over medium-high heat. When hot, add the tempeh and cook and stir for 15–20 minutes, or until browned all over. Add the carrots, bell peppers, and garlic, and cook and stir until the peppers are tender.

Drain the pineapple but reserve ½ cup of the juice. Place the reserved juice in a small bowl or measuring cup. Using a fork or mini-whisk, beat in the vinegar, water, soy sauce, sugar, cornstarch, and ginger. Mix until well combined. Pour over the tempeh and vegetables, then add the pineapple chunks. Cook, stirring constantly, for about 2 minutes, or until the sauce is just thickened. Serve hot, garnished with the optional green onions.

instead of
You can kill two birds with one stone.

use
You can slice two carrots with one knife.

"C" Is for Couscous

PER SERVING

calories: 344
protein: 11 g
fat: 14 g
carbohydrate: 45 g
fiber: 5 g

One evening, a group of friends and my husband and I decided to start the fictitious Universal Alphabetical Vegan Food Preparation League (UAVFPL) as a fun way of sharing food. We all felt it would be an enjoyable challenge (or perhaps ignite the next diet sensation) to try to create meals that include only foods that begin with a single letter of the alphabet. Starting with A and working our way through the alphabet letter by letter, we discovered new foods and learned that we could create exciting dishes by following this unusual method for meal planning and recipe invention. We began to extend the theme into activities that begin with the same letter, too (for example, bowling for B night, or dancing on D night), so our food and entertainment for the evening would be aligned. This particular recipe was devised for C night (well, obviously). You can add any other C foods to it that you like—you'll be amazed how well they all go together! By the way, anyone from any country, planet, or universe can join the League. They just have to have an alphabet!

2 tablespoons extra-virgin olive oil

1⅓ cups giant pearl couscous

2 cups boiling water

2 to 4 tablespoons freshly squeezed citrus juice (lime, lemon, or orange)

½ cup chopped raw or toasted cashews

1 cup cooked chickpeas, drained

1 cup diced English cucumbers

1 cup chopped fresh cilantro

1 carrot, peeled and finely diced or shredded (optional)

½ cup thinly sliced chives

1 teaspoon chili powder

¼ teaspoon cayenne

¼ teaspoon ground cumin

¼ teaspoon ground coriander

Pinch of ground cinnamon

Pinch of ground cloves

Salt

Pour 1 tablespoon of the olive oil into a medium saucepan and place over medium heat. Add the couscous and cook and stir until lightly browned, about 5 minutes. Slowly add the 2 cups boiling water and bring to a boil. Turn the heat down to medium-low, cover, and simmer for about 12 minutes, or until all the liquid is absorbed.

Transfer the couscous to a large bowl, and add the remaining 1 tablespoon olive oil and all the remaining ingredients. Season with salt to taste, and toss gently but thoroughly. Adjust the seasonings as needed and toss again. Serve warm or thoroughly chilled. Stored in a covered container in the refrigerator, "C" Is for Couscous will keep for 3–5 days.

Hearty Cabbage Casserole

Makes 4 to 6 servings | PER SERVING

This satisfying, "beefy" casserole tastes like traditional stuffed cabbage leaves, without all the work and hassle.

1 tablespoon extra-virgin olive oil

1 cup chopped onions

1 pound (16 ounces) vegan burger crumbles

1 cup cooked rice (any kind)

1 teaspoon salt

¼ teaspoon garlic powder

¼ teaspoon dried oregano

¼ teaspoon ground black pepper

¼ teaspoon dried thyme, crushed

6 cups coarsely shredded cabbage (about 1 small head)

2 cups vegan tomato soup

calories: 272
protein: 16 g
fat: 6 g
carbohydrate: 42 g
fiber: 10 g

Preheat the oven to 350 degrees F. Oil a medium casserole dish, or mist it with nonstick cooking spray.

Pour the olive oil into a large skillet, and place it over medium-high heat. Add the onions, and cook and stir until tender. Stir in the vegan burger crumbles, cooked rice, salt, garlic powder, oregano, pepper, and thyme. Mix well. Spread half the cabbage over the bottom of the prepared casserole dish. Cover it with the burger crumble mixture, and sprinkle with the remaining cabbage. Pour the tomato soup evenly over the top. Cover tightly and bake 1 hour, or until the cabbage is tender.

Southern-Fried Tofu

PER SERVING

calories: 284
protein: 24 g
fat: 12 g
carbohydrate: 18 g
fiber: 6 g

Makes 12 pieces (3 to 4 servings)

This dish is truly finger-lickin' good. Don't let the long list of seasonings fool you—this recipe is very simple to prepare. Serve it as an entrée along with a salad, steamed vegetables, and a grain or potato. It also makes a wonderful sandwich filling with vegan mayonnaise or ketchup, lettuce, and tomato.

TOFU

1 pound (16 ounces) firm regular tofu, rinsed and patted dry

SEASONING MIX

1½ cups nutritional yeast flakes

2 teaspoons salt

1 teaspoon garlic powder

1 teaspoon onion powder

1 teaspoon dried parsley flakes

½ teaspoon paprika

½ teaspoon dried tarragon

½ teaspoon dried dill weed

½ teaspoon dried basil

½ teaspoon dried oregano

½ teaspoon curry powder

¼ teaspoon dry mustard

¼ teaspoon ground rosemary

¼ teaspoon ground celery seeds

COATING

⅔ cup plain soymilk

2 teaspoons freshly squeezed lemon juice

⅔ cup flour (any kind), as needed

1 tablespoon vegetable oil, more or less as needed for browning

For the tofu: Cut the tofu horizontally into three equal slabs. If time permits, press the tofu according to the directions on page 33. If time does not allow you to press the tofu, wrap it in a clean tea towel or in paper towels, and press it gently all over with your hands to extract as much moisture as possible.

For the seasoning mix: Combine all the ingredients in a wide, shallow bowl. Stir until well blended.

For the coating: Combine the soymilk and lemon juice in a small bowl, and stir well. Place the flour in a separate small bowl.

To assemble and cook: Cut each slab of the pressed tofu into 4 triangles, making a total of 12 in all. Working with one piece at a time, dredge the tofu in the flour. Shake off any excess. Next, dip the tofu in the soured soymilk, submerging it completely. Immediately dredge the tofu in the seasoning mix, making sure it is well coated all over. (See notes.)

Coat a large, heavy skillet with a layer of vegetable oil, and place it over medium-high heat. When hot, add the tofu pieces in a single layer. Cook until the bottoms are well browned. Turn the pieces over and cook the other side until well browned. You will need to cook the tofu in several batches depending on the size of your skillet. Add a little more oil to the skillet between each batch, and adjust the heat as necessary.

As soon as you remove the tofu from the skillet, place it on a plate lined with a double thickness of paper towels to blot off any excess oil and keep the surface of the tofu crisp.

NOTES

- You may proceed cooking the tofu as soon as a few pieces have been coated, or you can place the coated tofu on a sheet of waxed paper and wait to begin the cooking process until all the pieces are ready. If the outside surface of the tofu becomes moist or sticky during the time it is resting prior to being cooked, dredge it again in the seasoning mix.

- Save the leftover seasoning mix, and store it in an airtight container at room temperature. It will keep for several months. Use it to make more Southern-Fried Tofu or as a flavorful coating for fried tomatoes or zucchini. Simply follow the breading and cooking directions above.

- Alternatively, the tofu can be sliced into slabs, sticks, cubes, or nuggets instead of triangles.

instead of
Cook someone's goose.
use
Burn someone's cookies.

Bread Stuffing Casserole

calories: 309
protein: 9 g
fat: 16 g
carbohydrate: 36 g
fiber: 6 g

*H*ere is the perfect holiday entrée or focal point for a cool-weather buffet. Serve it with your favorite gravy, cranberry sauce, winter squash, and steamed greens. Because it is effortless to make, this satisfying dish is also great for everyday meals.

4 cups whole grain bread cubes
¼ cup minced fresh parsley
2 tablespoons nutritional yeast flakes
1 teaspoon salt
¼ teaspoon dried marjoram
¼ teaspoon dried sage
¼ teaspoon dried thyme, crushed
⅛ teaspoon ground rosemary, or ¼ teaspoon dried rosemary, crushed
⅛ teaspoon ground black pepper
½ cup coarsely chopped walnuts
½ cup chopped onions
½ cup sliced mushrooms
½ cup finely diced celery
½ cup dried cherries, dried cranberries, seedless raisins, or chopped dried fruit (such as apricots, apples, or prunes)
½ cup boiling vegetable broth or water
2 tablespoons reduced-sodium soy sauce
1 to 2 tablespoons extra-virgin olive oil

Preheat the oven to 350 degrees F. Oil a two-quart casserole dish (that has a tight-fitting lid), or mist it with nonstick cooking spray.

Place the bread cubes in a very large bowl. Combine the parsley, nutritional yeast flakes, salt, marjoram, sage, thyme, rosemary, and pepper in a small bowl, and stir to mix well. Sprinkle over the bread cubes, and toss with a fork or wooden spoon until evenly distributed. Add the walnuts, onions, mushrooms, celery, and dried cherries, and toss again gently but thoroughly.

Stir the soy sauce and olive oil into the boiling broth and pour over the bread cube mixture to moisten it. Again, toss gently but thoroughly. Add a little additional broth or water if the mixture appears too dry. Transfer to the prepared casserole dish, cover, and bake for 20 minutes. Uncover and bake for 10 minutes longer.

Chickpeas à la King

Good! (handwritten)

*U*se chickpeas, not chicken, in this hearty old-fashioned entrée. You're bound to get compliments that will make you strut. Serve it over rice, toasted bread triangles, or split biscuits.

calories: 365
protein: 21 g
fat: 9 g
carbohydrate: 51 g
fiber: 14 g

1 tablespoon vegetable oil

1 cup sliced mushrooms

½ cup finely diced red bell peppers

½ cup flour (any kind)

¼ cup nutritional yeast flakes

½ teaspoon salt

½ teaspoon paprika

¼ teaspoon dried thyme, crushed

⅛ teaspoon ground black pepper

2 cups plain soymilk or other plain nondairy milk

1 can (15 or 16 ounces) chickpeas, rinsed and drained (about 1¾ cups)

½ cup thinly sliced green onions

Pour the oil into a medium saucepan, and place it over medium-high heat. When the oil is hot, add the mushrooms and bell peppers and cook, stirring almost constantly, for 3–4 minutes. Stir in the flour, nutritional yeast flakes, salt, paprika, thyme, and pepper. Cook, stirring constantly, for 1 minute longer.

Remove from the heat and gradually stir in the soymilk, adding about ½ cup at a time. Take care to keep the mixture smooth and free of lumps.

After all the soymilk has been added and the mixture is smooth, place over medium-high heat and cook, stirring constantly, until the sauce thickens and comes to a boil. Turn the heat down to low, and add the chickpeas and green onions. Heat, stirring almost constantly, for 3–5 minutes, or until the chickpeas are hot.

NOTE

- This recipe makes a sauce that is very thick. If you prefer a thinner sauce, gradually add a small amount of additional plain soymilk, light vegetable broth, or water after the sauce has thickened, stirring in 1 tablespoon at a time until the desired consistency is achieved.

Classic Quiche

PER SERVING

calories: 356
protein: 18 g
fat: 14 g
carbohydrate: 40 g
fiber: 8 g

his simple quiche is easily adapted to a number of different variations. It contains no eggs, cream, dairy milk, or cheese, yet it's very creamy and rich-tasting.

1 Perfect Pie Crust (page 216) or other uncooked pie crust of your choice, prebaked for 10 to 12 minutes

2 packages (about 12 ounces each) extra-firm silken tofu, crumbled

¾ cup plain soymilk, light vegetable broth, or water

½ cup flour (any kind)

¼ cup nutritional yeast flakes

1 teaspoon salt, or ¾ teaspoon if broth is salted (see note)

¼ teaspoon ground nutmeg

Scant ¼ teaspoon ground turmeric

⅛ teaspoon ground white pepper (optional)

1 tablespoon vegetable oil

1½ cups finely chopped onions

⅔ cup vegan bacon bits (optional)

Prepare and prebake the pie crust as directed. Cool on a wire rack for 10 minutes. Lower the oven temperature to 350 degrees F.

Combine the tofu, soymilk, flour, nutritional yeast flakes, salt, nutmeg, turmeric, and optional pepper in a blender or food processor, and process until the mixture is completely smooth. Stop the machine frequently to stir the mixture and scrape down the sides of the container with a rubber spatula. Set aside.

Pour the oil into a medium skillet, and place over medium-high heat. When hot, add the onions, lower the heat slightly, and cook and stir for about 8 minutes, or until tender and golden brown.

Stir the onions and optional vegan bacon bits into the blended mixture, and pour into the prepared pie crust. Bake on the center rack of the oven for 40–45 minutes, or until the top is firm, browned, and slightly puffed. Allow the quiche to rest for at least 15–30 minutes before slicing.

VARIATIONS

- **Broccoli Quiche:** Steam 2 cups bite-size broccoli florets until tender-crisp. Stir into the blended mixture before pouring into the pie crust.

- **Spinach Quiche:** Cook one package (10 ounces) frozen chopped spinach according to the package directions. Drain well in a wire mesh strainer. Cool. Press firmly with the back of a wooden spoon or squeeze it with your hands to expel as much liquid as possible. Stir into the blended mixture before pouring it into the pie crust.

- **Mushroom Quiche:** Add 2 cups sliced or coarsely chopped mushrooms to the onions once they are soft, and continue cooking and stirring until the mushrooms are tender and almost all of the liquid has evaporated. Stir into the blended mixture before pouring it into the pie crust.

- **Squash Quiche:** Omit the nutmeg. Add 2 cups diced zucchini or yellow summer squash to the onions once they are soft, and continue cooking and stirring until the squash is tender. Fold the squash and onions into the blended mixture along with 2 teaspoons dried basil before pouring it into the pie crust.

- **Green Onion Quiche:** Omit the onions and oil. Stir ½ to 1 cup thinly sliced green onions into the blended mixture before pouring it into the pie crust. This variation may be used in combination with any of the other variations listed above.

NOTE

- If vegan bacon bits are included, decrease the salt to ½ teaspoon. If using both vegan bacon bits and salted vegetable broth, reduce the salt to ¼ teaspoon.

Rumi

Rumi and his best friend, Studley, were rescued from an organic dairy farm. Used solely as breeding goats throughout their lives, both were getting old and less productive as "studs." The owner of the farm did not want them anymore. The future wasn't looking very bright for Rumi and Studley, until a kind woman offered to take the goats off the farmer's hands and bring them to Farm Sanctuary. They settled into their new home in no time and made many friends right away. Now distinguished leaders of the goat herd at Farm Sanctuary, these two handsome goats are living a life of leisure and teaching farm visitors the value of mercy and kindness.

Okonomiyaki

calories: 268
protein: 12 g
fat: 8 g
carbohydrate: 39 g
fiber: 8 g

*O*konomi means "as you like" and *yaki* means "grilled" or "cook" in Japanese, so this dish's name means "cook what you like, the way you like." Okonomiyaki is often compared to an omelet, pizza, or pancake because of the variety of ingredients it can contain as well as the way it is prepared. Hence it is sometimes referred to as "Japanese pizza" or "Japanese pancake." This tasty version is made with Eggless Omelets laced with flavorful vegetables. The omelets are then filled with a colorful mixture of red cabbage and green peas, topped with creamy vegan sour cream, and served with a splash of soy sauce. It's unbelievably delicious!

1 recipe Eggless Omelets (page 59), prepared as directed but not cooked

1 small carrot, peeled and shredded

¼ cup minced green onions

2 tablespoons minced fresh cilantro or parsley (optional)

1 teaspoon vegetable oil

2 cups thinly sliced or shredded red cabbage

½ cup frozen green peas, cooked according to the package directions, drained, and set aside

¼ cup Sour Dressing (page 209) or vegan sour cream

Reduced-sodium soy sauce

Stir the shredded carrot, green onions, and optional cilantro into the omelet batter, and cook the omelets as directed.

Meanwhile, pour the oil into a separate skillet, and place it over medium-high heat. When hot, add the cabbage and cook and stir for 8–10 minutes, or until it is tender-crisp. Add the cooked peas and toss the vegetables gently to combine. Continue to cook and stir for 1 minute longer.

Place the unfolded omelets onto dinner plates, with the most attractive side of each omelet facing the plate. Spoon one-quarter of the cabbage and pea mixture onto one half of each omelet. Fold the other side of the omelet over the vegetables. Garnish each omelet with a dollop of the Sour Dressing and serve with soy sauce on the side.

Hot-and-Sour Pad Thai Noodles

Makes 4 servings   **PER SERVING**

*T*his quick and easy dish employs a unique combination of flavors from Italy, Japan, and Thailand. The result is superb! For an ideal side dish, serve the noodles with a colorful medley of steamed vegetables, such as broccoli florets, diagonally sliced carrots, and water chestnuts.

calories: 206

protein: 7 g

fat: 5 g

carbohydrate: 35 g

fiber: 3 g

10 to 12 ounces fettuccine or similar long, flat noodles

1 to 2 teaspoons extra-virgin olive oil or toasted sesame oil (optional)

4 tablespoons tomato paste (no salt added)

¼ cup rice vinegar

¼ cup water

2 tablespoons granulated sugar or maple syrup

1 tablespoon reduced-sodium soy sauce

½ teaspoon crushed garlic

½ teaspoon crushed red pepper flakes

½ cup chopped fresh cilantro (optional)

¼ cup thinly sliced green onions

¼ cup chopped unsalted dry-roasted peanuts

Cook the fettuccine in a large pot of boiling water until tender to your liking. Drain well and return it to the pot. Add the optional oil and toss until the noodles are evenly coated. (The oil will help keep the noodles from sticking together.)

While the noodles are cooking, combine the tomato paste, vinegar, water, sugar, soy sauce, garlic, and red pepper flakes in a small mixing bowl, and stir to make a smooth sauce. Pour over the noodles and toss until they are evenly coated. Divide the pasta equally among four pasta bowls or dinner plates. Sprinkle the top of each serving with 2 tablespoons of the optional cilantro, 1 tablespoon of the green onions, and 1 tablespoon of the chopped peanuts. Serve at once.

instead of

The land of milk and honey.

use

The land of sweet abundance.

Macaroni and Cheez

PER SERVING

calories: 368
protein: 17 g
fat: 9 g
carbohydrate: 55 g
fiber: 6 g

Makes 4 to 6 servings

*P*asta tubes known as "macaroni" came from Italy more than two hundred years ago, but baking them with a cheese sauce didn't become popular in the United States until the nineteenth century. This cheese-less version has captured the rich taste and tang of traditional macaroni and cheese, yet it's totally dairy free.

2½ cups dry elbow macaroni

2 tablespoons extra-virgin olive oil

⅓ cup flour (whole wheat or unbleached white)

½ teaspoon dry mustard

Pinch of cayenne

1¾ cups plain soymilk, heated

½ cup nutritional yeast flakes

1 teaspoon salt

Ground black pepper

1 tablespoon finely chopped fresh parsley, or 1 teaspoon dried (optional)

½ cup fresh breadcrumbs (see page 109), packed

1 to 2 tablespoons nonhydrogenated vegan margarine (optional)

Preheat the oven to 375 degrees F. Mist an 8-inch square baking pan with non-stick cooking spray or coat it lightly with vegetable oil.

Cook the macaroni in a large pot of boiling water until tender to your liking. Drain well and return it to the pot. Cover with a lid to keep the macaroni warm and set aside.

While the macaroni is cooking, prepare the sauce. Pour the olive oil into a medium saucepan and place over medium-high heat. Stir in the flour, mustard, and cayenne, and cook for 1 minute, stirring constantly. Very gradually stir in the hot soymilk, a little at a time, whisking constantly. (It should take 5–7 minutes to add the soymilk. The sauce should continue to bubble as you add the soymilk; if it doesn't, you are adding the soymilk too quickly.) If necessary, cook the sauce 2–4 minutes longer, or until it is the consistency of thick cream. Remove from the heat and stir in the nutritional yeast flakes. Season with the salt and pepper to taste. Pour the sauce over the cooked macaroni, add the optional parsley, and mix well.

Transfer to the prepared baking pan. Sprinkle the breadcrumbs evenly over the top, and dot with the optional margarine. Bake for 25–30 minutes. Let stand for 5 minutes before serving.

NOTE

- Be sure to use only plain, unsweetened soymilk in this recipe for the best results.

Unrolled Cabbage Rolls

Makes 6 servings | PER SERVING

*T*his time-saving version of Eastern European cabbage rolls (called *golumpki*) has all the authentic original flavor without all the tedious work.

calories: 205
protein: 5 g
fat: 3 g
carbohydrate: 42 g
fiber: 6 g

2 teaspoons extra-virgin olive oil

1 cup chopped onions

1 cup sliced carrots

1 celery stalk, minced

½ teaspoon crushed garlic

6 cups chopped green cabbage

3½ cups cooked long-grain brown or white rice

1 cup unsalted vegetable broth or water

1½ cups tomato sauce, or more as needed

2 tablespoons granulated sugar or brown sugar

1 tablespoon paprika

1 teaspoon dried oregano

½ teaspoon salt

¼ teaspoon dried thyme, crushed

Pour the oil into a large, heavy pot and place over medium-high heat. When hot, add the onions, carrots, celery, and garlic, and cook and stir for 10 minutes.

Add the remaining ingredients and bring the mixture to a boil. Turn the heat down to medium-low, cover, and simmer for 30–35 minutes, or until the cabbage is very tender. If the mixture seems dry, add more vegetable broth, water, or tomato sauce to moisten.

Remove from the heat and let rest for 5 minutes. Stir to mix well. Serve hot.

Stuffed Omelets

PER OMELET

calories: 173
protein: 8 g
fat: 13 g
carbohydrate: 9 g
fiber: 2 g

Makes 4 omelets (2 to 4 servings)

This delightful dish makes a refreshing, light dinner or a pleasing lunch or brunch. Eggless Omelets are filled with a creamy, tempting tofu salad flecked with crunchy vegetables, and topped with a dollop of vegan sour cream. It's simple yet spectacular.

COTTAGE SALAD FILLING

½ pound (8 ounces) firm regular tofu, rinsed, patted dry, and mashed

1 cup diced English cucumbers

½ cup sliced red radishes, cut into half-moons

⅓ cup thinly sliced green onions

¼ cup vegan mayonnaise

½ teaspoon salt

½ teaspoon dried dill weed

¼ teaspoon garlic powder

¼ teaspoon ground black pepper

OMELETS AND TOPPINGS

1 recipe Eggless Omelets (page 59)

¼ cup Sour Dressing (page 209) or vegan sour cream

2 tablespoons chopped fresh parsley, for garnish

For the salad filling: Place the tofu, cucumbers, radishes, green onions, mayonnaise, salt, dill weed, garlic powder, and pepper in a medium bowl, and stir until well combined. If desired, the filling may be prepared a few hours in advance and stored in a covered container in the refrigerator.

To assemble: Prepare the Eggless Omelets as directed. Place the unfolded omelets onto dinner plates, with the most attractive side of each omelet facing the plate. Spoon one-quarter of the filling onto one half of each omelet. Fold the other side of the omelet over the salad. Garnish each omelet with a dollop of the Sour Dressing and a portion of the chopped parsley.

instead of

Go cold turkey.

use

Go cold tofu.

Chili Bean Macaroni   *Good!*

Makes 4 servings

PER SERVING

calories: 356
protein: 15 g
fat: 5 g
carbohydrate: 65 g
fiber: 7 g

Spicy beans and pasta make a hearty meal the whole family will enjoy. Serve this satisfying dish with a tossed green salad.

2 cups dry elbow macaroni

1 tablespoon extra-virgin olive oil

1½ cups chopped onions

1 green bell pepper, chopped

½ cup minced celery

1 teaspoon dried basil

1 teaspoon chili powder, or more to taste

1 teaspoon ground cumin

1 can (14 or 16 ounces) whole tomatoes, with juice

1 can (15 or 16 ounces) red kidney beans, rinsed and drained (about 1¾ cups)

¼ cup reduced-sodium soy sauce

Salt (optional)

Cook the macaroni in a large pot of boiling water until tender to your liking. Drain well and return it to the pot. Cover with a lid to keep the macaroni warm and set aside.

While the macaroni is cooking, pour the oil into a large, heavy skillet, and place over medium-high heat. When hot, add the onions, bell pepper, and celery, and cook and stir for 10–12 minutes, or until tender. Stir in the basil, chili powder, and cumin, and mix well. Cook for 1 minute longer, stirring constantly. Remove from the heat.

Add the tomatoes and their juice to the reserved pasta, breaking the tomatoes apart with your hands or the side of a wooden spoon. Stir in the beans, cooked vegetables, soy sauce, and optional salt to taste. Mix well. Place over medium-low heat, stirring often, until warmed through.

VARIATION

- **Curried Beans and Macaroni:** Replace the chili powder and basil with 1 teaspoon curry powder and 1 teaspoon dried dill weed.

Cauliflower Paprikash

calories: 348
protein: 20 g
fat: 12 g
carbohydrate: 44 g
fiber: 6 g

*I*n this recipe, a luscious sour cream-style sauce envelops a bed of tender cauliflower and noodles.

SOUR CREAM SAUCE

3 cups (about 24 ounces) crumbled firm silken tofu

1½ tablespoons extra-virgin olive oil

1½ tablespoons freshly squeezed lemon juice

1½ tablespoons apple cider vinegar

1 tablespoon reduced-sodium soy sauce

2 teaspoons granulated sugar

1 teaspoon salt

1 teaspoon vegetable oil

½ cup chopped onions

1½ cups sliced mushrooms

2 to 4 teaspoons paprika (preferably Hungarian)

½ teaspoon dried dill weed

Ground black pepper

CAULIFLOWER AND NOODLES

4 cups bite-size cauliflower florets

12 ounces long noodles of your choice (linguine, fettuccine, or spaghetti)

¼ cup finely chopped green onions

Paprika, for garnish (optional)

For the sauce: Combine the tofu, olive oil, lemon juice, vinegar, soy sauce, sugar, and salt in a food processor, and process several minutes until the mixture is very smooth and creamy. Transfer to a medium saucepan and set aside.

Pour the vegetable oil into a medium skillet, and place over medium-high heat. When hot, add the onions and cook and stir for 5 minutes. Add the mushrooms and continue to cook and stir for 3 minutes longer. Stir in the paprika and remove from the heat.

Add the onions and mushrooms to the tofu mixture in the saucepan. Stir in the dill weed and ground pepper, and mix well. Warm over very low heat, stirring often, for about 20 minutes, or until heated through. Do not boil!

For the cauliflower and noodles: While the sauce is warming, steam the cauliflower for 10–12 minutes, or until tender.

While the cauliflower is steaming, cook the noodles in a large pot of boiling water until tender to your liking. Drain well, return the noodles to the pot, and cover to keep warm. Set aside until the sauce has finished warming and the cauliflower is ready.

To serve: Divide the noodles equally among four dinner plates or pasta bowls. Distribute the cauliflower evenly over the noodles, then spoon the hot sauce equally over each serving. Garnish with the green onions and additional paprika, if desired. Serve at once.

VARIATION

- **Cauliflower Paprikash over Rice:** As an alternative, serve the Cauliflower Paprikash over hot cooked rice, using about 1 cup cooked rice per serving.

Stormy

Stormy was found abandoned behind a poultry exhibition show. Only a few days old at the time of her rescue, she and her friends had been dumped next to a trash receptacle and left to die. Fortunately, a woman found the tiny newborns and rushed them to Farm Sanctuary, where a rehabilitation pen was set up with heat lamps, baby turkey feed, and a big stuffed bear. Baby turkeys like to cuddle with a large animal for comfort and safety, and our surrogate teddy was happy to help. Now that Stormy and her sisters have grown up, they don't need the teddy bear anymore, but they do still enjoy receiving love and affection from the caregivers who raised them. They also enjoy having the run of the barnyard during the day and greeting visitors whenever they get the chance.

Not Your Mama's Meatloaf

PER SERVING

Makes 6 to 8 servings

calories: 271
protein: 29 g
fat: 8 g
carbohydrate: 25 g
fiber: 3 g

*T*his hearty, home-style favorite has the taste and texture of a ground beef meatloaf—without the meat, of course. Serve it plain or with tomato sauce or ketchup. Try sliced leftover loaf in sandwiches—it's marvelous.

2 teaspoons vegetable oil

1 large onion, chopped

1 medium carrot, peeled and shredded

½ teaspoon crushed garlic

4 cups Ground Seitan (page 50), coarsely ground seitan (see note), or vegan burger crumbles

1 cup fresh breadcrumbs (see page 109), firmly packed

½ cup rolled oats

⅓ cup smooth peanut butter or other nut butter of your choice

⅓ cup ketchup

1 tablespoon vegetarian Worcestershire sauce or reduced-sodium soy sauce

¼ teaspoon ground black pepper

¼ teaspoon dried thyme, crushed

¼ cup minced fresh parsley, or 2 tablespoons dried

½ cup tomato sauce

Additional ketchup or tomato sauce, for serving (optional)

Pour the oil into a medium skillet, and place over medium-high heat. When hot, add the onion and carrot and cook, stirring occasionally, for 6–8 minutes, or until the onion is translucent. Add the garlic and cook and stir for 1 minute longer. Remove from the heat and set aside to allow the vegetables to cool.

Preheat the oven to 350 degrees F. Mist an 8½ x 4½-inch loaf pan with nonstick cooking spray.

Place the ground seitan, breadcrumbs, rolled oats, and cooled vegetable mixture in a large bowl, and toss them together until they are thoroughly combined.

Place the peanut butter, ketchup, Worcestershire sauce, pepper, thyme, and dried parsley, if using, in a medium bowl, and stir vigorously until creamy and smooth. Add this mixture to the seitan along with the fresh parsley, if using, and combine thoroughly using your hands. Work the mixture well until it begins to hold together.

Pat the mixture firmly into the prepared loaf pan, and spread the tomato sauce evenly over the top. Bake for 1 hour and 15 minutes. Let the loaf cool in the pan (on a cooling rack) for at least 15–20 minutes.

To serve, cut the loaf into thick slices directly in the pan. Use a spatula to carefully lift the slices out of the pan. Serve warm or cold, accompanied with ketchup or tomato sauce, if desired.

NOTE

- To grind seitan, first cut it into 1½-inch chunks. Place the chunks in a food processor fitted with the S blade and pulse or process until it is the texture of ground beef.

Baked Stuffed Shells

Makes 16 stuffed shells (8 servings)   **PER SERVING**

hen you serve these pasta shells—brimming with nondairy ricotta, smothered in a savory marinara sauce, and topped with vegan Parmesan—who could resist?

calories: 335
protein: 13 g
fat: 12 g
carbohydrate: 44 g
fiber: 5 g

16 jumbo pasta stuffing shells

1 pound (16 ounces) firm regular tofu, rinsed, patted dry, and well mashed

⅔ cup vegan mayonnaise

1½ tablespoons minced fresh parsley, or 2 teaspoons dried

2 teaspoons dried basil

2 teaspoons onion powder

1 teaspoon garlic powder

Salt

Ground black pepper

6 cups well-seasoned tomato sauce

½ cup Parmezano Sprinkles (page 85) or vegan Parmesan

Preheat the oven to 350 degrees F. Oil a 9 x 13-inch baking dish, or mist it with nonstick cooking spray. Cook the pasta shells in a large pot of boiling water until tender to your liking. Drain well.

Combine the tofu, mayonnaise, parsley, basil, onion powder, garlic powder, and salt and pepper to taste in a large bowl, and mash into a finely grained paste. Stuff about 2 rounded tablespoonfuls into each shell.

Spread about 1 cup of the tomato sauce over the bottom of the prepared baking dish. Arrange the stuffed shells in a single layer over the sauce. Spoon the remaining sauce over the shells, and sprinkle the top with the Parmezano Sprinkles. Bake for 30–45 minutes, or until heated through.

Barbecued Buffalo Zings

calories: 197
protein: 22 g
fat: 3 g
carbohydrate: 25 g
fiber: 1 g

*T*hese spicy, chewy strips are the vegan version of buffalo wings. They make a great picnic or party treat. Just be sure to have plenty of napkins on hand! If you like, serve Bleu Cheez Dip and Dressing (page 210) as a dip on the side.

BARBECUE SAUCE

⅓ cup water

4 tablespoons tomato paste (no salt added)

¼ cup maple syrup

3 tablespoons reduced-sodium soy sauce

2 teaspoons vegetable oil

2 teaspoons dry mustard

½ teaspoon crushed garlic

¼ teaspoon ground black pepper

⅛ teaspoon crushed red pepper flakes, or several drops bottled hot sauce

2 to 3 drops liquid smoke (optional)

ZINGS

⅔ cup vital wheat gluten

2 teaspoons nutritional yeast flakes

¾ cup warm water

Preheat the oven to 350 degrees F. Mist a baking sheet with nonstick cooking spray, or line it with parchment paper (for the easiest cleanup), and set aside.

For the barbecue sauce: Place the water, tomato paste, maple syrup, soy sauce, oil, dry mustard, garlic, black pepper, crushed red pepper flakes, and optional liquid smoke in a small bowl, and stir until well combined.

For the zings: Combine the vital wheat gluten and nutritional yeast flakes in a large bowl. Stir in the water and mix well. The resulting gluten mixture will be moist. Place the gluten on a flat surface and roll it into a rectangle, keeping it as flat and thin as possible. Slice into 12–15 strips, about 5 inches long and 1 inch wide. Place on the prepared baking sheet at least 1 inch apart. Bake on the center rack of the oven for about 15 minutes, or until puffed, lightly browned, and crisp.

Remove from the oven and prick each strip all over with a fork. Turn the strips over, and pour or spoon the barbecue sauce evenly over them, covering the top and sides of each piece. Return to the oven and bake 10–15 minutes longer. Serve hot, room temperature, or cold. Covered tightly and stored in the refrigerator, leftover Barbecued Buffalo Zings will keep for about 1 week.

Unstuffed Shells

Makes 4 servings

PER SERVING

calories: 543
protein: 24 g
fat: 19 g
carbohydrate: 71 g
fiber: 6 g

*T*his recipe has generated an unprecedented amount of positive feedback over the years. Readers tell me that they receive compliments and requests for seconds from both vegans and nonvegans alike. Serve this dish with a tossed green salad and steamed kale or broccoli. It's beautiful enough for company, but easy enough for any night of the week.

1 pound (16 ounces) firm regular tofu, rinsed, patted dry, and well mashed

⅓ to ½ cup vegan mayonnaise

2 to 3 tablespoons minced fresh parsley, or 1 tablespoon dried

2 teaspoons dried basil

2 teaspoons onion powder

1 teaspoon garlic powder

½ teaspoon salt

1 can (16 ounces) tomato sauce (2 cups)

4 cups medium shell pasta

Parmezano Sprinkles (page 85) or vegan Parmesan (optional)

Place the tofu, mayonnaise, parsley, basil, onion powder, garlic powder, and salt in a medium bowl, and stir until thoroughly combined.

Pour the tomato sauce into a small saucepan and simmer over medium heat, stirring occasionally. When the sauce is hot, lower the heat and cover to keep the sauce warm.

While the tomato sauce is heating, cook the pasta in a large pot of boiling water until tender to your liking. Drain well and return it to the pot. Stir the tofu mixture into the hot pasta, tossing well until it is evenly distributed.

Divide the pasta mixture among four dinner plates. Top each serving with one-quarter of the hot tomato sauce (about ½ cup per serving). Serve at once. Pass Parmezano Sprinkles at the table, if desired.

Barbecue-Style Braised Short "Ribs"

PER SERVING

calories: 301
protein: 30 g
fat: 8 g
carbohydrate: 34 g
fiber: 5 g

Makes 6 servings

Tender and highly flavorful, these "ribs" are made from seitan instead of beef or pork. They're so delicious, you'll lick the plate clean! Serve them with mashed potatoes or sweet yams, steamed greens or coleslaw, and biscuits or cornbread. They are also great cold for picnics and parties.

DRY INGREDIENTS

1½ cups vital wheat gluten

¼ cup nutritional yeast flakes

½ teaspoon garlic powder

½ teaspoon onion powder

LIQUID INGREDIENTS

1 cup water

3 tablespoons reduced-sodium soy sauce

OIL FOR COOKING

3 tablespoons extra-virgin olive oil

LIP-SMACKIN' BARBECUE SAUCE

2 yellow onions, cut in half and thickly sliced

2 medium carrots, peeled and sliced

1 teaspoon crushed garlic

1 can (16 ounces) tomato sauce (2 cups)

1 cup bottled barbecue sauce

1 cup water

1 tablespoon reduced-sodium soy sauce

Salt

Ground black pepper

For the dry ingredients: Place all of the dry ingredients in a large bowl, and stir with a dry whisk until well combined.

For the liquid ingredients: Place all of the liquid ingredients in a small bowl, and stir until well combined. Pour into the dry ingredients, and mix well with a wooden spoon. If there is still flour around the edges, add a small amount of additional water (1–2 tablespoons only). You should now have a large, firm, spongy mass of gluten in the bowl.

Knead the gluten directly in the bowl for about 30 seconds only, just to blend. (Do not add any more flour. Kneading any longer than this will make the gluten fluffy, spongy, and breadlike, rather than dense, chewy, and meat-like!) Slice into 6 equal pieces.

Pour 2 tablespoons of the olive oil into a very large skillet or large, heavy pot and place over medium-high heat. When hot, add the gluten pieces and brown them evenly on all sides, taking care that they do not stick. Do not allow the "ribs" to touch. Transfer the "ribs" to a plate lined with several layers of paper towels to drain briefly. Lightly oil a large, heavy, ovenproof pot or deep baking dish, or mist it with nonstick cooking spray. Transfer the "ribs" to the prepared baking dish.

Preheat the oven to 325 degrees F.

For the barbecue sauce: Add the remaining 1 tablespoon olive oil to the skillet, and place over medium-high heat. When hot, add the onions and cook and stir for 15–20 minutes, or until they are lightly browned and starting to caramelize. Add the carrots, and cook and stir until they are softened, about 5 minutes. Add the garlic, and cook and stir for 1 minute. Then add the tomato sauce, barbecue sauce, water, soy sauce, and salt and pepper to taste, and stir until well combined. Bring to a boil, reduce the heat to medium-low, and simmer for 1 minute to blend the flavors.

Pour the sauce over the "ribs," and turn them so they are evenly coated. Bake the "ribs" uncovered for 1½ hours, turning them every 30 minutes.

Lassen

Adorable and sweet as pie, Lassen made a big splash when he arrived at Farm Sanctuary. Born into a 4-H hog project, he was the runt of the litter and was too sickly and weak to get enough milk from his mother. The participants in the project were going to let him die, but thankfully an animal control officer intervened to save his life. No longer a runt, but still small for his age and a bit hyperactive, Lassen occupies a very special place in the sanctuary herd. His antics occasionally get him in trouble with the older pigs, but he brings life and humor to the group as well. Beloved by staff, volunteers, and visitors alike for his sweet and excitable nature, he loves sanctuary life.

Pot Roast

calories: 214
protein: 29 g
fat: 8 g
carbohydrate: 13 g
fiber: 2 g

*T*his succulent, slowly braised seitan brisket is topped with a fabulous gravy. The roast takes a while to cook, but the actual preparation is far less work than it appears. This makes an impressive company or holiday dish.

DRY INGREDIENTS

1½ cups vital wheat gluten

¼ cup nutritional yeast flakes

½ teaspoon garlic powder

½ teaspoon onion powder

LIQUID INGREDIENTS

1 cup water

3 tablespoons reduced-sodium soy sauce

OIL FOR COOKING

3 tablespoons extra-virgin olive oil

VEGETABLES

2 medium onions, coarsely chopped

2 medium carrots, peeled and thinly sliced

COOKING BROTH

2½ cups dark vegetable broth or water

2 tablespoons tomato paste (no salt added)

2 tablespoons red wine vinegar

1½ tablespoons reduced-sodium soy sauce

½ teaspoon dried thyme, crushed

¼ to ½ teaspoon crushed garlic

¼ to ½ teaspoon liquid smoke (optional)

1 bay leaf

For the dry ingredients: Place all of the dry ingredients in a large bowl, and stir with a dry whisk until well combined.

For the liquid ingredients: Place all of the liquid ingredients in a small bowl, and stir until well combined. Pour into the dry ingredients, and mix well with a wooden spoon. If there is still flour around the edges, add a small amount of additional water (1–2 tablespoons only). You should now have a large, firm, spongy mass of gluten in the bowl.

Knead the gluten directly in the bowl for about 30 seconds only, just to blend. (Do not add any more flour. Kneading any longer than this will make the gluten fluffy, spongy, and breadlike, rather than dense, chewy, and meat-like!) Form into a loaf, and return it to the bowl.

Place 2 tablespoons of the olive oil in a large, heavy pot, and place over medium-high heat. When hot, add the gluten loaf and brown it evenly on all sides, taking care that it does not stick to the sides of the pot. Transfer the roast back to the large bowl and set aside.

For the vegetables: Pour the remaining 1 tablespoon olive oil into the pot and place over medium-high heat. When hot, add the onions and cook and stir for 15–20 minutes, or until they are lightly browned and starting to caramelize. Watch closely and adjust the heat as necessary so they do not burn. Add the carrots, and cook and stir until they are softened, about 5 minutes longer.

Add the broth, tomato paste, vinegar, soy sauce, thyme, garlic, optional liquid smoke, and bay leaf, and bring to a boil. Return the roast to the pot and turn the heat down to medium-low. Partially cover the pot (tilt the lid so there is room for steam to escape) and simmer for 1½ hours. Maintain the heat so that the liquid barely simmers, and turn the roast over about every 30 minutes.

When the roast is finished cooking, transfer it to a cutting board. Cover it loosely with foil and let rest for 15 minutes.

Remove the bay leaf from the pot and discard it. Transfer the cooking liquid and vegetables to a blender or food processor, and process into a smooth, thick gravy. Pour into a small saucepan and simmer over medium heat until warmed through.

To serve: Carve the roast on a slight diagonal into thin slices. Arrange the slices on a serving platter, overlapping them slightly, and spoon some of the hot gravy over the top. Pass the remaining gravy at the table.

instead of
Handle with kid gloves.

use
Handle with loving care.

Meaty Balls

PER SERVING

calories: 129
protein: 13 g
fat: 2 g
carbohydrate: 14 g
fiber: 3 g

Makes 12 balls (about 4 servings)

Serve these hearty, delectable, meatless balls the same way traditional meatballs are served—over spaghetti, with rice, in a casserole, or in a meatless meatball sub. They're delicious and satisfying.

1 cup TSP flakes or granules (see page 30)

¼ cup rolled oats

½ teaspoon dried basil

½ teaspoon dried oregano

½ teaspoon dried parsley flakes

½ teaspoon garlic powder

½ teaspoon onion powder

¼ teaspoon dry mustard

¾ cup boiling water

2 tablespoons ketchup

2 tablespoons reduced-sodium soy sauce

1 rounded tablespoon smooth peanut butter

¼ cup flour (any kind)

1 tablespoon nutritional yeast flakes (optional)

Preheat the oven to 350 degrees F. Mist a baking sheet with nonstick cooking spray, or line it with parchment paper (for the easiest cleanup).

Place the TSP, oats, basil, oregano, parsley, garlic powder, onion powder, and dry mustard in a medium bowl, and stir until evenly combined. In a small bowl, combine the boiling water, ketchup, and soy sauce, and stir until blended. Pour into the TSP mixture, and stir until well combined. Let rest for 5–10 minutes.

Add the peanut butter, and mix until it is well incorporated. Stir in the flour and optional nutritional yeast flakes, and mix thoroughly. Form into 12 walnut-size balls and arrange them on the prepared baking sheet. Mist the tops and sides with olive oil spray or nonstick cooking spray and bake for 25–30 minutes, turning them over midway in the cooking cycle.

Cool completely before storing. Packed into heavy-duty zipper-lock plastic bags or stored in an airtight container, leftover Meaty Balls will keep for about 1 week in the refrigerator, or up to 3 months in the freezer.

Good!

Seitan and Mushroom Stroganoff

Makes 4 servings

PER SERVING

calories: 223
protein: 22 g
fat: 7 g
carbohydrate: 23 g
fiber: 3 g

*T*his creamy stroganoff is perfect over rice, toast points, or wide noodles, and makes an impressive dish for vegan or nonvegan dinner guests. Just add a crunchy tossed salad on the side to complete your meal.

CREAMY GRAVY

2 tablespoons arrowroot, kuzu, or cornstarch

3 tablespoons reduced-sodium soy sauce

1⅓ cups dark vegetable broth or water

½ teaspoon garlic powder

2 tablespoons tahini

ONIONS, MUSHROOMS, AND SEITAN

2 teaspoons vegetable oil

2 cups thinly sliced onions

½ to 1 teaspoon crushed garlic

4 cups sliced mushrooms

2 cups thinly sliced seitan strips

Ground black pepper

For the gravy: Combine the arrowroot and soy sauce in a medium saucepan and stir well to make a thin, smooth paste. Gradually whisk in the vegetable broth and garlic powder. Place over medium-high heat and cook, stirring constantly with a whisk, until the mixture thickens and comes to a boil. Remove from the heat and beat in the tahini using the whisk. Cover and set aside.

For the onions, mushrooms, and seitan: Pour the oil into a large skillet, and place over medium-high heat. When hot, add the onions and garlic and cook and stir for 10 minutes.

Add the mushrooms and cook, stirring often, for 5–7 minutes. Add the seitan strips and the reserved gravy. Turn the heat down to low, and cook, stirring often, for 5–10 minutes, just until the seitan is heated through. Season with ground black pepper to taste. Serve at once.

Zucchini and Herb Calzones

Makes 4 calzones

calories: 384
protein: 19 g
fat: 7 g
carbohydrate: 60 g
fiber: 11 g

*T*he motto at the Farm Sanctuary chicken coop is "stuff bread not birds!" We couldn't agree more! If you like, top these scrumptious calzones with a spoonful or two of well-seasoned tomato sauce.

DOUGH

1 teaspoon active dry yeast

¾ cup lukewarm water (105–115 degrees F)

2 teaspoons granulated sugar or other sweetener of your choice

½ teaspoon salt

2 to 3 cups flour (whole wheat or unbleached white), more or less, as needed (see notes)

FILLING

1 teaspoon extra-virgin olive oil

1 cup diced zucchini, cut into ¼-inch cubes

½ teaspoon crushed garlic

½ pound (8 ounces) firm regular tofu, rinsed and patted dry

2 tablespoons minced fresh parsley

1 teaspoon dried basil

½ teaspoon dried oregano

½ teaspoon salt

⅛ teaspoon ground nutmeg

⅛ teaspoon ground black pepper

For the dough: Place the yeast in a large bowl, and pour the lukewarm water over it. Let rest for 5 minutes.

Add the sugar and salt to the yeast mixture. Then beat in enough flour to make a soft but pliable dough. Turn out onto a floured board and knead for 5 minutes. Lightly oil a clean, large bowl and place the dough in it. Turn the dough over so that it is lightly oiled on all sides. Cover the bowl with a clean, damp tea towel, and let the dough rise in a warm place for 1 hour (see page 69).

For the filling: While the dough is rising, pour the olive oil into a medium skillet, and place over medium-high heat. When hot, add the zucchini and garlic and cook and stir for 3–5 minutes, until the zucchini is just tender. Remove from the heat.

Place the tofu in a medium bowl and mash it well. Add the parsley, basil, oregano, salt, nutmeg, and pepper, and mix well. Fold in the zucchini and set aside.

Preheat the oven to 400 degrees F. Mist a baking sheet with nonstick cooking spray, or line it with parchment paper (for the easiest cleanup).

Punch down the dough and divide it into 4 equal balls. Keep the dough covered with the same tea towel that covered the bowl, and work with 1 ball of dough at a time. Place each ball of dough on a lightly floured board and roll it into a 6-inch round. Place one-quarter of the filling (about ½ cup for each calzone) slightly off-center, and fold the dough over. Seal the edges of the calzone by crimping them with your fingers or with the tines of a fork dipped in flour. Prick each calzone in a few places on top with the tines of the fork.

Place the calzones on the prepared baking sheet as soon as they are formed. Bake on the center rack of the oven for about 20 minutes, or until they are lightly browned.

NOTES

- Bread flour or all-purpose flour will provide the best results.
- If desired, spray, brush, or rub the tops of the calzones with a little olive oil before baking and/or after they emerge from the oven.

Kathy

Kathy was rescued from a cruel Thanksgiving promotion at a salvage yard. The owners were charging customers a quarter to chase down and catch frightened turkeys for their holiday dinners. But this was not to be Kathy's fate. Farm Sanctuary was able to convince the salvage yard owner to halt the promotion and surrender dozens of the turkeys into their care. Ten hours after staff and volunteers took the turkeys from the salvage yard, they arrived at Farm Sanctuary's California Shelter. Seeming to sense that she was now safe and sound, Kathy settled in right away. The next morning, after a good night's rest, she and her friends awoke to a new beginning—and a delicious Thanksgiving dinner of cranberry sauce, pumpkin pie, and stuffed squash.

Macaroni with Tomatoes and Cheez

PER SERVING

calories: 361
protein: 13 g
fat: 9 g
carbohydrate: 57 g
fiber: 6 g

Makes 8 servings

This stove-top casserole is customarily prepared with lots of butter and processed cheese. With a few adaptations, the butter and cheese were removed, while the flavor and consistency were enhanced. It's a hearty and filling dish that is especially appealing to children.

2 tablespoons extra-virgin olive oil

2 large onions, finely chopped

½ cup water

½ cup tomato juice

½ cup raw cashews, or ⅓ cup cashew butter or tahini

2 tablespoons freshly squeezed lemon juice

2 tablespoons rolled oats or flour (any kind)

½ cup nutritional yeast flakes

1 teaspoon onion powder

½ teaspoon garlic powder

½ teaspoon dry mustard

1 pound (16 ounces) elbow macaroni

1 can (32 ounces) chopped tomatoes, with juice

Salt

Ground black pepper

Pour the oil into a large pot and place over medium-high heat. When hot, add the onions and cook and stir for 30–60 minutes, or until they are tender, deep brown, and caramelized. Watch closely and adjust the heat as necessary so the onions don't burn.

Combine the water, tomato juice, cashews, lemon juice, oats, nutritional yeast flakes, onion powder, garlic powder, and dry mustard in a blender. Process several minutes until completely smooth.

Cook the macaroni in a large pot of boiling water until tender to your liking. Drain well and stir into the cooked onions. Add the tomatoes and their juice. Then stir in the blended mixture. Season with salt and plenty of pepper to taste. Cook and stir over medium heat for 10–20 minutes, or until hot, thickened, and bubbly.

Stuffed Green Peppers

*T*here's something about stuffed peppers that makes dinner guests feel well cared for and family members feel special. Use your favorite tomato sauce—homemade or store-bought. This recipe will have everyone praising your culinary skills!

4 very large green bell peppers

1 cup white basmati or long-grain white rice

1 cup almost-boiling water

3 cups well-seasoned tomato sauce

1 cup cooked or canned chickpeas, rinsed and drained

¼ cup pine nuts or walnuts

¼ cup seedless raisins

1 teaspoon salt

½ teaspoon crushed garlic

¼ teaspoon ground cinnamon

¼ teaspoon ground allspice

1½ cups water

1 to 2 tablespoons extra-virgin olive oil (optional)

Select very large green peppers that can stand upright without toppling. Cut off the tops (and reserve them) and carefully hollow out the peppers, removing the seeds and ribs with your hands. Rinse well and drain. Combine the rice, almost-boiling water, 1 cup of the tomato sauce, chickpeas, raisins, salt, garlic, cinnamon, and allspice in a large bowl. Stir until well mixed. Carefully fill the cavities of the green peppers, taking care not to overstuff them. They should be about two-thirds full.

Combine the remaining 2 cups tomato sauce, 1½ cups water, and optional olive oil in a large, deep pot that has room for all 4 peppers. Trim the pepper flesh from around the reserved tops, cut it into large pieces, and add it to the sauce. Stand the peppers upright in the sauce, and bring to a boil. Lower the heat to a simmer, cover, and cook over medium-low heat for 60–70 minutes, or until the rice is plump and very tender. To serve, place a pepper upright on each dinner plate and ladle some of the sauce around it.

Lasagne Roll-Ups

PER SERVING

calories: 439
protein: 25 g
fat: 10 g
carbohydrate: 64 g
fiber: 8 g

Makes 4 to 5 servings

*Y*ou'll impress your friends and family (and even yourself!) with this beautiful dish. The presentation makes it look like it is complicated and time-consuming to prepare, so don't let on how easy it is!

10 lasagna noodles

1 pound (16 ounces) fresh spinach (see note)

1 tablespoon extra-virgin olive oil

½ cup chopped onions

1 cup mashed firm regular tofu

1 tablespoon nutritional yeast flakes

1 teaspoon dried oregano

½ teaspoon salt

½ teaspoon dried basil

½ teaspoon dried dill weed

¼ teaspoon ground black pepper

2 tablespoons flour (any kind)

2 cups well-seasoned tomato sauce

Preheat the oven to 350 degrees F. Lightly oil a large, shallow, oblong casserole dish or baking pan, or mist it with nonstick cooking spray.

Cook the lasagna noodles in a large pot of boiling water until tender. Drain and set aside in a bowl of cold water. Wash the spinach well, remove the stems, and chop.

Pour the olive oil into a large skillet, and place over medium-high heat. When hot, add the onions and cook and stir for 5–10 minutes, or until translucent. Add the chopped spinach, and cook and stir until it is wilted. Add the tofu, nutritional yeast flakes, oregano, salt, basil, dill weed, and black pepper, and mix well. Turn off the heat and stir in the flour.

Remove the lasagna noodles from the water and hang them over the edge of the sink to drain. Working with one noodle at a time, lay it flat. Spread it with 2–3 tablespoons of the tofu mixture along its entire length, and roll it up like a pinwheel. Repeat until all the noodles are filled and rolled. Place them spiral-side up in the prepared casserole dish. Pour the tomato sauce evenly over the roll-ups. Cover and bake for about 45 minutes, or until bubbly and hot.

NOTE

- If you prefer, replace the fresh spinach with 1 package (10 ounces) frozen chopped spinach. Thaw the spinach in a colander in the sink, squeeze out the excess liquid with your hands, and add it directly to the tofu mixture.

Potatoes Gruyère

*T*his is a hearty *au gratin* potato casserole. Serve it with a steamed vegetable, salad, and crusty rolls.

calories: 259
protein: 10 g
fat: 6 g
carbohydrate: 42 g
fiber: 4 g

1¼ cups water

1 package (about 12 ounces) firm silken tofu, crumbled

½ cup raw cashews

⅓ cup nutritional yeast flakes

2 tablespoons freshly squeezed lemon juice

1 tablespoon onion powder

½ teaspoon garlic powder

⅛ teaspoon ground nutmeg

1 small onion, finely chopped

½ cup sliced green onions

6 medium white or gold potatoes, peeled and thinly sliced

Salt

Ground black pepper

Preheat the oven to 350 degrees F. Oil a large, deep casserole dish, or mist it well with nonstick cooking spray. Combine the water, tofu, cashews, nutritional yeast flakes, lemon juice, onion powder, garlic powder, and nutmeg in a blender, and process several minutes until completely smooth. Stir in the onion and green onions.

Arrange a layer of the potato slices in the prepared casserole dish, and sprinkle with salt and a generous amount of pepper. Drizzle on some of the blended sauce, then layer more of the potatoes, salt, and pepper, more of the sauce, and so on, finishing with a layer of sauce. Cover and bake for 1 hour. Uncover and bake 45 minutes longer, or until the top is golden brown and the potatoes are very soft and tender. Let stand 10 minutes before serving. Serve hot.

Quinoa Primavera *Good!*

PER SERVING

calories: 282
protein: 10 g
fat: 8 g
carbohydrate: 46 g
fiber: 9 g

Makes 2 to 3 servings

Quinoa cooks so quickly that this healthful grain-based entrée can be on the table in under thirty minutes. If you have a large household or are serving guests, this recipe is easily doubled.

1¼ cups water

½ cup quinoa, rinsed well

1 cup frozen green peas, thawed in hot water and drained

1 tablespoon extra-virgin olive oil

1 medium carrot, peeled and thinly sliced on the diagonal

1 medium zucchini, thinly sliced on the diagonal

1 small red bell pepper, chopped

1 large leek, thinly sliced

½ teaspoon crushed garlic

1 teaspoon dried dill weed

Salt

Ground black pepper

Pour the water into a medium saucepan and bring to a boil. Stir in the quinoa. Cover, turn the heat down to low, and cook for 15–18 minutes. Remove from the heat and scatter the peas on top of the grain; do not stir. Cover and let rest for 8 minutes.

Meanwhile, pour the oil into a large, heavy skillet, wok, or pot, and place over medium-high heat. Add the carrot, zucchini, red bell pepper, leek, and garlic. Cook and stir for about 8 minutes, or until the carrot is tender-crisp.

How to Clean Leeks

Rinse leeks thoroughly to remove the sandy grit and dirt. One way to do this is to slice halfway through each bulb lengthwise and separate the leaves gently so the inner sections of the leek are exposed and can be readily rinsed clean under running water. Another method is to slice the unwashed leeks and put them in a colander. Separate the slices into rings using your fingers, and rinse them thoroughly under running water. Remember to use only the white bulb and the tender green part of the leek. The dark green upper portion is too tough to eat, but it makes an excellent addition to homemade vegetable broth.

Add the quinoa, peas, and dill weed, and toss until thoroughly combined. Place over medium-high heat, tossing constantly until the peas are heated through, about 2 minutes. Season with salt and pepper to taste. Serve hot.

Igor's Special *Good! Easy!*

*T*his quick pasta dish is different and delicious. It's ideal for busy schedules because it can be on the table in a flash.

12 to 16 ounces pasta (any kind)

4 cups bite-size broccoli florets

2 large ripe tomatoes, chopped

½ cup chopped red onions or sliced green onions

½ cup coarsely chopped walnuts

2 tablespoons freshly squeezed lemon or lime juice

2 tablespoons balsamic or wine vinegar

1½ tablespoons extra-virgin olive oil

½ teaspoon crushed garlic

½ teaspoon curry powder

Pinch of ground black pepper

Pinch of cayenne

Pinch of salt

Dash of reduced-sodium soy sauce

calories: 334

protein: 10 g

fat: 16 g

carbohydrate: 43 g

fiber: 3 g

Cook the pasta in a large pot of boiling water until just tender. Do not drain. Remove the pot from the heat and add the broccoli florets. Cover and let the pasta and broccoli rest for 5–8 minutes. Then drain the pasta and broccoli well in a colander.

Meanwhile, combine the tomatoes, onions, and walnuts in a large bowl. Add the lemon juice, vinegar, olive oil, garlic, curry powder, pepper, cayenne, salt, and soy sauce, and toss to combine.

When the pasta and broccoli are ready, add them to the tomato and onion mixture and toss well. Adjust the seasonings, if necessary, and toss again. Serve at once.

Sensational Stuffed Squash

PER SERVING

calories: 202
protein: 5 g
fat: 6 g
carbohydrate: 37 g
fiber: 9 g

Makes 1 large stuffed squash (5 to 6 servings)

Vegans enjoy having something to stuff and carve for a celebration, and there's nothing better for stuffing than winter squash. Although other large winter squashes may be used, I recommend buttercup (also known as turban squash) for this recipe. Its flat bottom, round shape, beautiful dark green shell, and succulent, deep orange flesh make it an impressive, edible showpiece for any special occasion. Buttercup squash also is sweeter, more dense, and less watery than other winter squashes, and its skin is very tender when cooked. Serve it with Savory Chickpea Gravy (page 185); if you like, pass cranberry sauce at the table.

1 large buttercup squash (about 3 pounds)

1 cup water

½ large onion, chopped

¼ cup white basmati rice, rinsed and drained

¼ cup quinoa, rinsed well and drained

¼ cup toasted sunflower seeds or chopped nuts

¼ cup drained and chopped oil-packed sun-dried tomatoes

2 tablespoons chopped flat-leaf parsley

1½ teaspoons extra-virgin olive oil

½ teaspoon dried basil

¼ teaspoon dried oregano

¼ teaspoon crushed garlic

Salt

Ground black pepper

Preheat the oven to 350 degrees F. Pierce the top of the squash with a sharp knife at a 45-degree angle. Pushing the knife blade away from your body, rotate the blade around the top of the squash, and remove the cone-shaped top piece. Slice off any fibrous material from the cone and set the top aside. Using a large spoon, scoop out the seeds and all the fibrous pulp from the cavity of the squash and discard. Place the squash and top on a baking sheet and bake for 30 minutes. Remove from the oven and set aside to cool for 15 minutes.

While the squash is baking, place the water, onion, rice, and quinoa in a large pot and bring to a boil. Lower the heat to medium, cover, and simmer for 15 minutes. Remove from the heat and let rest, covered, for 10 minutes.

Fluff with a fork and add the sunflower seeds, sun-dried tomatoes, parsley, olive oil, basil, oregano, garlic, and salt and pepper to taste.

Spoon the stuffing into the cavity of the squash until it is almost full. Put the squash top in place and bake for 50–60 minutes, or until a toothpick can be inserted easily into the side of the squash. If there is leftover stuffing, place it in a separate small pan, sprinkle it with 2–3 tablespoons water, cover, and heat through for the last 20 minutes of the squash cooking time. Remove the squash from the oven and place it on a warm serving platter. Slice into wedges to serve.

Cicero

Cicero was rescued from a factory farm ravaged by Hurricane Katrina in rural Mississippi. A tornado spawned by the hurricane destroyed the warehouse where he lived, and because he and his friends were considered an "acceptable loss" to the poultry company, they were left to die in the wreckage. Thankfully, a Farm Sanctuary rescue team found the chickens before it was too late and brought them to safety in New York, where they could begin a new life. Grateful to have been given a second chance, Cicero lives each new day to the fullest. He has even appointed himself as official flock flycatcher and spends most of his waking hours chasing down the buzzing insects.

instead of

He who steals a calf steals a cow.

use

He who crushes an acorn kills an oak.

Moroccan Millet

calories: 350
protein: 10 g
fat: 12 g
carbohydrate: 53 g
fiber: 7 g

*T*his pilaf is great as a one-dish meal or served with a fresh green salad.

2 tablespoons extra-virgin olive oil

1 large red bell pepper, sliced into strips

1 large green bell pepper, sliced into strips

1 large onion, sliced into half-moons

2 tablespoons crushed garlic

2 teaspoons paprika

½ teaspoon salt

1 teaspoon ground cumin

½ teaspoon ground cinnamon

¼ teaspoon ground turmeric

¼ teaspoon ground ginger

⅛ teaspoon cayenne

1½ cups millet

3 cups light vegetable broth

1 can (15 or 16 ounces) chickpeas, rinsed and drained (about 1¾ cups)

¼ cup pine nuts

¼ cup seedless raisins or chopped dates

Salt

Ground black pepper

Preheat the oven to 450 degrees F. Place 1 tablespoon of the oil in a 9 x 13-inch casserole dish or large roasting pan. Add the peppers, onion, garlic, paprika, and salt. Toss until everything is evenly coated with the oil and well combined. Place in the oven to roast for 20 minutes, stirring two or three times partway through the cooking cycle. Remove from the oven and allow the vegetables to cool until they can be safely handled; then chop them coarsely.

Meanwhile, heat the remaining 1 tablespoon oil in a large saucepan. Add the cumin, cinnamon, turmeric, ginger, and cayenne. Raise the heat to medium-high and stir constantly until the spices are uniform in color and well combined, about 30 seconds. Add the millet and stir quickly to coat, about 1 minute. Immediately pour in the vegetable broth and bring to a boil. Lower the heat, cover, and cook for 20 minutes, or until all the liquid is absorbed.

Transfer to a large bowl and fluff with a fork. Add the roasted vegetables, chickpeas, pine nuts, and raisins. Season with salt and pepper to taste. Toss gently, and serve.

Mahvelous Millet Loaf

Makes about 8 servings | **PER SERVING**

*W*hen millet is cooked with abundant water, it becomes soft and tender, with a texture similar to polenta. It makes an ideal foundation for a meatless loaf. Because the millet is cooked on the stove top and the loaf is not baked, it's very easy to prepare.

calories: 224
protein: 7 g
fat: 11 g
carbohydrate: 27 g
fiber: 3 g

1 cup millet

2½ cups water

1 cup finely chopped onions

1 cup finely chopped or shredded carrots

1 cup finely diced celery

1¼ teaspoons salt

½ teaspoon crushed garlic

½ teaspoon dried thyme, crushed

2 tablespoons extra-virgin olive oil

½ to 1 cup chopped pistachios

Oil a large loaf pan and set it aside. Rinse the millet well and place it in a large, heavy pot along with the water, onions, carrots, celery, salt, garlic, and thyme. Bring to a boil. Cover, turn the heat down to medium-low, and simmer for 30 minutes. Remove from the heat and let stand, covered, for 10 minutes.

Stir in the oil and pistachios and mix well. Spoon into the prepared loaf pan, packing the mixture down firmly. Place on a cooling rack and allow the loaf to rest in the pan at room temperature for 15–30 minutes. The longer the loaf rests, the firmer it will become. Carefully turn the loaf out of the pan onto a cutting board or attractive serving platter. Cut into slices and serve.

Red Hot Green Curry

PER SERVING

calories: 132
protein: 4 g
fat: 4 g
carbohydrate: 22 g
fiber: 4 g

This recipe looks like a lot of work, but it moves along surprisingly fast if you have all your spices ready to go. There are no hard-and-fast rules regarding which vegetables to use, so feel free to replace any of these with ones you may have on hand, such as frozen peas, cauliflower, broccoli, and/or Swiss chard. This dish is well worth the effort, as it turns out much like a good restaurant curry. For an authentic presentation, serve it with basmati rice and chutney.

2½ cups diced peeled potatoes

2½ cups cut green beans, in 1-inch pieces

2 tablespoons extra-virgin olive oil

2 cups chopped onions (about 2 large)

1 tablespoon crushed garlic

2 teaspoons ground turmeric

1½ teaspoons salt

1 teaspoon ground coriander

1 teaspoon ground cumin

½ teaspoon hot paprika

½ teaspoon cayenne

½ teaspoon ground black pepper

¼ teaspoon ground cinnamon

4 cups fresh spinach, washed, dried, and stems removed

1½ cups thickly sliced zucchinis

¾ cup water

½ cup seedless raisins (optional)

4 tablespoons chopped hot green chiles, or 2 teaspoons red or green Thai curry paste

1½ tablespoons grated fresh ginger

2 tablespoons freshly squeezed lemon juice

Boil the potatoes and green beans in a large pot of salted water for 5 minutes only. Drain and set aside.

Pour the olive oil into a large, heavy skillet or pot and place over medium-high heat. When hot, add the onions and garlic and cook and stir until the onions are soft. Add the turmeric, salt, coriander, cumin, hot paprika, cayenne, black pepper, and cinnamon. Cook and stir for about 2 minutes. Add the potatoes, green beans, spinach, zucchinis, water, optional raisins, chiles, ginger, and lemon juice. Mix well. Simmer uncovered, stirring often, until most of the water has cooked off and the vegetables are tender to your liking. Serve hot with rice and chutney.

Fettuccine with Lemony Vegetables

Makes 6 servings

PER SERVING

*S*oothing noodles in a rich, sour cream-style sauce form a sumptuous bed for crisp, tangy vegetables.

calories: 289

protein: 17 g

fat: 11 g

carbohydrate: 34 g

fiber: 5 g

3 cups (about 24 ounces) crumbled firm silken tofu

½ cup freshly squeezed lemon juice

¼ cup water

2 tablespoons tahini

½ cup sliced green onions

½ teaspoon crushed garlic

1 pound (16 ounces) fettuccine

1 to 2 tablespoons extra-virgin olive oil

3 cups broccoli florets or asparagus spears, cut into bite-size pieces

2 medium zucchinis, thinly sliced on the diagonal

1 tablespoon grated lemon zest

Lemon wedges

Combine the tofu, lemon juice, water, tahini, green onions, and garlic in a food processor or blender, and process into a smooth, creamy sauce. Set aside.

Cook the fettuccine in a large pot of boiling water until tender to your liking. Drain well and return to the pot. Cover and set aside.

Pour the oil into a large skillet, and place over medium-high heat. When hot, add the broccoli and zucchinis and cook and stir 8–10 minutes, or until tender-crisp. Remove from the heat, add the lemon zest, and toss gently. Cover and set aside.

Pour the reserved sauce over the warm pasta and toss well. Top each serving of pasta and sauce with a portion of the reserved vegetables. Garnish with lemon wedges or pass them at the table.

Gardener's Pie

calories: 341
protein: 22 g
fat: 10 g
carbohydrate: 44 g
fiber: 10 g

This power-packed casserole relies on convenience foods to re-create a vegan version of shepherd's pie, which is typically made with lamb or mutton. Mixed vegetables are combined with an herb-seasoned sauce, then topped with a mashed potato crust, and baked to a delectable golden brown. This is stick-to-your-ribs food—the kind that gives you the stamina to accomplish amazing feats of compassion, generosity, and peace.

CASSEROLE FILLING

2 packages (16 ounces each) frozen mixed vegetables (any kind)

2 teaspoons extra-virgin olive oil

2 medium onions, finely chopped

½ to 1 teaspoon crushed garlic

½ cup flour (any kind)

2 teaspoons dried thyme, crushed

1 teaspoon dried basil

1½ cups plain soymilk

1 pound (16 ounces) firm regular tofu, rinsed, patted dry, and cut into bite-size cubes

1 teaspoon salt

Ground black pepper

POTATO TOPPING

1½ cups water

2 teaspoons extra-virgin olive oil

1½ cups plain soymilk

2½ cups instant potato flakes

½ teaspoon garlic powder (optional)

½ teaspoon salt

Ground black pepper

Paprika, for garnish

Preheat the oven to 400 degrees F. Oil a deep 2-quart casserole dish, or mist it with nonstick cooking spray, and set aside.

For the filling: Cook the vegetables according to the package instructions. Drain well and place in a large bowl.

Pour the oil into a medium saucepan, and place over medium-high heat. When hot, add the onions and garlic. Lower the heat to medium, and cook and stir for about 10 minutes, or until the onions are tender. Remove from the heat and stir in the flour, thyme, and basil. Gradually stir in the soymilk, about ½ cup at a time, beating vigorously after each addition to avoid lumps. When all the soymilk has been added, place over medium heat and cook and stir until the sauce is very thick.

Stir the sauce into the reserved vegetables. Fold in the cubed tofu and salt, and season with pepper to taste. Spoon into the prepared casserole dish.

For the topping: Place the water and oil in a medium saucepan and bring to a boil. Remove from the heat and stir in the soymilk. Using a fork, stir in the potato flakes, optional garlic powder, salt, and pepper to taste. Mix well with the fork until the potatoes are smooth. If the potatoes are too thick, stir in a little more soymilk or water. If they are too thin, add more potato flakes.

Spoon the potatoes over the filling in the casserole dish, spreading the potatoes out to the edges using a fork. If desired, create an attractive design on the top of the potatoes using the tines of the fork. Dust the potatoes lightly with paprika.

Bake for 35–40 minutes, or until hot and bubbly and the top is golden brown. Remove from the oven and let rest for 5–10 minutes before serving.

Queenie

Queenie took her fate into her own four hooves and escaped from a live meat market in New York City. She ran from slaughterhouse workers, surprised dozens of motorists and pedestrians, and managed to evade NYPD officers for several blocks before she was captured. At first, it seemed Queenie would be taken back to the market to be butchered, but hundreds of New Yorkers spoke up for her, asking that her life be spared. Eventually, the owner of the meat market agreed and Queenie was transported to Farm Sanctuary. When she arrived, she was greeted with heartfelt cheers from the sanctuary staff and loud, welcoming moos from the shelter cows. Queenie is now a part of the sanctuary family, but she remains fiercely independent. And that's the way it should be.

Vegetables and side dishes

Ethiopian Potatoes and Green Beans

This delectable, highly seasoned dish is a classic in Ethiopian restaurants. Now you can make your own authentic version at home.

2 large gold or white potatoes, peeled and diced

2 cups cut green beans, in 1-inch pieces

2 teaspoons vegetable oil

1 small onion, minced

½ teaspoon crushed garlic

½ teaspoon ground cumin

½ teaspoon ground turmeric

½ teaspoon salt

Cayenne

1 can (15 ounces) stewed tomatoes

½ teaspoon freshly squeezed lime juice

Place the potatoes in a large saucepan, cover with water, and bring to a boil. Lower the heat and simmer for 10 minutes. Add the green beans and simmer for 5 minutes longer. Drain the potatoes and green beans in a colander and set aside.

Heat the oil in a large, heavy skillet or saucepan (nonstick will work best). Add the onion and garlic, and cook and stir for 5–10 minutes. Stir in the cumin, turmeric, salt, and cayenne to taste, and cook and stir for 1 minute longer. Add the potatoes, green beans, stewed tomatoes, and lime juice, and simmer over medium heat for 10–15 minutes, stirring often.

PER SERVING   *calories: 153*, protein: 6 g, fat: 8 g, carbohydrate: 19 g, fiber: 4 g

Twice-Baked Potatoes

N ow you can make tantalizing, restaurant-style, twice-baked potatoes at home, with no animal ingredients and a fraction of the fat.

4 large russet potatoes, scrubbed and baked (see page 22)

⅓ cup nutritional yeast flakes

1½ to 2 tablespoons dried chives

1 tablespoon dried onion flakes

1 teaspoon garlic powder

Large pinch of cayenne

Salt

Ground black pepper

1 cup plain soymilk, more or less as needed

1 can (4 ounces) sliced mushrooms, drained

3 tablespoons vegan bacon bits (optional)

Paprika, for garnish

calories: 243

protein: 10 g

fat: 2 g

carbohydrate: 48 g

fiber: 7 g

Do not turn off the oven after baking the potatoes (it should be at 375 degrees
F). Slice the hot potatoes in half lengthwise. Carefully scoop out the flesh to
create 8 potato shells (take care not to damage or puncture the skin). Place the
flesh in a large bowl. Set the shells aside.

Mash the potatoes well with a potato masher or sturdy fork. Add the
nutritional yeast flakes, chives, onion flakes, garlic powder, cayenne, and salt
and pepper to taste. Stir in ⅓ cup of the soymilk, adding more as needed to
make a smooth, thick mixture. (Too much soymilk will make the potatoes too
thin, so add just a little at a time.) Stir in the mushrooms and optional vegan
bacon bits.

Fill the reserved potato shells with the mashed potato mixture, forming it
into a mound. Sprinkle the tops with paprika. Place on a baking sheet and
bake for 20 minutes, or until hot. If you want a crispy, golden crust on top,
place under the broiler for 5 minutes.

instead of

"Almost" never killed a fly.

use

"Nearly" never saved a life.

Garlicky Greens

PER SERVING

calories: 153
protein: 6 g
fat: 8 g
carbohydrate: 19 g
fiber: 4 g

*T*his is a spectacular way to serve greens! Don't be intimidated by the large quantity of garlic. Thinly sliced cooked garlic is surprisingly mild because very little of its pungent oil is released.

2 tablespoons extra-virgin olive oil

6 to 8 cloves garlic, sliced lengthwise very thinly

1½ pounds dark leafy greens (collards, kale, mustard greens, turnip greens, and/or beet greens)

½ cup water, more or less as needed

Bottled hot sauce (optional)

Freshly squeezed lemon juice (optional)

Salt

Ground black pepper

Rinse the greens well, taking care to wash off any sand or grit. Remove the thick center ribs, and finely tear or chop the leaves into small pieces. You should have about 8 cups.

Heat the oil in a very large saucepan or pot. When hot, add the garlic and cook, stirring constantly, for 30 seconds. Add the greens, toss to coat with the oil, and cook and stir for 2–5 minutes, or until slightly wilted.

Pour in just enough water to cover the bottom of the pan, and bring to a boil. Lower the heat, cover, and steam, stirring occasionally, for 20–30 minutes, or until the greens are tender to your liking. There should be very little liquid left in the saucepan. If there is liquid, uncover and simmer briefly until it cooks off. Add a little more water during cooking only if necessary. Do not let the greens cook dry or they will scorch.

Stir in the optional hot sauce and lemon juice to taste, if desired. Season with salt and pepper to taste.

instead of

The straw that broke the camel's back.

use

The drop that made the cup spill over.

Roasted Butternut Squash and Bell Peppers

Makes 4 servings   **PER SERVING**

his dish has become a staple in our household. The aroma is intoxicating, and the delectable flavor of roasted winter squash, bell peppers, garlic, and herbs is irresistible.

calories: 168
protein: 3 g
fat: 7 g
carbohydrate: 28 g
fiber: 7 g

1 medium or large butternut squash

1 onion, coarsely chopped

1 red bell pepper, thinly sliced

1 green bell pepper, thinly sliced

2 tablespoons extra-virgin olive oil

1½ teaspoons dried thyme, crushed

1½ teaspoons dried rosemary, crushed

½ to 1 teaspoon crushed garlic

½ teaspoon salt

½ teaspoon ground black pepper

Preheat the oven to 375 degrees F. Slice the squash in half lengthwise from top to bottom. Scoop out the seeds and pulp and discard them. Slice the squash horizontally into ½-inch-thick half circles. Using a paring knife, slice away the thick rind. Cut the squash into bite-size cubes (this will make about 4 cups) and place into a 9 x 13-inch casserole dish or large roasting pan. Add the remaining ingredients, and mix thoroughly so all the vegetables are well coated with the olive oil, herbs, and garlic.

Bake uncovered for 30–45 minutes, stirring occasionally, until the squash is tender and the vegetables have browned.

VARIATIONS

■ **Roasted Butternut Squash, Bell Peppers, and Leek:** Stir 1 leek (see page 166), thinly sliced, into the vegetables after they have roasted for 15–20 minutes.

■ **Roasted Butternut Squash, Bell Peppers, and White Beans:** After the vegetables have finished roasting, stir in 1 can (15 or 16 ounces) white beans (such as Great Northern, cannellini, or navy), rinsed and drained. Lower the oven temperature to 350 degrees F, and return the mixture to the oven for about 10 minutes to let the beans heat through. This makes a delicious main dish.

Perfect Brown Rice

PER ½ CUP

Makes about 3½ cups

calories: 109
protein: 3 g
fat: 1 g
carbohydrate: 23 g
fiber: 2 g

Brown rice takes a little longer to cook than white rice, but its chewy, nutty, whole grain goodness is worth it. Cooked brown rice freezes beautifully, so make a double batch and freeze it in heavy-duty zipper-lock plastic bags. Simply thaw it in a bowl of hot water. The secret to perfect brown rice is to not lift the lid as it cooks, since heat will be lost when the steam escapes.

2 ¼ cups water
1 cup brown rice
Pinch of salt

Pour the water into a medium saucepan and bring to a boil. Add the rice slowly so the boiling doesn't stop. Add the salt and stir. Lower the heat, cover, and simmer for 40–50 minutes, or until the rice is tender and almost all the water has been absorbed. Remove from the heat and let rest for 10–15 minutes, covered. Fluff with a fork before serving.

Green Grits

PER SERVING

Makes 4 servings

calories: 105
protein: 2 g
fat: 4 g
carbohydrate: 16 g
fiber: 1 g

Broccoli adds flavor, nutrition, and beautiful flecks of green to this delicious recipe. Serve it as a side dish in place of rice or potatoes. Do not be tempted to substitute cornmeal for the grits, as you will not have good results. Use only the more coarsely ground corn grits, also called polenta.

2 cups water
½ to 1 cup finely chopped broccoli
½ cup yellow corn grits
1 tablespoon extra-virgin olive oil
½ teaspoon salt, or a dash of umeboshi vinegar

Combine the water and broccoli in a heavy-bottomed saucepan (nonstick will work best) and bring to a boil. Reduce the heat to medium and simmer for 5 minutes. Remove from the heat and stir in the grits with a long-handled wooden spoon. Return to a boil. Turn the heat down to low, cover, and cook, stirring occasionally, for about 20 minutes. Stir well. Add the olive oil and salt, and mix thoroughly. Serve hot.

Coconut Rice

*T*his is an utterly scrumptious way to prepare rice. The optional curry paste sparks a bit of heat, though it is mellowed by the coconut milk.

calories: 197
protein: 3 g
fat: 13 g
carbohydrate: 19 g
fiber: 2 g

1 cup white or brown rice

1 cup water

1 cup lite or full-fat coconut milk

½ to 2 teaspoons red or green Thai curry paste

Salt

2 tablespoons unsweetened shredded dried coconut, toasted
(optional; see note)

Place the rice, water, coconut milk, and curry paste in a saucepan with a tight-fitting lid. Bring to a boil, cover, and turn the heat down to low. If using white rice, cook for 18–20 minutes; if using brown rice, cook for about 40 minutes. Remove from the heat and let rest, covered, for 5–10 minutes. Season with salt to taste. Transfer to a serving dish, fluff with a fork, and sprinkle with the optional toasted coconut.

NOTE

- To toast the coconut, place it in a small saucepan over medium to medium-high heat, stirring constantly until it just begins to brown. This will take just a few minutes; watch closely so it doesn't burn.

VARIATION

- **Coconut Rice with Veggies:** Cut your favorite vegetables into bite-size pieces, and scatter them on top of the rice during cooking. Longer-cooking vegetables can be added to white rice at the start, or added to brown rice after about 20 minutes, depending on the vegetables, how thick they are cut, and how tender you like them. Shorter-cooking vegetables can be added 5–10 minutes before the rice has finished cooking, or you can add them during the resting time, after the rice is done cooking and has been removed from the heat. This will lightly steam them.

instead of

Dumb as a cow.

use

Thick as a brick.

Rosemary Red Ribbon Rice

PER ½ CUP

Makes about 3 cups

calories: 188
protein: 4 g
fat: 6 g
carbohydrate: 32 g
fiber: 2 g

*T*his rice dish is fragrant, festive, and easy to prepare, making it ideal for everyday meals or for entertaining.

1½ cups light vegetable broth or water

½ cup seedless raisins

1 teaspoon crushed garlic

½ teaspoon salt

¼ to ½ teaspoon dried rosemary, crushed

1 cup white basmati rice

1 small red bell pepper, cut into thin matchsticks

½ cup roasted and peeled chestnuts (see note), coarsely broken, or chopped walnuts

1 tablespoon extra-virgin olive oil (optional)

Combine the broth, raisins, garlic, salt, and rosemary in a medium saucepan and bring to a boil. Stir in the rice, cover, and turn the heat down to low. Cook for 18–20 minutes, or until almost all the liquid has been absorbed.

Remove from the heat, add the red bell pepper, chestnuts, and optional olive oil, and toss gently with a fork until evenly distributed. Cover and let stand for 5–10 minutes (this will lightly steam the red bell pepper). Fluff with a fork and serve.

NOTE:

- Used jarred or tinned chestnuts for the easiest preparation.

instead of
Never fish in troubled waters.

use
Never fly a kite in a storm.

Sauces, gravies, and condiments

Velvety Cheez Sauce

Use this velvety, cheddar-style sauce on vegetables, pasta, rice, or toast points.

1 medium potato, peeled and coarsely chopped

¾ cup water

½ cup chopped carrots

½ cup chopped onions

¾ cup crumbled silken tofu (any firmness)

⅓ cup nutritional yeast flakes

1 tablespoon freshly squeezed lemon juice

1 teaspoon salt

¼ teaspoon garlic powder

Combine the potato, water, carrots, and onions in a medium saucepan, and bring to a boil. Lower the heat to medium, cover, and simmer for 10 minutes, stirring once or twice, until the vegetables are tender.

Place the cooked vegetables, their cooking liquid, and the remaining ingredients in a blender, and process several minutes until completely smooth. Depending on the size of your blender, you may need to do this in several batches (see page 38).

Rinse out the saucepan and return the blended mixture to it. Warm over low heat, stirring often, until the sauce is hot. Stored in a covered container in the refrigerator, leftover Velvety Cheez Sauce will keep for about 3 days.

PER ½ CUP *calories: 88,* protein: 7 g, fat: 2 g, carbohydrate: 12 g, fiber: 3 g

Rich Brown Gravy

calories: 94
protein: 4 g
fat: 5 g
carbohydrate: 10 g
fiber: 1 g

This versatile gravy is terrific on everything from beans and tofu to veggies, grains, and mashed potatoes.

2 tablespoons cornstarch, arrowroot, or kuzu

3 tablespoons reduced-sodium soy sauce

1½ cups dark vegetable broth (no salt added) or water

½ teaspoon garlic powder

2 tablespoons tahini

Combine the cornstarch and soy sauce in a medium saucepan. Mix well to make a smooth paste. Gradually whisk in the vegetable broth and garlic powder. Cook over medium-high heat, stirring constantly with the whisk, until the gravy thickens and comes to a boil. Remove from the heat and beat in the tahini using the whisk. Serve at once.

Creamy Raw Spinach Sauce

calories: 89
protein: 3 g
fat: 7 g
carbohydrate: 5 g
fiber: 1 g

This sauce is so incredibly rich-tasting and delicious, it will force even avowed vegetable avoiders to have a change of heart. We pour it over pasta (instead of traditional tomato sauce), baked spuds, rice, and whole grains. It's lick-the-bowl-clean good!

2 cups baby spinach leaves, lightly packed

½ cup raw cashews

½ cup water

½ teaspoon crushed garlic

½ teaspoon dried dill weed

½ teaspoon dried tarragon

¼ teaspoon salt

Combine all the ingredients in a blender, and process several minutes until completely smooth and creamy. Stored in a covered container in the refrigerator, Creamy Raw Spinach Sauce will keep for about 3 days. Stir well before serving.

Savory Chickpea Gravy

| Makes 3 to 3½ cups | PER ½ CUP |

*T*his handy sauce is a delicious way to enhance even the simplest meals. Folks who swear they don't like beans will love it. Since it is made with toasted chickpea flour, they'll never know they are eating beans!

calories: 112
protein: 3 g
fat: 7 g
carbohydrate: 9 g
fiber: 2 g

3 tablespoons extra-virgin olive oil

1 cup chickpea flour

1 teaspoon dried sage

½ teaspoon dried thyme, crushed

½ teaspoon dried rosemary, crushed

¼ teaspoon ground black pepper

3½ cups hot water

1 tablespoon umeboshi vinegar

1 tablespoon reduced-sodium soy sauce

Salt

Pour the oil into a large saucepan and place over medium heat. When hot, stir in the flour, sage, thyme, rosemary, and pepper, stirring constantly to form a smooth, thick paste. Cook over medium heat for 5–10 minutes, or until lightly browned and the flour no longer tastes raw. Remove from the heat.

Gradually whisk in the hot water, stirring constantly and mixing carefully to avoid lumps. Add the vinegar, soy sauce, and salt to taste. Warm over medium heat, whisking occasionally, until hot, thick, and bubbly. Whisk in more water, if needed, to achieve the desired consistency. Stored in a covered container in the refrigerator, leftover Savory Chickpea Gravy will keep for about 5 days.

instead of
I have a bone to pick with you.
use
I have a stone to pick with you.

Pizza and Pasta Sauce

Makes about 1 cup

TOMATO SAUCE

calories: 63
protein: 4 g
fat: 0 g
carbohydrate: 14 g
fiber: 2 g

RED BELL PEPPERS

calories: 20
protein: 1 g
fat: 0 g
carbohydrate: 4 g
fiber: 1 g

*T*his flavorful sauce is great for last-minute pizzas or pasta dishes. It's so quick, easy, and low in fat that you may never resort to jarred sauce again!

1 can (8 ounces) tomato sauce, or 1 jar (8 ounces) roasted red bell peppers, drained

2 teaspoons granulated sugar

½ teaspoon dried oregano

½ teaspoon dried basil

½ teaspoon dried rosemary, crushed

½ teaspoon ground fennel

½ teaspoon salt

¼ teaspoon garlic powder

If using the roasted red peppers, remove any seeds and skin, and blend them in a food processor or blender until smooth. Combine all the ingredients in a small saucepan, and bring to a boil over medium heat. Reduce the heat to low and simmer for 15 minutes.

How to Roast Bell Peppers

Choose heavy peppers with a thick, meaty flesh. Light, thin peppers will burn before their skin chars.

Preheat the oven to 400 degrees F. Wash and dry the peppers but do not slice them. Place the whole peppers on a baking sheet, and roast them on the center rack of the hot oven, turning them over frequently until they are softened and the skin is charred and blistered all over.

Transfer to a bowl and cover the bowl with a lid or plate. Allow the peppers to steam this way for 20–30 minutes.

Peel off the loosened skin with your fingers. Do not rinse the peppers under water, as this will wash away much of the flavor. Remove and discard the stems, seeds, and ribs. Stored in a covered container in the refrigerator, Roasted Peppers will keep for about 5 days.

Tomato Rarebit

Rarebit is a thick, sumptuous sauce with a delectable "cheddar and beer" flavor. Try it with Welsh Rarebit (page 97), or simply spoon it over split and toasted English muffins or bagels topped with mild red onion rings, or baked potatoes topped with steamed broccoli florets or asparagus spears. Impressive!

calories: 151
protein: 6 g
fat: 6 g
carbohydrate: 20 g
fiber: 3 g

1½ cups (12 ounces) nonalcoholic lager beer

½ cup water

⅓ cup raw cashews, or 4 tablespoons cashew butter

5 to 6 tablespoons tomato paste (no salt added)

¼ cup nutritional yeast flakes

3 tablespoons arrowroot, kuzu, or cornstarch

1½ teaspoons onion powder

½ teaspoon crushed garlic or garlic powder

½ teaspoon hot or sweet paprika

½ teaspoon dry mustard

¼ teaspoon salt

Several drops bottled hot sauce

Combine all the ingredients in a blender, and process several minutes until completely smooth. Pour into a medium saucepan and bring to a boil, stirring constantly. Turn the heat down to low and continue to cook and stir a few minutes longer until the mixture is thick and smooth. Serve immediately.

Cool any leftover Tomato Rarebit before storing. Stored in a covered container in the refrigerator, leftover Tomato Rarebit will keep for 5–7 days.

instead of

[Someone] is no spring chicken.

use

[Someone] is no spring onion.

Warm Tahini-Miso Sauce

*N*o cooking is required to make this luscious sauce! It boosts the flavor and protein of any meal. Try it on baked winter squash, steamed cabbage wedges, or hot brown rice—it's divine!

⅔ cup tahini

⅓ cup light or chickpea miso

2 teaspoons grated fresh ginger (optional)

Large pinch of cayenne (optional)

⅔ cup almost-boiling water, more or less as needed

Combine the tahini, miso, optional ginger and cayenne, and half the water in a bowl. Mash and beat with a spoon until the mixture forms a smooth paste. Gradually beat in the remaining water, using just enough to form a thick but pourable sauce.

VARIATION

- **Warm Almond-Miso Sauce:** Replace the tahini with an equal amount of smooth or crunchy almond butter.

Tartar Sauce

*S*erve this incredible sauce instead of mayonnaise on all your favorite veggie burgers.

1 cup vegan mayonnaise

1 green onion, thinly sliced (optional)

2 tablespoons chopped pickles

2 tablespoons chopped fresh parsley

2 tablespoons chopped capers (see page 196)

2 to 3 teaspoons freshly squeezed lemon juice

1 to 3 teaspoons Dijon mustard

Salt

Ground black pepper

Combine all the ingredients in a small bowl, and stir until well blended. Stored in a covered container in the refrigerator, Tartar Sauce will keep for 5–7 days.

Hollandaze Sauce

| | Makes 2 cups | PER ¼ CUP |

This rich, creamy, lemony sauce will remind you of hollandaise, and you won't miss the butter or eggs. It's wonderful and festive over steamed broccoli or baked potatoes.

calories: 109
protein: 4 g
fat: 9 g
carbohydrate: 3 g
fiber: 1 g

- 1 package (about 12 ounces) firm silken tofu, crumbled
- ½ cup plain soymilk
- 1 tablespoon nutritional yeast flakes
- 1 tablespoon tahini
- 1 tablespoon freshly squeezed lemon juice
- 1 teaspoon ground turmeric (for a buttery yellow color)
- ½ teaspoon dried tarragon
- ¼ cup extra-virgin olive oil

Combine the tofu, soymilk, nutritional yeast flakes, tahini, lemon juice, turmeric, and tarragon in a blender, and process until very smooth and creamy. With the machine running, slowly drizzle in the olive oil through the cap opening in the lid.

Transfer to a small saucepan, and place over medium-low heat. Warm, stirring often, until the sauce is heated through. Do not boil! Stored in a covered container in the refrigerator, leftover Hollandaze Sauce will keep for about 3 days.

NOTE

- The sauce may be made in advance and refrigerated. Heat it gently before serving.

instead of

You can't make an omelet without breaking eggs.

use

You can't make wine without crushing grapes.

Incredible Cashew Cheez Sauce

PER ¼ CUP

Makes about 2⅔ cups

calories: 88
protein: 4 g
fat: 6 g
carbohydrate: 5 g
fiber: 1 g

I always keep veggie broth on hand just to make this simple but compelling sauce. It's a staple in our household because it contains no added oil, is quick and easy to prepare, and can be spooned on almost everything. Unlike other nuts, cashews have an uncanny ability to thicken when they are blended and heated. Drizzle this delectable sauce over casseroles or pizza (before or after baking), or pour it over macaroni for a speedy mac-and-cheez delight. When chilled, it becomes very thick, turning it from a sauce to a convenient cold dip or sandwich spread.

2¼ cups light vegetable broth

1 cup raw cashews

1 tablespoon freshly squeezed lemon juice (optional)

¼ cup nutritional yeast flakes

2 teaspoons salt, or 1 teaspoon if broth is salted

2 teaspoons onion powder

½ teaspoon dry mustard

¼ teaspoon garlic powder

Combine all the ingredients in a blender, and process until completely smooth. Pour into a medium saucepan and place over medium heat. Cook, stirring almost constantly, for 18–20 minutes, or until the sauce is very thick, smooth, and creamy. Stored in a covered container in the refrigerator, leftover Incredible Cashew Cheez Sauce will keep for 5–7 days.

NOTE

- This sauce will thicken when chilled. The cold sauce makes a delicious spread for crackers or chips, or it can be used as a sandwich filling. If you want to reheat the sauce, warm it gently over low heat. It will thin out a bit as it warms.

Cashew Pimiento Cheez Sauce

Makes about 3 cups | **PER ½ CUP**

*T*his sauce is a snap to make and oh-so-luscious. Use it to top grains, baked corn chips, baked potatoes, all your favorite veggies, and, of course, macaroni. It's even great as a dipping sauce.

calories: 145
protein: 5 g
fat: 11 g
carbohydrate: 9 g
fiber: 1 g

2 cups water

1 cup raw cashews

½ cup drained pimientos or roasted red bell peppers (skin and seeds removed)

2½ tablespoons freshly squeezed lemon juice

¼ cup nutritional yeast flakes (optional)

2 teaspoons salt

2 teaspoons onion powder

½ teaspoon dry mustard

¼ teaspoon garlic powder

Combine all the ingredients in a blender, and process until completely smooth and no orange flecks remain. Pour into a medium saucepan and place over medium heat. Cook, stirring almost constantly, for 18–20 minutes, or until the sauce is very thick, smooth, and creamy. Stored in a covered container in the refrigerator, leftover Cashew Pimiento Cheez Sauce will keep for 5–7 days.

NOTES

- This sauce will thicken when chilled. The cold sauce makes a delicious spread for crackers or chips, or it can be used as a sandwich filling. If you want to reheat the sauce, warm it gently over low heat. It will thin out a bit as it warms.

- If you prefer, you can replace the pimientos with ½ cup well-cooked carrots.

instead of
Opening a can of worms.
use
Opening a can of spaghetti.

Last-Minute Sauce

PER ¼ CUP

calories: 170
protein: 8 g
fat: 11 g
carbohydrate: 10 g
fiber: 2 g

Makes about 1¼ cups

*T*his delectable sauce is a terrific way to inspire anyone to eat their veggies. Serve it as a dipping sauce for lightly steamed vegetables; it's also great over rice, pasta, whole grains, salad, or cooked greens. It's so easy and quick to prepare, you can make it in a moment's notice.

½ cup peanut butter

2 to 3 tablespoons reduced-sodium soy sauce

¼ cup ketchup

½ cup water, as needed

Combine the peanut butter, soy sauce, and ketchup in a small bowl, and stir until well blended. Whisk in just enough water to create a pourable sauce. Stored in a covered container in the refrigerator, Last-Minute Sauce will keep for about 5 days. Bring to room temperature before serving.

Tangy White Bean Sauce

PER ¼ CUP

calories: 111
protein: 5 g
fat: 4 g
carbohydrate: 14 g
fiber: 3 g

Makes about 1¼ cups

*T*his well-seasoned cold sauce is ideal for topping steamed greens, grains, or pasta.

1 can (15 or 16 ounces) white beans, rinsed and drained (about 1¾ cups)

2 tablespoons freshly squeezed lemon juice

4 teaspoons extra-virgin olive oil

1½ teaspoons Dijon mustard

1 teaspoon dried tarragon

½ teaspoon salt

¼ to ½ teaspoon crushed garlic

Ground white or black pepper

⅓ cup light vegetable broth or water, more or less as needed

Place all the ingredients in a blender, and process until very smooth and creamy. Use just enough broth or water to create a thick sauce. Serve at room temperature or thoroughly chilled. Stored in a covered container in the refrigerator, Tangy White Bean Sauce will keep for 3–5 days.

NOTES

- For the beans, choose among Great Northern, cannellini, navy, or any other white bean you prefer.
- This sauce will thicken somewhat when refrigerated. If desired, thin it with a little more broth or water before using.

Mushroom Gravy

Makes about 1¼ cups | **PER ½ CUP**

This gravy is fabulous on meatless loaves, burgers, and grains.

3 tablespoons flour (any kind)

1 cup water or dark vegetable broth

2 tablespoons reduced-sodium soy sauce

1 teaspoon extra-virgin olive oil

¼ teaspoon garlic powder

¼ to ½ cup thinly sliced or chopped mushrooms

Pinch of ground black pepper

calories: 63
protein: 4 g
fat: 2 g
carbohydrate: 9 g
fiber: 1 g

Place the flour in a small saucepan, and toast it over very low heat, stirring occasionally, until it is lightly browned and fragrant. Remove from the heat.

Gradually whisk in the water, soy sauce, olive oil, and garlic powder. Beat vigorously with the whisk until the sauce is smooth.

Place the saucepan over medium heat and cook, stirring constantly with the whisk, until the gravy thickens and comes to a boil. Add the mushrooms, turn the heat down to medium-low, and simmer for 1–2 minutes longer, stirring constantly. Season with pepper to taste. Serve at once.

instead of

Lay an egg.

use

Launch a dud.

Golden Gravy

calories: 105
protein: 7 g
fat: 4 g
carbohydrate: 12 g
fiber: 3 g

*N*utritional yeast flakes impart a captivating flavor to this gravy, imbuing it with homey warmth. Spoon this lovely sauce over vegetables, potatoes, croquettes, grains, or biscuits.

¼ cup nutritional yeast flakes

¼ cup flour (any kind)

1½ cups water or light vegetable broth

2 tablespoons reduced-sodium soy sauce

2 teaspoons extra-virgin olive oil

¼ teaspoon onion powder

Pinch of ground white or black pepper

Place the nutritional yeast flakes and flour in a small saucepan, and toast them over medium heat, stirring constantly, until lightly browned and fragrant.

Remove from the heat. Gradually whisk in the water, soy sauce, and olive oil, whisking vigorously until the gravy is very smooth. Then whisk in the onion powder and pepper to taste.

Cook over medium heat, stirring almost constantly with the whisk, until the gravy is thickened, smooth, and bubbly. Serve at once.

Green Martian Sauce

calories: 70
protein: 2 g
fat: 4 g
carbohydrate: 9 g
fiber: 3 g

*E*ven people who look askance at kale will like this sauce, but those who love kale will adore it! It is so simple, healthful, delicious, and versatile. It's also very low in fat. You can use it as a sauce for rice or pasta, as a luscious topping for baked potatoes, or as a dip or spread. Kids get a kick out of the title of this sauce, aptly named for its dark, unearthly shade of green.

2 cups water

1 bunch lacinato (dinosaur) kale, rinsed well and chopped

1 pound carrots, scrubbed and chopped

1 to 2 teaspoons crushed garlic

¼ to ⅓ cup pecans

Salt (optional)

Place the water, kale, carrots, and garlic in a large pot. Bring to a boil, cover, turn the heat down to medium-low, and cook for 30–40 minutes, or until very tender. Transfer the vegetables and remaining liquid to a blender. Add the pecans and process until completely smooth. (Unless you own a very large blender, you will need to process the mixture in several batches.) Pour into a clean saucepan and stir in the optional salt to taste. Warm through gently. Stored in a covered container in the refrigerator, leftover Green Martian Sauce will keep for 5–7 days.

Spicy Peanut Sauce

Makes about 1⅓ cups | **PER ¼ CUP**

*T*his delectable sauce is always a phenomenal hit. Serve it over pasta, grains, salad, greens, or steamed vegetables. It's exceedingly flavorful, so a little goes a long way.

½ cup smooth peanut butter

2 tablespoons reduced-sodium soy sauce

1 teaspoon rice vinegar

1 teaspoon maple syrup

½ teaspoon ground ginger

¼ to ½ teaspoon crushed garlic

⅛ to ¼ teaspoon cayenne

½ to ⅔ cup water, as needed

calories: 150
protein: 8 g
fat: 11 g
carbohydrate: 7 g
fiber: 2 g

Place the peanut butter in a small bowl. Stir in the soy sauce, vinegar, maple syrup, ginger, garlic, and cayenne, beating vigorously with a wooden spoon. Gradually whisk in just enough water to achieve the desired consistency. Stored in a covered container in the refrigerator, Spicy Peanut Sauce will keep for about 5 days.

NOTE

▪ This sauce will thicken somewhat when refrigerated. If desired, thin it with a little more water before using.

Ravigote

PER ¼ CUP

Makes about 2 cups

calories: 62
protein: 3 g
fat: 5 g
carbohydrate: 2 g
fiber: 1 g

A robust combination of capers, dill pickle, and mustard make this thick and zesty cold sauce unique. It is an exceptionally versatile topping, ideal for potatoes, salads, cooked vegetables, beans, grains, tofu, tempeh, or pasta.

1 package (about 12 ounces) firm silken tofu, crumbled

3 tablespoons chopped dill pickles or drained dill pickle relish

2 tablespoons extra-virgin olive oil

2 tablespoons minced flat-leaf parsley

1 large green onion, sliced

1 tablespoon reduced-sodium soy sauce

1 tablespoon freshly squeezed lemon juice

1 tablespoon red wine vinegar

1 tablespoon water

2 teaspoons Dijon mustard

2 teaspoons drained capers

2 teaspoons dried tarragon

½ teaspoon salt

Combine all the ingredients in a blender, and process until very smooth, thick, and creamy. Serve at once or thoroughly chilled. Stored in a covered container in the refrigerator, Ravigote will keep for 3–5 days.

What Are Capers?

Capers are the cured flower buds of a bush indigenous to the Mediterranean and parts of Asia. The small buds are picked, dried in the sun, and then pickled in a vinegar brine. If desired, capers may be rinsed before using to remove excess salt and brine. Their peppery flavor lends a piquant tartness wherever they are used. Capers will keep indefinitely when stored in the refrigerator.

Tunisian Cream Sauce

Makes about 1½ cups	**PER ¼ CUP**

calories: 77
protein: 4 g
fat: 6 g
carbohydrate: 2 g
fiber: 1 g

*I*nspired by the fiery seasonings of the Tunis region of North Africa, this simple, spicy sauce is superb over a mixture of hot potato chunks, steamed vegetables, and/or cooked beans. The caraway adds a distinctive flavor that is especially delightful on steamed cabbage, brussels sprouts, or cauliflower.

1 package (about 12 ounces) firm silken tofu, crumbled

¼ cup freshly squeezed lemon juice

2 tablespoons extra-virgin olive oil

1 teaspoon ground caraway seeds, or 1½ teaspoons whole caraway seeds

1 teaspoon ground coriander

¾ teaspoon salt

½ teaspoon crushed garlic

Cayenne

Combine the tofu, lemon juice, olive oil, caraway seeds, coriander, salt, garlic, and cayenne to taste in a blender, and process until very smooth and creamy. Serve at once or thoroughly chilled. Stored in a covered container in the refrigerator, Tunisian Cream Sauce will keep for 3–5 days.

Basil

Basil was rescued after being shipped through the mail and abandoned at a post office in Pennsylvania. Shipped via U.S. postal mail from hatcheries to farms across the country, day-old chicks routinely die from illness, exposure, or improper handling. Males, like Basil, who were improperly sexed and thought to be female, are even more at risk because they are often discarded or killed once the customer realizes they are roosters. Happily, Basil did not have to face such a fate. A caring postal worker found the abandoned chicks and wanted them to live. Once powerless to control the course of his own destiny, Basil now spends his days doing what *he* wants to do. Each morning, he happily ventures outdoors, relaxes in the sun, and grooms his lady friends. Then, again and again throughout the day, when the time feels right, he throws back his head, shakes his feathers, and crows loudly enough to be heard in the neighboring county.

Salads and salad dressings

Musabaha

Pronounced moo-SAH-ba-ha, this simple but delectable Middle Eastern chickpea salad makes a lovely side dish or satisfying entrée. Use the freshest tomato you can find, as its flavor will be the soul of the dish.

1 can (15 or 16 ounces) chickpeas, rinsed and drained (about 1¾ cups)

1 small ripe tomato, seeded and chopped (see page 126)

¼ cup chopped sweet onions or thinly sliced green onions, or ¼ to ½ teaspoon crushed garlic

Hot chili oil, crushed red pepper flakes, cayenne, or chipotle chili powder

Salt

Ground black pepper

¾ cup Tahina (page 208), or more as desired

Paprika, for garnish (optional)

Dried oregano, for garnish (optional)

Combine the chickpeas, tomato, onions, and hot chili oil, salt, and pepper to taste in a serving bowl, and toss together gently. Top with the Tahina, spreading it evenly over the salad, and garnish with paprika and oregano, if desired. Serve at once.

PER SIDE   *calories: 307,* protein: 12 g, fat: 18 g, carbohydrate: 28 g, fiber: 7 g

Warm Salad Niçoise

*T*raditionally, one of the main components of salad niçoise is tuna fish. In this modified version, the tuna fish has been replaced with chickpeas, and the large quantity of olive oil typically called for has been greatly reduced. Nevertheless, this lightened rendition retains all the flavor for which salad niçoise is renowned.

calories: 236
protein: 8 g
fat: 7 g
carbohydrate: 37 g
fiber: 8 g

NIÇOISE DRESSING

2 tablespoons extra-virgin olive oil

2 tablespoons freshly squeezed lemon juice

1 tablespoon red wine vinegar

1 teaspoon Dijon mustard

½ teaspoon granulated sugar

½ teaspoon crushed garlic

¼ teaspoon dried basil

¼ teaspoon dried oregano

¼ teaspoon salt

SALAD MIX

3 medium red skin potatoes, cut into bite-size chunks

2 cups fresh green beans, trimmed and cut into 1- to 2-inch pieces

1 can (15 or 16 ounces) chickpeas, rinsed and drained (about 1¾ cups)

2 ripe tomatoes, each cut into 8 wedges

¼ cup minced red onions

2 to 4 tablespoons green nori flakes (see page 26)

4 cups mixed salad greens, torn

For the dressing: Place the olive oil, lemon juice, vinegar, mustard, sugar, garlic, basil, oregano, and salt in a small bowl, and whisk until well combined. Set aside.

For the salad: Steam the potatoes and green beans until tender. Place in a large bowl with the chickpeas, tomato wedges, and onions. Drizzle the dressing over the vegetables and beans. Sprinkle the nori flakes on top, and toss gently to mix.

To serve: Divide the salad greens among four to six salad plates. Top with the salad mix and serve.

Hot-and-Sour Seitan Steak Salad

calories: 236
protein: 24 g
fat: 8 g
carbohydrate: 22 g
fiber: 5 g

*T*he flavor of this hearty salad is reminiscent of Thai cuisine, uniquely characterized by the use of peanuts, ginger, basil, mint, and hot pepper.

HOT-AND-SOUR DRESSING

2 tablespoons peanut butter (crunchy or smooth)

5 teaspoons reduced-sodium soy sauce

½ teaspoon ground ginger

2 tablespoons frozen apple juice concentrate, rice syrup, or agave syrup

¼ cup freshly squeezed lime juice

2 tablespoons water

1 teaspoon dried basil

½ teaspoon garlic powder

½ teaspoon dried spearmint

⅛ teaspoon crushed red pepper flakes

SEITAN STEAK SALAD

1 cup seitan strips

1 medium bell pepper (red, yellow, or orange), sliced into thin, bite-size strips

½ cup thin, bite-size cucumber strips (peel the cucumber if it is waxed)

2 cups torn romaine lettuce, in bite-size pieces

2 cups torn leaf lettuce, in bite-size pieces

For the dressing: Combine the peanut butter, soy sauce, and ginger in a small bowl, and stir to make a paste. Stir in the juice concentrate. Gradually stir in the lime juice, water, basil, garlic powder, spearmint, and crushed red pepper flakes. Mix well and set aside.

For the salad: Mist a medium skillet with nonstick cooking spray, or coat it with a thin layer of vegetable oil, and place over medium-high heat. When hot, add the seitan strips in a single layer, and brown them well on both sides, turning them once with a fork.

Remove from the heat and pour the dressing over the seitan in the skillet. Add the bell pepper and cucumber strips, and toss gently.

To serve: Toss the lettuce greens together and divide them between two large salad bowls or dinner plates. Spoon the warm seitan mixture over the greens. Serve immediately.

NOTE

■ Do not substitute lemon juice for the lime juice, as the flavor will not be correct.

Fiesta Coleslaw

Makes about 5 cups | **PER ¾ CUP**

*N*o vegan picnic or barbecue would be complete without coleslaw. This recipe incorporates a variety of hues for a tasty and eye-appealing twist on an old standby.

calories: 60

protein: 2 g

fat: 4 g

carbohydrate: 5 g

fiber: 2 g

SALAD MIX

3 cups finely chopped or shredded green cabbage

1 cup finely chopped or shredded red cabbage

2 medium carrots, peeled and shredded (about 1 cup)

⅓ cup thinly sliced green onions

8 pimiento-stuffed green olives, sliced

CREAMY DRESSING

½ cup vegan mayonnaise

2 teaspoons prepared yellow mustard

¼ teaspoon ground black pepper

Salt

For the salad: Place the cabbage, carrots, green onions, and olives in a medium bowl, and toss until well combined.

For the dressing: Place the vegan mayonnaise, mustard, and pepper in a bowl, and whisk until smooth. Pour over the cabbage mixture and toss to mix thoroughly. Season with salt to taste, and toss once more.

NOTE

■ A food processor fitted with the S blade or a shredding disc will greatly speed the work of preparing the cabbage and carrots.

Vegan Antipasto

PER SIDE

Makes 2 main dish servings, or 4 side dish servings

calories: 225
protein: 6 g
fat: 13 g
carbohydrate: 22 g
fiber: 5 g

Vegetables and beans take the place of the traditional luncheon meats and cheeses in this beautiful antipasto. It makes a filling meal for two hungry adults. Serve it with a good-quality Italian bread or a crusty sourdough, and your meal will be complete.

1 cup fresh green beans, trimmed and cut into 1-inch pieces,
    or 1 cup frozen cut green beans

4 cups torn romaine lettuce, in bite-size pieces

¾ cup cooked or canned chickpeas, rinsed and drained

½ cup water-packed artichoke hearts, drained and quartered

¼ cup pitted whole black olives or pimiento-stuffed green olives

1 small ripe tomato, seeded and chopped (see page 126)

4 or 5 thin slices red onion, separated into rings or cut
    into bite-size pieces

⅔ cup bottled Italian dressing

Salt

Ground black pepper

Steam the fresh green beans until tender-crisp, or cook the frozen green beans according to the package directions and drain. Chill for several hours in the refrigerator.

Place the torn lettuce in a large bowl along with the chilled green beans, chickpeas, quartered artichoke hearts, olives, tomato, and onion. Pour the dressing over the vegetables and toss gently. Season with salt and pepper to taste and toss gently again. Divide the salad between two large salad bowls or dinner plates (or four smaller ones, if serving the salad as a side dish), and serve.

NOTE

- For a richer flavor, combine the green beans, chickpeas, artichoke hearts, olives, and dressing in a large bowl, cover tightly, and let marinate in the refrigerator for up to 48 hours. Add the tomato, lettuce, salt, and pepper just before serving.

instead of
Talk turkey.
use
Speak vegan.

Greek Salad

S alty, marinated tofu chunks mimic feta cheese and lend an authentic Mediterranean taste to this enticing salad. Serve it with a crusty whole grain bread for a complete and satisfying meal.

VEGAN FETA

½ pound (8 ounces) firm regular tofu, rinsed and patted dry (press if time permits; see page 33)

2 tablespoons red wine vinegar

4 teaspoons extra-virgin olive oil

1 tablespoon freshly squeezed lemon juice

½ teaspoon dried basil

½ teaspoon dried oregano

½ teaspoon salt

¼ teaspoon garlic powder

¼ teaspoon ground black pepper

SALAD MIX

4 cups torn romaine lettuce, in bite-size pieces

1½ cups sliced English cucumber, cut into half-moons

1 ripe tomato, cut in half and thinly sliced into half-moons

⅓ cup whole kalamata olives

¼ cup chopped red onions

For the vegan feta: Cut the tofu into ¾-inch cubes and place it in a wide, shallow ceramic or glass bowl. Combine the vinegar, olive oil, lemon juice, basil, oregano, salt, garlic powder, and pepper in a small measuring cup or bowl, and whisk until well blended. Pour over the tofu chunks and toss gently until they are evenly coated. Cover the bowl tightly and let the tofu marinate in the refrigerator for 12–48 hours, tossing gently every few hours.

To serve: Just before serving, prepare the salad ingredients and place them in a large bowl. Add the tofu and marinade and toss gently but thoroughly. Serve at once, with additional salt and pepper on the side to season as desired.

Caesar Salad

calories: 149
protein: 7 g
fat: 6 g
carbohydrate: 18 g
fiber: 4 g

egend has it that this renowned salad was created in 1924 by Italian chef Caesar Cardini, who owned a restaurant in Tijuana, Mexico. Classically, the salad is tossed with a garlic vinaigrette dressing made with Worcestershire sauce, lemon juice, grated Parmesan, croutons, a raw or coddled egg, and anchovies. This healthful vegan version tastes incredibly like the original, but it contains no eggs, dairy products, or anchovies, and it's simple to make using basic pantry staples.

CROUTONS

1½ cups French or sourdough bread, cubed
(remove crusts, if desired)

CAESAR DRESSING

3 tablespoons nutritional yeast flakes

2 tablespoons tahini

2 tablespoons Dijon mustard

¼ to ½ teaspoon crushed garlic

3 tablespoons freshly squeezed lemon juice

1 tablespoon reduced-sodium soy sauce

⅓ cup water

SALAD MIX

6 to 8 cups torn romaine lettuce (about 1 medium head)

Ground black pepper

Green nori flakes (see page 26; optional)

Lemon wedges (optional)

For the croutons: Preheat the oven to 350 degrees F. Spread the bread cubes in a single layer on a baking sheet and bake for 15 minutes, or until dry and lightly toasted. (The croutons will not reach their full crispness until they have cooled.) Set aside.

For the dressing: Place the nutritional yeast flakes, tahini, mustard, and garlic in a medium bowl, and stir to make a paste. Gradually add the lemon juice, soy sauce, and water, stirring vigorously with a whisk until the dressing is completely smooth.

To assemble: Place the lettuce leaves in a large bowl. (The larger the bowl the better to facilitate tossing.) Pour the dressing over the lettuce, and toss until all the leaves are well coated. Add the croutons and toss again, making sure that the dressing and croutons are well distributed.

Scoop the salad equally onto two or four salad plates. Sprinkle each portion with ground black pepper and optional green nori flakes to taste. Garnish with lemon wedges, if desired. Serve immediately.

VARIATION

- **Sea-Sar Salad:** Replace the Caesar Dressing with ½ to 1 cup Sea-Sar Dressing (below).

Sea-Sar Dressing

Makes 2 cups | **PER 2 TBSP**

*T*his divine vegan version of the classic Caesar dressing is provided courtesy of It's Only Natural Restaurant. The olives give the dressing bite, while the nori replaces the anchovies. It has a very rich flavor, so a little goes a long way.

calories: 79
protein: 2 g
fat: 8 g
carbohydrate: 1 g
fiber: 0 g

1 package (about 12 ounces) firm silken tofu, crumbled

10 to 12 pitted green olives

3 tablespoons water

2 tablespoons green nori flakes (see page 26)

2 tablespoons freshly squeezed lemon juice

1 tablespoon nutritional yeast flakes

1 tablespoon olive brine (from the olives)

1 tablespoon Dijon mustard

1 teaspoon crushed garlic

1 teaspoon ground black pepper

½ teaspoon salt

½ cup extra-virgin olive oil

Combine the tofu, olives, water, nori flakes, lemon juice, nutritional yeast flakes, olive brine, mustard, garlic, pepper, and salt in a blender, and process until completely smooth. With the blender running, slowly drizzle in the olive oil through the cap opening in the lid. Serve at once or thoroughly chilled. Stored in a covered container in the refrigerator, Sea-Sar Dressing will keep for 5–7 days.

VARIATION

- **Reduced-Fat Sea-Sar Dressing:** If you need to curb your fat intake, you can still savor the piquant flavor of this magnificent recipe. Just increase the water to ⅓ cup and reduce the olive oil to 2 to 3 tablespoons.

Fatoosh

PER SERVING

Makes 4 servings

calories: 142

protein: 4 g

fat: 8 g

carbohydrate: 16 g

fiber: 3 g

This special Middle Eastern vegetable salad includes pieces of toasted pita triangles. What an ingenious way to use up slightly stale bread!

SALAD MIX

1 large pita bread

2 cups finely torn romaine lettuce, lightly packed

2 ripe tomatoes, chopped

1 small cucumber, peeled, seeded, and chopped

2 green onions, thinly sliced

2 tablespoons minced fresh parsley

½ to 1 teaspoon dried spearmint or oregano

LEMON-GARLIC DRESSING

2 tablespoons freshly squeezed lemon juice

2 tablespoons extra-virgin olive oil

½ teaspoon crushed garlic

Pinch of salt

Ground black pepper

For the salad: Slice the pita bread into 8 triangles. Separate each triangle into 2 thin triangles to make 16 pieces in all. Place on a baking sheet and toast briefly under the broiler, just until crisp and lightly brown. Watch closely so the bread does not burn (this will only take a few minutes). Break the triangles into large pieces and set aside. Combine the remaining salad ingredients in a large bowl.

For the dressing: Combine the lemon juice, olive oil, garlic, salt, and pepper to taste in a small bowl, and whisk until well combined. Pour over the salad and toss gently. Add the toasted pita pieces just before serving (so they stay crispy) and toss once more. Serve at once.

instead of

As easy as duck soup.

use

As easy as boiling water.

Best-of-the-House Dressing

Everyone appreciates a great signature recipe that is unique yet universally beloved. Here is yours! It's simple and quick to make and perks up everything from salads and steamed veggies to rice, pasta, and potatoes. This "house dressing" stores well, so you can use it throughout the week, not just on special occasions. It's rich, so a little goes a long way!

calories: 63
protein: 1 g
fat: 6 g
carbohydrate: 2 g
fiber: 0 g

½ cup tahini

¼ cup extra-virgin olive oil

1½ teaspoons dried spearmint

1¼ teaspoons salt

1 teaspoon garlic powder

1¼ cups water

½ cup freshly squeezed lemon juice

In a food processor, blender, or medium bowl, blend or whisk the tahini, olive oil, spearmint, salt, and garlic powder until creamy and smooth. Blend or whisk in the water in a slow, gradual stream. When smooth, blend or vigorously beat in the lemon juice until well combined. Stored in a covered container in the refrigerator, Best-of-the-House Dressing will keep for 10–14 days. Stir well before serving.

Thousand Island Dressing

Indulge your cravings with this thick and luxurious temptation.

calories: 52
protein: 1 g
fat: 3 g
carbohydrate: 5 g
fiber: 0 g

1 cup vegan mayonnaise

½ cup ketchup

6 tablespoons pickle relish, lightly drained

1 slightly heaping teaspoon onion powder

½ teaspoon salt

Combine all the ingredients in a small bowl, and stir until creamy and well combined. Stored in a covered container in the refrigerator, Thousand Island Dressing will keep for 5–7 days.

Deli Dressing *(Vegan Mayonnaise)*

calories: 58
protein: 2 g
fat: 5 g
carbohydrate: 1 g
fiber: 0 g

*T*his is the perfect low-fat alternative to traditional egg-laden mayonnaise. It's rich-tasting without being high in fat, and creamy without containing any eggs or dairy products.

1 package (about 12 ounces) firm silken tofu, crumbled

3 tablespoons freshly squeezed lemon juice

½ teaspoon salt

¼ teaspoon dry mustard

¼ cup extra-virgin olive oil

Place the tofu, lemon juice, salt, and dry mustard in a blender or food processor, and process until very smooth and creamy. With the appliance running, drizzle in the oil in a slow, steady stream through the cap opening in the lid. Stored in the refrigerator, Deli Dressing will keep for about 7 days.

Tahina

calories: 64
protein: 2 g
fat: 5 g
carbohydrate: 3 g
fiber: 1 g

*T*his luscious creamy sauce is served as a dip or dressing. Use it sparingly, as it is very rich.

1 cup tahini

2 to 4 tablespoons freshly squeezed lemon juice

⅔ cup water, more or less as needed

¼ teaspoon crushed garlic (optional)

Salt

Paprika (optional)

Minced fresh parsley (optional)

Place the tahini in a medium bowl. Very gradually beat in the lemon juice and just enough water to make a thick, light-colored cream. At first the sauce will thicken into grainy lumps, but keep beating. It will continue to thicken and become smooth and creamy. Season with garlic, if desired, and salt to taste. To use as a dip, garnish with paprika and parsley. To use as a dressing, thin with a little more water.

Sour Dressing *(Vegan Sour Cream)*

calories: 39
protein: 2 g
fat: 3 g
carbohydrate: 1 g
fiber: 0 g

*U*se this delicious creamy topping wherever you would use dairy sour cream. It's low in fat, cholesterol free, and contains no gums or gelatins, which are typically found in the "real" thing.

1 package (about 12 ounces) firm silken tofu, crumbled

2 tablespoons freshly squeezed lemon juice

1 tablespoon white wine vinegar or golden balsamic vinegar

½ teaspoon salt

⅛ teaspoon ground coriander

2 tablespoons organic canola oil

Place the tofu, lemon juice, vinegar, salt, and coriander in a blender or food processor, and process until smooth and creamy. With the appliance running, drizzle in the oil in a slow, steady stream through the cap opening in the lid. Stored in the refrigerator, Sour Dressing will keep for about 7 days.

Classic Ranch Dressing

calories: 58
protein: 2 g
fat: 5 g
carbohydrate: 1 g
fiber: 0 g

*E*njoy all the rich taste and allure of creamy ranch dressing, with a fraction of the calories and none of the objectionable dairy fat.

1 package (about 12 ounces) firm silken tofu, crumbled

¼ cup extra-virgin olive oil

2 tablespoons umeboshi vinegar

2 tablespoons freshly squeezed lemon juice

2 tablespoons water

1 teaspoon dried tarragon

½ teaspoon dried dill weed

½ teaspoon crushed garlic

¼ teaspoon dry mustard

Combine all the ingredients in a blender or food processor, and process until very smooth and creamy. Stored in a covered container in the refrigerator, Classic Ranch Dressing will keep for about 5 days.

Bleu Cheez Dip and Dressing

PER 2 TBSP		Makes 2 cups

calories: 31
protein: 2 g
fat: 2 g
carbohydrate: 2 g
fiber: 0 g

*T*his rich, flavorful dressing is delightful as a dip for raw or steamed vegetables or Barbecued Buffalo Zings (page 152). It also makes a great topping for crunchy salads, especially ones with beans. Try it with chopped fresh vegetables over split baked potatoes.

1 package (about 12 ounces) firm silken tofu, crumbled

½ cup plain soymilk

4 teaspoons umeboshi plum paste (see page 31)

1 to 2 tablespoons tahini

1 to 2 tablespoons extra-virgin olive oil (optional)

1 teaspoon nutritional yeast flakes

½ teaspoon crushed garlic

Pinch of ground white pepper (optional)

1 tablespoon chopped fresh parsley, or 1½ teaspoons dried

Combine the tofu, soymilk, umeboshi plum paste, tahini, oil, nutritional yeast flakes, garlic, and optional white pepper in a blender. Process until very smooth and creamy. Stir in the parsley and mix well. Chill several hours before serving to allow the flavors to blend. Stored in a covered container in the refrigerator, Bleu Cheez Dip and Dressing will keep for 3–5 days.

Christy

Christy was rescued from a man who was keeping his rabbits in miserable, unhealthful conditions outside his trailer home. When he was confronted about his treatment of the rabbits, he agreed to relinquish the animals in order to avoid getting in trouble. Now, instead of living in a barren wire cage, Christy spends her days in the rabbit refuge at Farm Sanctuary. With all of the pellets, fresh grass, and veggies she could ask for, it's no wonder she frolics and plays the way she does! When she's not engaged in a game of chase with her bunny friends, Christy can be found sunning herself outside in the cool grass.

Granola Nut Crust

*T*ry this spectacular crust for any sweet pie, including cream pies, fruit pies, or cheezcakes.

1 cup rolled oats

½ cup flour (any kind)

½ cup finely ground walnuts or pecans

1 teaspoon ground cinnamon

½ teaspoon salt

¼ cup vegetable oil

¼ cup maple syrup

1 teaspoon vanilla extract

Preheat the oven to 350 degrees F. Combine the oats, flour, ground nuts, cinnamon, and salt in a large bowl, and mix well. In a small bowl or measuring cup, combine the oil, maple syrup, and vanilla extract. Pour into the oat mixture and stir well until evenly blended. Press into the bottom and sides of a 9- or 10-inch pie plate or the bottom of an 8- to 10-inch springform pan.

For pies that require further baking, bake for about 8 minutes, or just until set. For refrigerator pies (i.e., pies that do not require baking), fully bake for 10–12 minutes, or until lightly browned. Cool completely before filling.

PER SERVING   *calories: 183,* protein: 4 g, fat: 11 g, carbohydrate: 18 g, fiber: 2 g

Rich Chocolate Pudding or Pie Filling

PER SERVING

calories: 231
protein: 7 g
fat: 13 g
carbohydrate: 23 g
fiber: 1 g

Makes 10 servings

*T*his dessert is so decadently rich that no one will guess it's made with tofu. Serve it on special occasions when you really want to impress your guests. For an attractive presentation, you can serve the pudding in small parfait glasses. Try a graham cracker crust or chocolate cookie crust, if you prefer to make a pie.

2 packages (about 24 ounces) extra-firm silken tofu, crumbled

1 teaspoon vanilla extract

1 package (12 ounces) vegan semisweet chocolate chips

1 ripe banana (optional)

1 (9-inch) pie crust (regular, graham cracker, or chocolate cookie), fully baked (optional)

¼ cup sliced or slivered almonds, or ¼ to ½ cup fresh red raspberries

Combine the tofu and vanilla extract in a blender or food processor, and process until very smooth and creamy. Melt the chocolate chips over water in a double boiler, or in a heavy saucepan over very low heat, or in a microwave oven. Pour the melted chocolate into the tofu in the food processor, and process until thoroughly combined, stopping to scrape down the sides of the blender jar or work bowl as necessary.

Have ready ten small pudding cups or parfait glasses, or 1 fully-baked pie crust. Slice the optional banana and layer it with the pudding in each pudding cup. For pie, arrange the banana slices in a layer over the bottom of the pie crust and top with the pudding. Refrigerate 1–3 hours before serving. Garnish with the sliced almonds or raspberries.

instead of

He/she is a bad egg.

use

He/she is a rotten apple.

Peach Kuchen

This heirloom confection consists of a rich shortbread crust layered with juicy peach halves and a sweet golden cream topping. It's the ideal dessert when you want to dazzle your guests—it's extraordinary!

SHORTBREAD CRUST

1 cup whole wheat pastry flour

1 cup unbleached white flour or additional whole wheat pastry flour

¼ cup granulated sugar

½ teaspoon salt

¼ teaspoon baking powder

½ cup vegetable oil

PEACH FILLING

9 large peach halves (peeled fresh peaches or canned peach halves, drained)

2 tablespoons granulated sugar

1 teaspoon ground cinnamon

GOLDEN CREAM TOPPING

1 cup Sour Dressing (page 209) or vegan sour cream

2 tablespoons maple syrup

Tiny pinch of ground turmeric

Preheat the oven to 350 degrees F.

For the crust: Place the flours, sugar, salt, and baking powder in a large bowl, and stir with a dry whisk until well combined. Cut in the oil using a pastry blender or fork until evenly distributed and the mixture is crumbly. Pat an even layer of this mixture over the bottom and halfway up the sides of an 8-inch square glass baking pan.

For the filling: Arrange the peach halves in three rows, cut-side down, over the pastry. Combine the sugar and cinnamon and sprinkle evenly over the peaches. Place on the center rack of the oven and bake for 15 minutes.

Meanwhile, place the Sour Dressing, maple syrup, and turmeric in a small bowl, and stir until well combined. After the kuchen has baked for 15 minutes, remove it from the oven and spoon the Sour Dressing mixture evenly over the top of the peaches. Return to the oven to continue baking for 30 minutes longer. Serve warm or thoroughly chilled.

Creamy Pumpkin Pie

PER SERVING

calories: 274
protein: 8 g
fat: 7 g
carbohydrate: 47 g
fiber: 5 g

Makes 8 servings

Enjoy your favorite holidays with egg-free, dairy-free pumpkin pie. The spirit of your celebration will be enhanced by your compassion. Vegan whipped topping artistically piped around the edge of the pie or spooned atop each serving would make a lovely presentation.

1 Perfect Pie Crust (page 216) or other 9-inch pie crust, unbaked

1 package (about 12 ounces) firm silken tofu

1 can (15 ounces) unsweetened pumpkin (about 1¾ cups)

¾ cup dark brown sugar

⅓ cup cornstarch

1 teaspoon ground cinnamon

½ teaspoon salt

¼ to ½ teaspoon ground ginger

¼ to ½ teaspoon ground nutmeg

⅛ to ¼ teaspoon ground cloves

Preheat the oven to 400 degrees F. Prebake the pie crust for 10–12 minutes. Transfer to a cooling rack, and let cool for 10 minutes. Lower the oven temperature to 350 degrees F.

While the crust is cooling, crumble the tofu into a food processor or blender. Add the remaining ingredients, and process until completely smooth and very creamy. (Use the larger amount of spices for a more strongly spiced filling.) Pour into the cooled crust. Smooth out the top. Bake on the center rack of the oven for 45 minutes.

Remove from the oven, and let cool on a wire rack for at least 1 hour before cutting. Tightly covered and stored in the refrigerator, Creamy Pumpkin Pie will keep for about 3 days.

instead of
Walking on eggshells.

use
Walking on broken glass.

Lemon Cloud Pie

Lemon lovers, get ready to pucker up for this tart and tangy treat. This is the vegan response to lemon meringue pie.

calories: 312
protein: 7 g
fat: 9 g
carbohydrate: 52 g
fiber: 4 g

1 Perfect Pie Crust (page 216) or other 9-inch pie crust, unbaked

2 cups water

1 cup granulated sugar

½ package (about 6 ounces) firm silken tofu, crumbled

6 tablespoons cornstarch

¼ teaspoon salt

½ cup freshly squeezed lemon juice

1 tablespoon nonhydrogenated vegan margarine

2 teaspoons finely grated lemon zest (optional)

¾ cup vegan whipped topping

Preheat the oven to 400 degrees F. Fully bake the pie crust for 20 minutes. Transfer to a cooling rack, and let cool for 10 minutes.

Place the water, sugar, tofu, cornstarch, and salt in a blender, and process until completely smooth. Pour into a medium saucepan. Place over medium-high heat and bring to a boil, stirring constantly with a whisk. After the mixture thickens, turn the heat down to low and continue to cook, stirring constantly with the whisk, for 1 minute longer. Remove the saucepan from the heat, and beat in the lemon juice, margarine, and optional lemon zest. Pour the hot filling into the cooled pie crust.

Cover the top of the pie with a sheet of waxed paper, pressing it against the filling very gently to prevent a skin from forming. The edges of the waxed paper will fan out. Chill the pie in the refrigerator for 8–24 hours.

Just before serving, carefully remove the waxed paper. Spread the top of the chilled pie evenly with the whipped topping or pipe it in a decorative pattern. Alternatively, spoon a dollop of the topping on each slice as it is served.

VARIATION

- **Lime Cloud Pie:** Replace the lemon juice with an equal amount of freshly squeezed lime juice or bottled key lime juice, and use lime zest instead of lemon zest.

Perfect Pie Crust

PER SERVING

calories: 185
protein: 8 g
fat: 7 g
carbohydrate: 22 g
fiber: 4 g

*P*reparing flaky, whole grain pastry is not particularly difficult—the secret is in the technique. Work quickly, and handle the dough as little as possible, to guarantee the flakiest results. Use this simple, delicious crust for any sweet or savory pie.

1½ cups whole wheat pastry flour

¼ teaspoon salt

¼ cup vegetable oil

3 to 4 tablespoons cold soymilk, rice milk, or water, more or less as needed

Have ready one 9-inch pie plate. Place the flour and salt in a large bowl, and stir with a fork or dry whisk. Cut in the oil with a pastry blender or fork until the mixture resembles coarse crumbs. Sprinkle the soymilk over the flour mixture, tossing gently with a fork to lightly moisten the dry ingredients. The flour should be evenly moistened, not damp or soggy. With your hands, quickly form the dough into a ball, handling it as little as possible.

Place the dough between two sheets of waxed paper, and roll it out into a circle about one inch larger than your pie plate. Remove the top sheet of waxed paper. Carefully flip the crust over, and lay it in the pie plate with the dough against the plate. Working very carefully and gently, remove the second sheet of waxed paper. Ease the crust into the pie plate without stretching or tearing it. Trim the edges, or turn them under to within ¼ inch of the rim and flute them.

Thoroughly prick the sides and bottom of the crust with the tines of a fork to keep air bubbles from forming under the surface.

To prebake the crust (for pies that will be filled and then baked), place it in a preheated 400 degree F oven for 12–15 minutes, or until it turns a deep golden brown. Remove the crust from the oven and allow it to cool on a wire rack before filling it.

To fully bake the crust (for pies that will be filled and chilled, or baked very briefly), place it in a preheated 400 degree F oven for about 20 minutes, or until it turns a rich brown color and is crisp. Remove the crust from the oven, and allow it to cool on a wire rack before filling it.

NOTE

- Lightly moistening your countertop with water will help to keep the waxed paper from sliding when you are rolling out the crust.

Ultra-Fudgey Fudge Brownies

Brownies are not health food, but they can certainly boost the spirits and feed the soul. Here is the ultimate fudge brownie experience, minus the guilt. Indulge!

calories: 199
protein: 4 g
fat: 7 g
carbohydrate: 32 g
fiber: 3 g

1¼ cups whole wheat pastry flour or unbleached white flour

1 cup granulated sugar

¼ teaspoon baking powder

¼ teaspoon salt

½ package (about 6 ounces) firm silken tofu

½ cup unsweetened cocoa powder

½ cup water

½ cup maple syrup

2 tablespoons vegetable oil

1 tablespoon vanilla extract

½ to 1 cup chopped walnuts

Preheat the oven to 350 degrees F. Mist an 8-inch square glass baking pan with nonstick cooking spray.

Place the flour, sugar, baking powder, and salt in a medium bowl, and stir with a dry whisk until well combined.

Crumble the tofu into a blender or food processor. Add the cocoa powder, water, maple syrup, oil, and vanilla extract, and process until completely smooth. Pour into the flour mixture and stir until well combined. Fold in the walnuts.

Pour the batter evenly into the prepared baking pan. Bake on the center rack of the oven for 40 minutes, or until a toothpick inserted in the center comes out clean. Cool the brownies in the pan on a wire rack. Cut and serve.

instead of

It's raining cats and dogs.

use

It's raining rice and beans.

Fruit Butter Bars

Makes 12 to 16 bars

calories: 215
protein: 4 g
fat: 5 g
carbohydrate: 38 g
fiber: 3 g

This old-fashioned favorite is easy to make. It's a lunchbox staple, a wholesome afternoon snack, or a welcome dessert. Because these bars are made with a small amount of vegetable oil rather than saturated dairy fats, they are a bit crumbly; so serve them on a plate, and use a fork.

1½ cups whole wheat pastry flour or unbleached white flour

1½ cups quick-cooking rolled oats (not instant)

½ cup granulated sugar

½ teaspoon baking soda

¼ teaspoon salt

½ cup maple syrup

¼ cup vegetable oil

1½ cups thick apple butter or prune butter

Preheat the oven to 350 degrees F. Mist an 8-inch square glass baking pan with nonstick cooking spray, and set aside.

To make the crust, place the flour, oats, sugar, baking soda, and salt in a large bowl, and stir with a dry whisk until well combined. In a small bowl, stir together the maple syrup and oil. Pour into the flour-oat mixture, and mix thoroughly until everything appears evenly moistened. The mixture will be crumbly.

Press half the crust mixture evenly into the prepared baking pan, packing it down very firmly with your hands. Carefully spread the fruit butter evenly over this base. Sprinkle or crumble the rest of the crust mixture evenly over the fruit butter, and pat it down lightly.

Bake for 20–25 minutes, or until lightly browned. Cool on a wire rack. Slice into bars or squares.

instead of

You can't make a silk purse out of a sow's ear.

use

You can't make granola out of gravel.

Lemon Date Squares

*T*he exotic flavors of lemon, coconut, and dates mingle harmoniously in this tempting confection.

1 cup whole wheat pastry flour

1 cup quick-cooking rolled oats (not instant)

¼ cup unsweetened shredded dried coconut

2 tablespoons granulated sugar

¼ teaspoon salt

½ cup maple syrup

¼ cup vegetable oil

3 tablespoons freshly squeezed lemon juice

1 tablespoon grated lemon zest

1 teaspoon vanilla extract

½ cup chopped soft dates

calories: 152

protein: 2 g

fat: 6 g

carbohydrate: 22 g

fiber: 3 g

Preheat the oven to 350 degrees F. Mist an 8-inch square glass baking pan with nonstick cooking spray, and set aside.

Combine the flour, oats, coconut, sugar, and salt in a large bowl, and stir with a dry whisk. Combine the maple syrup, oil, lemon juice, lemon zest, and vanilla extract in a separate small bowl, and stir until well blended. Pour into the flour-oat mixture, and mix well. Add the dates and mix again.

Pack the dough into the prepared baking dish, patting it out evenly using water-moistened fingertips. Bake for 20–25 minutes, or until lightly browned. Cool on a wire rack. Slice into squares or bars while warm. Cool completely before serving.

instead of

It's no use beating a dead horse.

use

It's no use watering a dead rose.

The Ultimate Chocolate Chip Cookies

Makes about 32 small (2-inch) cookies

One bite and chocolate lovers will know they have met their match! These are the best chocolate chip cookies I've ever had. I think you will agree.

1½ cups quick-cooking rolled oats (not instant)

1 cup whole wheat pastry flour

1 cup coarsely chopped walnuts, lightly toasted (see note)

1 cup vegan semisweet chocolate chips

½ teaspoon salt

¼ teaspoon baking soda

½ cup vegetable oil

½ cup maple syrup

2 tablespoons water

2 teaspoons vanilla extract

Preheat the oven to 350 degrees F. Line two baking sheets with parchment paper (for the easiest cleanup), or mist them with nonstick cooking spray.

Place the oats, flour, walnuts, chocolate chips, salt, and baking soda in a large bowl. Stir with a dry whisk until well combined. Place the oil, maple syrup, water, and vanilla extract in a small bowl, and beat vigorously with a whisk until well combined. Stir into the flour mixture, mixing just until everything is evenly moistened. Let rest for 5 minutes so the oats can absorb some of the moisture.

Drop slightly rounded tablespoons of dough onto the prepared baking sheets, about 1 inch apart. The dough will be crumbly. Flatten with your hand to one-third inch thick. Smooth the edges to make each cookie uniformly round, gently pressing the dough so the cookies hold together.

Bake one sheet at a time on the center rack of the oven for 18 minutes, or until the cookies are lightly browned. Transfer the cookies to a cooling rack, and let cool completely. Store in an airtight container in the refrigerator. (The cookies will taste best after they have been chilled.)

NOTE

■ To toast the walnuts, preheat the oven to 350 degrees F. Spread the nuts in a single layer on a baking sheet. Bake on the center rack of the oven for 8–10 minutes, or until fragrant and lightly browned.

Oatmeal Chocolate Chip Cookies

Makes 36 cookies	PER COOKIE

*T*hese cookies are decadently rich-tasting and satisfying.

1 cup whole wheat pastry flour

1 cup quick-cooking rolled oats (not instant)

1 cup granulated sugar

½ teaspoon baking powder

¼ teaspoon salt

⅓ cup water

¼ cup vegetable oil

1½ teaspoons vanilla extract

½ cup vegan semisweet chocolate chips

⅓ cup coarsely chopped walnuts

calories: 70

protein: 1 g

fat: 3 g

carbohydrate: 10 g

fiber: 1 g

Preheat the oven to 350 degrees F. Coat one or two baking sheets with non-stick cooking spray, or line them with parchment paper (for the easiest cleanup), and set aside.

Place the flour, oats, sugar, baking powder, and salt in a medium bowl, and stir with a dry whisk.

Place the water, oil, and vanilla extract in a separate small bowl, and stir until well blended. Pour into the flour-oat mixture, and mix well to make a stiff dough. Stir in the chocolate chips and walnuts, and mix until they are evenly distributed.

Drop the dough by small rounded spoonfuls onto the prepared baking sheet(s), about 12–15 per sheet, spacing the cookies at least 2 inches apart. Do not flatten the cookies, as they will spread out when they bake. Bake for 15–18 minutes, or until lightly browned. Let the cookies rest on the baking sheet for 5 full minutes. Then carefully loosen them and transfer them to a cooling rack using a metal spatula. Cool completely before storing.

instead of

On a wild goose chase.

use

Out chasing rainbows.

Lemon Apricot Thumbprint Cookies

Makes 24 cookies

calories: 93
protein: 2 g
fat: 3 g
carbohydrate: 15 g
fiber: 2 g

*T*hese elegant cookies make a lovely gift, tea-time snack, or company dessert.

1½ cups whole wheat pastry flour

1¼ cups oat flour (see note on page 101)

½ teaspoon baking powder

¼ teaspoon salt

½ cup maple syrup

¼ cup freshly squeezed lemon juice

¼ cup vegetable oil

8 teaspoons fruit-sweetened apricot jam

Preheat the oven to 350 degrees F. Lightly oil a large baking sheet, mist it with nonstick cooking spray, or line it with parchment paper (for the easiest cleanup), and set aside.

Combine the whole wheat flour, oat flour, baking powder, and salt in a medium bowl and stir with a dry whisk. Combine the maple syrup, lemon juice, and oil in a separate bowl, and mix well. Pour into the flour mixture, and stir until thoroughly combined. The dough should be stiff. If it is too soft to roll into balls, add a little more of either flour.

Using your hands, form the dough into 24 walnut-size balls, and place on the prepared baking sheet about 1 inch apart. Make an indentation in the center of each ball with your thumb, pressing down lightly. Bake for 14–18 minutes, or until very lightly browned on the bottom.

Transfer the cookies to a cooling rack and fill the cavities with a rounded ¼ teaspoon of apricot jam while the cookies are still hot. Cool completely before storing.

NOTES

- If your thumb sticks to the dough when you are making the impressions, moisten it with a little water.
- Raspberry, blackberry, or strawberry jam may be substituted for the apricot jam, if you prefer.

instead of

What a crab!

use

What a sour cherry!

Crispy Rice Chews

Everyone enjoys this easy, no-bake confection—including the cook!

calories: 102
protein: 2 g
fat: 4 g
carbohydrate: 16 g
fiber: 1 g

½ cup rice syrup

¼ cup crunchy almond butter or peanut butter

¼ cup tahini

¼ teaspoon ground cinnamon

1 teaspoon vanilla extract

Tiny pinch of salt (optional; omit if nut butter or cereal contains salt)

2 cups crisped rice cereal

⅓ cup seedless raisins, chopped nuts, or vegan semisweet chocolate chips

Mist an 8-inch square glass baking pan with nonstick cooking spray, and set aside.

Place the rice syrup, almond butter, tahini, and cinnamon in a medium saucepan, and place over low heat until the mixture is softened. Remove from the heat and stir in the vanilla extract and salt, if using. Mix well.

Fold in the cereal and raisins, and mix gently until everything is evenly distributed. The mixture will be extremely stiff.

Press the mixture evenly into the prepared pan using lightly water-moistened fingertips or a piece of waxed paper. Cut into 16 squares. Cover the pan with plastic wrap, and chill the squares in the refrigerator for 1–2 hours before serving.

Marino

Marino was rescued from a man who hatched 200 turkey eggs at home in hopes of making a quick profit on the Internet. Badly neglected at the hands of this would-be turkey breeder, Marino was lucky to find his way to Farm Sanctuary when he did. At the sanctuary he has all the nourishing food, quality health care, and affection he'll ever need—and he is making a big difference in the world. As an ambassador for his species, he is teaching sanctuary visitors just how intelligent and companionable turkeys really are. He hopes his human guests leave knowing that turkeys have feelings too.

Grandmother's Spice Cake

Makes 8 to 9 servings

PER SERVING

calories: 225
protein: 5 g
fat: 4 g
carbohydrate: 43 g
fiber: 5 g

*D*ark, dense, and delicately spiced. Try a slice topped with fresh fruit and Very Vanilla Maple Cream Sauce (page 232).

WET INGREDIENTS

1¼ cups unsweetened applesauce

½ cup maple syrup

2 tablespoons vegetable oil

DRY INGREDIENTS

1¾ cups whole wheat pastry flour

2 tablespoons unsweetened cocoa powder, sifted

1 tablespoon baking powder

1 teaspoon baking soda

1 teaspoon ground cinnamon

¼ teaspoon ground nutmeg

⅛ teaspoon ground cloves

⅛ teaspoon ground ginger

½ cup seedless raisins

½ cup coarsely chopped or broken walnuts (optional)

Preheat the oven to 350 degrees F. Lightly oil an 8-inch square glass baking pan, or mist it with nonstick cooking spray, and set aside.

Place the wet ingredients in a large bowl, and stir until well blended. Place the dry ingredients, except the raisins and walnuts, in a separate large bowl, and stir with a dry whisk. Gradually stir the dry ingredients into the wet ingredients, sprinkling in about one-third at a time and mixing well after each addition. The batter will be thick. Stir in the raisins and optional walnuts.

Spoon the batter into the prepared baking pan. Bake on the center rack of the oven for 35–40 minutes, or until a toothpick inserted in the center comes out clean.

Cool in the pan on a wire rack. Let the cake cool completely before cutting it. Covered tightly and stored in the refrigerator, leftover Grandmother's Spice Cake will keep for 3–5 days.

Aunt Bunny's Carrot Cake

arrot cake aficionados will hop for joy over this recipe!

calories: 328
protein: 6 g
fat: 9 g
carbohydrate: 58 g
fiber: 5 g

WET INGREDIENTS

1 cup granulated sugar

1 can (8 ounces) unsweetened crushed pineapple in juice

2 tablespoons vegetable oil

1½ cups grated carrots, lightly packed

½ cup seedless raisins

½ cup coarsely chopped or broken walnuts

DRY INGREDIENTS

2 cups whole wheat pastry flour

1 tablespoon baking powder

1 teaspoon baking soda

1 teaspoon ground cinnamon

½ teaspoon salt

¼ teaspoon ground allspice

Preheat the oven to 350 degrees F. Lightly oil an 8-inch square glass baking pan, or mist it with nonstick cooking spray, and set aside.

Place the sugar, pineapple and its juice, and the oil in a large bowl, and stir until well combined. Add the carrots, raisins, and walnuts, and mix well.

Place the dry ingredients in a separate large bowl, and stir with a dry whisk. Gradually stir the dry ingredients into the wet ingredients, sprinkling in about one-third at a time and mixing well after each addition. The batter will be thick.

Spoon the batter into the prepared baking pan. Bake on the center rack of the oven for 35–40 minutes, or until a toothpick inserted in the center comes out clean.

Cool in the pan on a wire rack. Let the cake cool completely before cutting it. Covered tightly and stored in the refrigerator, leftover Aunt Bunny's Carrot Cake will keep for 3–5 days.

Golden White Cake

PER SERVING

calories: 297
protein: 4 g
fat: 8 g
carbohydrate: 53 g
fiber: 1 g

Makes 10 to 12 servings (two 9" layer cakes, or one 9" x 13" sheet cake)

Light, fluffy, and moist, this basic but divine cake is ideal for every special occasion. It is surprisingly low in fat, rich in flavor, and not too sweet. Because it is made with unbleached flour, the color is more golden than white. Unbleached sugar will also contribute to a golden hue and a slight molasses flavor. (The only way to obtain a snowy-white cake is to use bleached flour and sugar.) Spread your favorite filling between the layers and frost the top and sides, or simply top the sheet cake with your favorite frosting or my favorite frosting alternative, a thin coating of fruit-sweetened jam. If you prefer to top each serving individually, try a drizzle of chocolate syrup, a dollop of applesauce or apple butter, or a spoonful of fruit pie filling.

1½ cups granulated sugar

6 tablespoons vegetable oil or nonhydrogenated vegan margarine

¼ cup unsweetened applesauce

1½ tablespoons grated lemon zest (optional)

3 cups unbleached white flour

1½ teaspoons baking powder

1 teaspoon baking soda

¼ teaspoon salt

1 cup water or vanilla soymilk or rice milk

2 tablespoons freshly squeezed lemon juice

1½ teaspoons vanilla extract

Preheat the oven to 350 degrees F. Lightly oil two 9-inch round cake pans or one 9 x 13-inch baking pan, or mist with nonstick cooking spray, and set aside.

Place the sugar, oil, and applesauce in a large bowl, and blend using an electric mixer on medium speed until light and fluffy. Add the optional lemon zest, and mix briefly.

Whisk together the flour, baking powder, baking soda, and salt in a medium bowl. Combine the water, lemon juice, and vanilla extract in a small bowl. On low speed, beat the dry ingredients into the sugar mixture, alternating with the lemon water, beginning and ending with the dry ingredients. Mix until just combined, scraping down the sides of the bowl with a rubber spatula as necessary. The batter will be thick. Pour or spoon into the prepared pan(s) and smooth the top(s).

Bake for 20–25 minutes for the layers, or 30–35 minutes for the sheet cake, or until the top is golden brown and a toothpick inserted into the cen-

Storing Frosted Cakes

Leftover frosted cakes should be covered and stored in the refrigerator. The best storage container for layer cakes is called a cake saver, which is designed specifically for this purpose. If you do not own a cake saver, you can improvise one simply by inverting a large mixing bowl over the cake plate.

ter(s) comes out clean. Cool in the pan(s) on a wire rack for 5 minutes. Then remove the layers from the pans and cool completely on a wire rack. The sheet cake can be cooled completely in the pan. Covered tightly and stored at room temperature or in the refrigerator, leftover Golden White Cake will keep for 3–5 days.

VARIATION

- **Chocolate Chip Cake:** Stir 1 cup vegan semisweet mini or regular chocolate chips into the batter before pouring or spooning it into the pan(s).

The World's Best (and Easiest) Chocolate Pudding

Makes 1½ cups | **PER ½ CUP**

Great homemade chocolate pudding in under five minutes? You'll be an instant believer with this remarkable recipe.

calories: 201
protein: 9 g
fat: 4 g
carbohydrate: 35 g
fiber: 4 g

1 package (about 12 ounces) firm silken tofu, crumbled

⅓ to ½ cup granulated sugar

⅓ cup unsweetened cocoa powder

2 teaspoons vanilla extract

Tiny pinch of salt (optional)

Combine all the ingredients in a food processor or blender, and process until very smooth, creamy, and thick. Start with the smaller amount of sugar and add more to taste. Chill thoroughly before serving. Stored in a covered container in the refrigerator, The World's Best (and Easiest) Chocolate Pudding will keep for about 5 days.

Fantastic Chocolate Cake

PER SERVING

Makes 8 to 9 servings

calories: 239
protein: 3 g
fat: 9 g
carbohydrate: 39 g
fiber: 2 g

Serve this incredible cake on its own, or top it with fresh berries, orange marmalade, cherry pie filling, sifted confectioners' sugar, or chocolate frosting. It's the most delicious chocolate cake around, and best of all, it's easy to make and calls for inexpensive ingredients that you are likely to always have on hand.

1½ cups unbleached white flour

1 cup granulated sugar

⅓ cup unsweetened cocoa powder, sifted

1 teaspoon baking soda

1 cup water

⅓ cup vegetable oil

1 tablespoon vanilla extract

½ cup chopped walnuts or vegan semisweet mini chocolate chips (optional)

2 tablespoons apple cider vinegar

Preheat the oven to 375 degrees F. Lightly oil an 8-inch square glass baking pan, or mist it with nonstick cooking spray, and set aside.

Place the flour, sugar, cocoa powder, and baking soda in a large bowl, and stir with a dry whisk until evenly combined. In a separate small bowl, combine the water, oil, and vanilla extract. Pour into the flour mixture and beat with the whisk until well blended. Stir in the walnuts or chocolate chips, if using. Add the vinegar, and quickly whisk until it is evenly distributed. Pour immediately into the prepared baking pan, and immediately put the cake into the oven (this is essential). Bake for about 35 minutes, or until a toothpick inserted in the center of the cake tests clean.

Cool in the pan on a wire rack. Let the cake cool completely before cutting it. Covered tightly and stored at room temperature, leftover Fantastic Chocolate Cake will keep for 3–5 days.

Banana Cake

This popular snack cake is delicious plain or spread with your favorite chocolate frosting.

calories: 332

protein: 8 g

fat: 13 g

carbohydrate: 48 g

fiber: 6 g

WET INGREDIENTS

1½ cups mashed ripe bananas (about 3 to 4 medium)

½ cup maple syrup

2 tablespoons vegetable oil

2 teaspoons vanilla extract

DRY INGREDIENTS

2¼ cups whole wheat pastry flour

1 tablespoon baking powder

1 teaspoon baking soda

1 cup coarsely chopped or broken walnuts

Preheat the oven to 350 degrees F. Lightly oil an 8-inch square glass baking pan, or mist it with nonstick cooking spray, and set aside.

Place the wet ingredients in a large bowl, and stir until well blended. Place the dry ingredients in a separate large bowl, and stir with a dry whisk. Gradually stir the dry ingredients, except the walnuts, into the wet ingredients, sprinkling in about one-third at a time and mixing well after each addition. The batter will be thick. Stir in the walnuts.

Spoon the batter into the prepared baking pan. Bake on the center rack of the oven for 30–35 minutes, or until a toothpick inserted in the center comes out clean.

Cool in the pan on a wire rack. Let the cake cool completely before cutting it. Covered tightly and stored in the refrigerator, leftover Banana Cake will keep for 3–5 days.

instead of

Packed in like sardines.

use

Packed in like pickles.

Poppy Seed Cake

calories: 248
protein: 7 g
fat: 8 g
carbohydrate: 37 g
fiber: 5 g

*P*oppy seeds lend a unique texture to this delicious cake.

WET INGREDIENTS

1 cup plain or vanilla soymilk or rice milk

½ cup poppy seeds

½ cup maple syrup

2 tablespoons vegetable oil

1 tablespoon vanilla extract

DRY INGREDIENTS

2 cups whole wheat pastry flour

1 tablespoon baking powder

1 teaspoon baking soda

Preheat the oven to 350 degrees F. Mist an 8-inch square glass baking pan with nonstick cooking spray, and set aside.

If time permits, soak the poppy seeds in the soymilk in a large bowl for 1 hour at room temperature. Add the maple syrup, oil, and vanilla extract, and stir until well blended. If time does not permit soaking, simply place all the wet ingredients in a large bowl, and stir until well blended.

Place the dry ingredients in a separate large bowl, and stir with a dry whisk. Gradually stir the dry ingredients into the wet ingredients, sprinkling in about one-third at a time, and mixing well after each addition.

Pour the batter into the prepared baking pan. Bake on the center rack of the oven for 35–40 minutes, or until a toothpick inserted in the center tests clean.

Cool in the pan on a wire rack. Let the cake cool completely before cutting it. Covered tightly and stored in the refrigerator, leftover Poppy Seed Cake will keep for 3–5 days.

instead of

Sweating like a pig.

use

Sweating like a politician.

Lemon Teasecake *(Vegan Cheesecake)*

Makes 8 to 10 servings

PER SERVING

This scrumptious signature dessert was developed by acclaimed vegan chef and restaurateur Francis Janes.

1 Granola Nut Crust (page 211), fully baked (use an 8-inch springform pan)

½ cup uncooked millet

2 cups water

½ cup raw cashews

⅓ cup freshly squeezed lemon juice

⅓ cup maple syrup

2 teaspoons vanilla extract

1 teaspoon lemon extract

TOPPINGS (OPTIONAL; CHOOSE ONE)

1 cup (8 ounces) cherry preserves

2 kiwifruit, peeled and sliced into thin rounds

with CHERRY TOPPING

calories: 374
protein: 6 g
fat: 15 g
carbohydrate: 55 g
fiber: 4 g

with KIWI TOPPING

calories: 312
protein: 7 g
fat: 15 g
carbohydrate: 40 g
fiber: 3 g

Fully bake the pie crust as directed and cool completely. Set aside.

Combine the millet and water in a medium saucepan with a tight-fitting lid and bring to a boil. Cover and simmer over low heat for 50 minutes, or until the water is absorbed and the millet is soft.

While the millet is cooking, place the cashews, lemon juice, maple syrup, vanilla extract, and lemon extract in a blender. Process several minutes until perfectly smooth. If necessary, scrape down the sides of the blender jar with a spatula and process for another minute or two. Add the warm cooked millet to the mixture in the blender, and process for 3 minutes until creamy. Pour into the cooled crust.

Cool the pie for 30 minutes at room temperature. Then chill it in the refrigerator for at least 4 hours before serving. Place plastic wrap over the surface to prevent excess cracking. Decorate with the optional topping of your choice before serving. Covered and stored in the refrigerator, Lemon Teasecake will keep for about 3 days.

VARIATION

- **Lime Teasecake:** Replace the lemon juice and lemon extract with an equal amount of freshly squeezed lime juice or key lime juice and lime extract.

Tofu Whipped Topping

PER ¼ CUP   *Makes about 1½ cups*

calories: 97
protein: 4 g
fat: 5 g
carbohydrate: 10 g
fiber: 1 g

*T*his incredibly easy whipped topping has a mesmerizing flavor. Let it be the crowning touch to all your vegan confections.

1 package (about 12 ounces) firm silken tofu, crumbled

¼ cup maple syrup

4 teaspoons hazelnut oil, walnut oil, or organic canola oil

2 teaspoons vanilla extract

⅛ teaspoon ground nutmeg

Combine all the ingredients in a blender or food processor, and process several minutes until completely smooth and very creamy. Stored in a covered container in the refrigerator, Tofu Whipped Topping will keep for about 5 days.

Very Vanilla Maple Cream Sauce

PER 2 TBSP   *Makes about 1½ cups*

calories: 60
protein: 1 g
fat: 3 g
carbohydrate: 8 g
fiber: 0 g

*T*his sweet dessert sauce may be served warm or chilled. It makes a delicious topping when drizzled over cakes, pies, fruits, berries, and frozen desserts. You can even enjoy a spoonful on your morning oatmeal! Because it contains no soy products, it is an excellent alternative to tofu-based whipped toppings.

1 cup water

½ cup raw cashews

¼ cup maple syrup

2 tablespoons granulated sugar

2 teaspoons vanilla extract

½ teaspoon freshly squeezed lemon juice

Combine the water, cashews, maple syrup, and sugar in a blender, and process several minutes until completely smooth. Pour into a small saucepan and place over medium heat. Cook, stirring almost constantly, for 18–20 minutes, or until the sauce is very thick, smooth, and creamy. Remove from the heat and vigorously stir in the vanilla extract and lemon juice. Serve warm or thoroughly chilled. Stored in a covered container in the refrigerator, Very Vanilla Maple Cream Sauce will keep for 5–7 days.

Heavenly Coconut Frosting

Makes about ¾ cup (enough for one 8" square cake, one 9" round cake, or 6 cupcakes)

PER ⅙ RECIPE

calories: 164
protein: 2 g
fat: 13 g
carbohydrate: 12 g
fiber: 3 g

Here is a luxurious frosting for any vegan baked goods that need a crowning touch.

½ cup plus 2 tablespoons plain or vanilla soymilk

½ cup unsweetened finely shredded dried coconut

¼ cup frozen apple juice concentrate

4 teaspoons cornstarch

Pinch of salt

Place ½ cup of the soymilk along with the coconut and juice concentrate in a small saucepan. Bring to a simmer over medium-high heat. Turn the heat down to low, cover, and simmer for 10 minutes, stirring occasionally.

Place the cornstarch in a small glass measuring cup. Add the remaining 2 tablespoons soymilk and stir until the cornstarch is dissolved. Stir into the simmering coconut along with the salt. Simmer uncovered, stirring constantly, for 2–5 minutes, or until the mixture is thickened. Remove from the heat and let cool slightly before using.

NOTE

- If the coconut you are using is not very fine, transfer the frosting to a food processor and pulse it briefly into a coarse paste.

Jay Jay

Jay Jay was fortunate enough to begin his life at Farm Sanctuary. His mother was one of nine sheep surrendered by a Pennsylvania farmer who had decided he could no longer slaughter his sheep. Jay Jay is as happy as can be living at Farm Sanctuary. Having never known anything but kindness in his life, he prances and parades around his pasture without a care in the world, just trying to make sure everyone else is having as good a time as he is. Gifted with many good friends and loving brothers and sisters, Jay Jay is living each day to the fullest, ever grateful for having been given the chance to live.

Rich Fudge Frosting

PER ⅙ RECIPE

Makes about ¾ cup (enough for one 8" square cake, one 9" round cake, or 6 cupcakes)

calories: 143
protein: 4 g
fat: 11 g
carbohydrate: 8 g
fiber: 1 g

*D*ark and creamy, this frosting has a deep, chocolaty flavor.

4 tablespoons smooth almond butter, at room temperature

2 tablespoons maple syrup

1 teaspoon vanilla extract

2 tablespoons unsweetened cocoa powder, sifted

1 to 1½ tablespoons plain or vanilla soymilk or rice milk, as needed

Place the almond butter in a small bowl. Add the maple syrup and vanilla extract and mix well. Stir in the cocoa powder and mix well. Gradually stir in just enough soymilk to achieve a spreadable consistency.

Use at once or store in the refrigerator. Bring to room temperature before using, and thin with additional soymilk, if necessary, to spread more easily. Stored in a covered container in the refrigerator, Rich Fudge Frosting will keep for about 1 week.

VARIATION

■ **Ultra-Creamy Fudge Frosting:** Increase the maple syrup to 3 tablespoons and replace the soymilk with ½ cup crumbled firm silken tofu. Place all the ingredients in a food processor, and process until very smooth and creamy. Makes about ¾ cup.

Sifting Cocoa Powder

When used in baking, cocoa powder should be sifted because it tends to lump, and once it is mixed with a liquid, the lumps are almost impossible to smooth out. Sifting will eliminate any lumps from the start. If you do not own a sifter, simply measure out the quantity of cocoa powder you need, place it in a wire mesh strainer, and stir it through the strainer directly into your mixing bowl.

Mail order sources

FOR VEGAN FOOD PRODUCTS

The companies listed below sell a multitude of foods and ingredients that make compassionate cooking as easy as vegan pie. Although the list is by no means complete, it will help you locate the basic items you'll need to embark on the vegan path. Many sell a wide variety of other vegan products, so be sure to check out their Web sites to see all that they offer.

BOB'S RED MILL NATURAL FOODS
www.bobsredmill.com
5209 SE International Way, Milwaukie, OR 97222
800-349-2173
Unique grains, beans, stone-ground flours (including gluten-free flours), vital wheat gluten, and specialty grain products sold in small, prepackaged sizes and bulk sizes.

COSMO'S VEGAN SHOPPE
www.cosmosveganshoppe.com
1860 Sandy Plains Road, Suite 204–208, Marietta, GA 30066
800-260-9968 or 678-921-0102
info@cosmosveganshoppe.com
Snacks, gluten-free foods, and sweets.

FOOD FIGHT! VEGAN GROCERY
www.foodfightgrocery.com
4179 SE Division Street, Portland, OR 97202
503-233-3910
info@foodfightgrocery.com
Vegan cheese, baked goods, chips, and exotic foods.

FRANKFERD FARMS FOODS
www.frankferd.com
717 Saxonburg Boulevard, Saxonburg, PA 16056
724-352-9500
Organic farm and flour mill offering a wide range of whole grain flours, grains, and packaged vegan products, including excellent vital wheat gluten.

GOLD MINE NATURAL FOOD COMPANY
www.goldminenaturalfood.com
7805 Arjons Drive, San Diego, CA 92126
800-475-3663 or 858-537-9830
sales@goldminenaturalfood.com
Hard-to-find organic and heirloom foods, macrobiotic specialty items, and top-quality kitchenware.

MAIL ORDER CATALOG
www.healthy-eating.com
PO Box 180, Summertown, TN 38483
800-695-2241
A wide range of food products and ingredients including TSP, tempeh starter, and Vegetarian Support Formula nutritional yeast flakes.

PANGEA
www.veganstore.com
2381 Lewis Avenue, Rockville, MD 20851
800-340-1200
info@veganstore.com
Pantry essentials and specialty items.

VEGAN ESSENTIALS
www.veganessentials.com
1701 Pearl Street, Unit B, Waukesha, WI 53186
866-88-VEGAN or 262-574-7761
questions@veganessentials.com
Baking mixes, quick meals, and pantry essentials.

Index

WS. 3/17

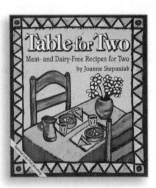